THE VIKING

THE VIKING

This work is the result of comprehensive teamwork by scientists and specialists from a number of countries.

BERTIL ALMGREN

Professor at Uppsala University, Sweden, archeologist and specialist in Ancient History, has been the chief contributor to and advisory expert for this work.

CHARLOTTE BLINDHEIM

Norway. Curator, Museum of Antiquities, University of Oslo.

YVES DE BOUARD

France. Professor at the University of Caen.

TORSTEN CAPELLE

Germany. Ph. D. University of Göttingen.

ARNE EMIL CHRISTENSEN JR. M. A.

Norway. Curator, Museum of Antiquities, University of Oslo.

KRISTJÁN ELDJÁRN

Ph. D. Iceland. National Custodian of Icelandic Antiquities, Reykjavik.

RICHARD M. PERKINS

Iceland. Lecturer at Reykjavik University

THORKILD RAMSKOU

Denmark. Curator, National Museum of Antiquities, Copenhagen.

PETER SAWYER

Great Britain. Lecturer in Early Medieval History. University of Leeds.

Contributors;

INGA HENNING

Sweden. B. A. Uppsala.

SUNE LINDQVIST

Sweden. Prof. Em., University of Uppsala

KJELL LUNDHOLM

Sweden. M. A. Uppsala.

T. R. NICHOLSON

Great Britain. M. A. (Oxon.). Supervising editor of the English text.

KERSTIN PETTERSSON

Sweden. M. A. Uppsala University. Institution of Scandinavian Archeology.

JAMES STEWART

Sweden. Lecturer at Uppsala University.

Main illustrations;

ÅKE GUSTAVSSON

ISBN: 91 7442 003 8

Printed in Italy, 1984, by New Interlitho S.P.A.

THE VIKING

NORDBOK

CONTENTS

could be bitterly cold, and two men would lie together in the same sleeping-bag in order to keep warm. Everyone relieved himself over the rails. "Going to board", it was called, when less polite expressions were not used. Knowledge of navigation was just as necessary as knowledge of seamanship. Justifiably, the Norse discoveries in the North Atlantic have excited much admiration. The Vikings were, in fact, the only sailors of early medieval Europe prepared to sail far away from landmarks. The original discoveries in the North Atlantic are remarkable enough, but they are not miraculous. In the spring the existence of land far away is betrayed to those with keen sight by the flight of nesting sea birds. Sailors who observed the pattern of flight of birds like gannets each evening would know where land probably lay. The regular navigation of the Atlantic did not, of course, depend on sea birds. On starry nights the Vikings used the North Star, but astral navigation was difficult in the light northern summer nights. At night in the summer, therefore, they navigated by the sun. They could do this because, thanks to countless observations taken during the year, just before dawn and after sunset, they knew the motion of the sun across the sky. A table compiled by a man called Stjerne-Oddi (Star-Oddi) and who lived at Flatey in Iceland, has been preserved. It gives the altitude of the sun for the whole year, and also a table showing the direction of dawn and twilight; that is, of the light on the horizon at the sun's going up and down. All the measurements of angles were made in what was called a "half wheel", a kind of half sun-diameter, which corresponds to about sixteen seconds of an arc. This was something which was known to every skipper at that time, or by the "long-voyage pilot" or "kendtmand" (man who knows) who sometimes went along on voyages when the skipper was himself unfamiliar with the route. When the sun was in the sky, it was not, therefore, difficult to find the four points of the compass, and the determining of latitude did not cause any problems either. For establishing the altitude of the sun, and thereby latitude, Norse writing indicates there was a "solbrädt" (sun-board) divided into "half wheels", though an example of these has unfortunately never yet been found. However, a bearing-plate or pelorus similar in principle to those used today has been discovered. It was used partly for coastal navigation, and partly to find the four points of the compass, which could be done because the position of the sun was known at sunrise and sunset.

In bright weather, it was thus possible to keep a pretty straight course on a voyage along a latitude. The course could be regulated every noon by means of the "sun-board". If the angle to the sun had grown larger, the ship had drifted southwards; if it was smaller, the course had slipped too far north. But

THE DANGEROUS ROAD

In the drawing above, a small fleet of Viking ships has shipped oars and set its sails, as the last of the sheltering islands of the North Sea coast of Scandinavia are left behind. The crews are resting, while they can. The sea in its fierce moods was always the Vikings' enemy, especially off rocky shores like those of western Sweden, shown in the colour photograph on the next pages. The Saga of Torfinn Karlsevne *tells of a battle lost to the sea. " . . . Because of the tempest, Bjarne Grimolfsön drifted with his ship to the Irish Sea, and they met a breaker, and the ship began to go down. They had a small boat greased with tar which protects against the seaworms. They entered the boat but realized that it could not carry all of them. Then said Bjarne, 'Whereas the boat cannot carry more than half of our men, it is my advice that lots should be cast to settle who shall go into the boat, because this cannot be settled by rank.' They all thought this very fair, so nobody objected. So they drew lots, and it fell to Bjarne's share to go in the boat with half of the men, because the boat could not carry any more."*

A HAVEN FROM THE ATLANTIC

Lying glass-still between high, snow-tipped mountains, and rimmed with fields and fir trees, the fjord of Skei i Jölster is one of thousands that indent the Atlantic coast of Norway. Vikings farmed these lands a thousand years ago just as a handful of Norwegian farmers do today, and rowed in from the stormy sea to shelter here. But good land, then as now, was scarce. And the long, narrow waterway which led the longships in became the sea road over which Viking families migrated to find homes in England and Iceland.

Most of the towns that perished during the Viking period or shortly afterwards have been located and more or less thoroughly excavated. Other towns proved more vigorous, and many modern towns can trace their history back to Viking days. This is not the case with the settlements in the country. Only a few Viking farms and outbuildings have been found. One reason may be that the present villages are placed on top of the old ones, so that the foundations of early Viking buildings lie too deep to find. Other archaeological finds, especially the burials, have helped locate Viking settlements. Men and women were buried with their most valued possessions around them, so that they should be properly equipped for their journey into the next world. The great majority of graves found so far seem to be quite modestly furnished. They represent the broad middle classes, the farmers, who were the nucleus of the population. The graves of the thralls or slaves have not been found, as it is hardly likely that they were provided with grave-goods of a durable sort. Finally, there are a few very rich interments, which must belong to members of the small ruling class. These include the famous ship-burials, which have been found in all the Scandinavian countries. Another kind of find, which also helps to throw light on the question of settlement, is buried treasure. Most Viking treasure consists of fortunes which were buried during a period of heavy fighting and then abandoned for one reason or another. They suggest that many people were far richer than the burials seem to indicate. A third kind of relic are the rune-stones, standing stones which were inscribed with characters in the old Norse (runic) alphabet. Most of them were erected in connection with an interment, and are really, therefore, tombstones. But some rune-stones were set up in memory of certain notable events or good deeds. Finally, the churches should be taken into account, for the majority of them are situated in areas which were inhabited in the Viking period.

The material at our disposal is not often derived from systematic investigation. This, indeed, would be impossible. The most numerous finds are the tombs, which are found under flat fields, and have nearly always been revealed by accident during agricultural work. Only when this is finished may the archaeologist come and make his investigations. The same is true of the treasure. Only rune-stones and grave mounds are always to be seen and recognized for what they are. And yet there is no doubt that even if a lot more material is found in the future, it will not affect the assessments which have been made so far. Archaeology is a science of long standing in Scandinavia, and the existing material is sufficient to map out the settlements in all essentials.

FOREST, LAKE AND RIVER

There was probably little cultivation of land in the wilder parts of Finland in Viking times, but otherwise the picture at left, showing the Kuopio district, gives a good idea of the country which favoured Viking expansion into the land east of the Baltic, with its innumerable waterways.

WHY THE VIKINGS LEFT HOME —
THE POLITICS, POVERTY AND OVERCROWDING
THAT FORCED THEM OUT INTO THE WORLD

The little scene on the picture-stone above, left, shows how the Vikings looked to the people they encountered in the world when they left their own countries. Swinging their newly-sharpened swords, their appearance alone terrified their enemies.

People at the time were hardly aware that several different forces were driving the Scandinavians out into the world. They probably distinguished only between the peaceful Norse traders and the rest of the Vikings, who brought war and destruction with them. At times, however, the traders were not as peaceful as all that. They themselves had to beware of pirates, and were therefore armed to the teeth. If they came across a smaller ship with an attractive cargo, it was tempting to throw away the scales, grab the sword, make a quick assault and thus augment their own cargo. When acting in this way, the trader placed himself in the other category: that of the real Vikings who undertook occasional predatory expeditions with the sole purpose of enriching themselves, but who otherwise usually spent their lives on their home farms. Of course a freebooter's life is sometimes pleasantly habit-forming, and many Vikings settled down abroad in the new places they had found, where they would be surrounded by other Scandinavian colonists. Such people came to make up a third Viking category.

The traders are known to us from the story of a Norwegian called Ottar, or Ohthere, who came from Hålgoland in the northernmost part of Norway, where the Lapps lived. He described his life to King Alfred of Wessex, and Alfred had his story written down. "He [Ottar] was very rich in those things that their [*i.e.* the Scandinavians'] riches consist of, that is, wild animals. When he came to the King [Alfred], he still had 600 unsold tame animals. He called those animals reindeer, and among them were six bait reindeer, which are very expensive among the Lapps, as they are used for catching wild reindeer. He was one of the greatest men in that neighbourhood, and yet he only had twenty oxen, twenty sheep and twenty pigs, and the little he ploughed, he ploughed with horses. And most of his income came from the taxes that the Lapps pay

Accordingly the servants of God, when they saw that matters had turned out propitiously as they had desired, began eagerly to preach the word of salvation to the people of that place. There were many who were well disposed towards their mission, and who willingly listened to the teaching of the Lord. There were also many Christians who were held captive amongst them, and who rejoiced that now at last they were able to participate in the divine mysteries. It was thus made clear that everything was as their [the Swedes'] messengers had declared to the king, and some of them desired earnestly to receive the grace of baptism. These included the prefect of this town, named Herigar, who was counsellor of the king and much beloved by him. He received the gift of holy baptism and was strengthened in the Catholic faith. A little later he built a church on his own ancestral property and served God with the utmost devotion. Several remarkable deeds were accomplished by this man, who afforded many proofs of his invincible faith."

In his account, Rimbert also notes many significant details about Birka, such as the fact that it was governed by an assembly or *thing*, and establishes that Birka merchants had contacts with the trading town of Dorestad in Holland. Rimbert also tells of an attack on Birka, during which the citizens and merchants sheltered in a nearby fortification.

The remains of this fort are easily located today. It stands in a commanding position about a hundred feet above the lake's edge to the south of the town. From the fort's summit it is possible to see great distances along the waterways that lead to the island. The position of this fort in relation to the town is very reminiscent of the arrangement at Hedeby, another Viking town, and a further similarity is the wall that surrounds the site. The walls were late additions at both Hedeby and Birka, and the Birka wall can be roughly fixed in time by the discovery under it of a coin dated 925 A.D. This wall originally enclosed all of the landward side of the town that was unprotected by the fort. There were a number of gaps in it, probably for entrances, which would have been important because some of the anchorages lay beyond the town.

The east end of the wall is nowadays quite a long way from the water's edge, but this was not always so. Since the Viking Age the water level in this part of Sweden has dropped by about eighteen feet, and this has greatly altered the shape of the island. In the ninth and tenth centuries it was very much smaller than it is now, and the anchorages and beaches for landing small boats were better than they seem today. Two of the anchorages have names that go back several centuries and are probably survivals from the days of Birka's existence as a town. They are Korshamn and, opposite the end of the wall, Kugghamn (see the illustration on pages 38-39). The latter may preserve a memory of the

A RELIC OF AN EARLY CHRISTIAN CONVERT

The oldest known crucifix found in Sweden was unearthed in a grave at Birka which dates from about 900 A.D.

Frisian cogs or merchant ships which, with their greater draught, needed deeper water than the local boats. In front of the town the ground shelved gently into the water, and timbers which have been discovered in this part of the lake are probably the remains of jetties. Another shelving beach beyond the fort to the south of the town may also have been used.

Present-day knowledge of Birka and its trade connections depend mainly on the graves that surround the town. There are at least 2000 of them, and over 1100 have been excavated. There are four main types. First, a number of richly furnished burials of the ninth century contain objects from western Europe — glass and pottery from the Rhineland, Frankish jewellery, Anglo-Irish bronzes — and therefore confirm the impression given by the *Life of St. Anskar* that the western trade routes of the town were important. This view is further strengthened by the rare "Birka coins", a few of which seem to have been minted in the town during the ninth century. They are modelled on Carolingian coins, the currency of the empire of the Franks.

There is little evidence of trade connections with the west in the tenth-century graves. Some are richly furnished, but their contents come from the region of the middle Volga in Russia, and beyond. Apart from these rich graves, there are a great many more modest ones that are typical of the Viking Age in this part of Sweden, and also a number of graves that, being sparsely furnished, are difficult, if not impossible, to date. These graves of uncertain date make it difficult to be certain when Birka began to function as a trading centre. It is possible, however, to be more confident about the date of Birka's end. This is determined by the complete absence of any English coins of the reign of King Ethelred (978 - 1016 A.D.) or of contemporary German coins. Both are so common elsewhere in Scandinavia that their absence from Birka makes us believe that the town ceased to exist before the end of the tenth century, possibly before 980 A.D.

A HOLY MAN FROM FAR AWAY

This bronze statuette of Buddha, which dates from about the fifth century, was brought more than 5000 miles — from northern India to Helgö, the trading centre which flourished before its neighbour, Birka, rose to importance (*see page 44*).

THE RICH TRADE-GOODS OF BIRKA

Because it was short of agricultural land, the town had to live mostly by trade, and as a result it trafficked in some of the finest goods the workmen of the age could fashion. How rich and varied they were can be seen by the assortment shown here. Merchants from far and wide met at Birka, bargained, bought and sold on a scale that is hard to comprehend. Even so, only those who were welcome were allowed to come to town: traders who were known to bring only good merchandise. Others were not guided through the gigantic labyrinth of the Stockholm archipelago and the islands of Lake Mälar, a journey which was even more difficult then than it is today. Because of the destructive effects of time on fibres, the picture does not show the fine wool cloth which was the most popular imported article in Scandinavia. But apart from that, a fair sampling appears, including furs, like the highly popular grey miniver (left foreground), the colourful winter coat of the squirrel. Even today, furs are one of the most important trade articles at the large market which still exists in the Mälar Valley, at Distingen near Uppsala. Pottery customarily came from the Rhineland, and included the characteristic blue-black jug-like pitchers (with handles) decorated with metal-bright patterns. Whether pottery itself was a major article of trade, or mainly served as containers for liquids and other commodities, is still a matter for argument. The Scandinavian word köpa *(meaning to buy), deriving from the latin* caupo *and used to denote a public-house landlord, gives some idea, however, of the importance of wine as an article of trade in ancient times. The glass mugs and funnel-shaped drinking glasses shown here came from the Rhineland too. The only domestic glass which appears to have been manufactured on Björko Island consisted of beads used in necklaces. The round gaming counters (centre) usually found as grave-goods, are of uncertain origin; they may even come from as far away as Egypt. The oval silver ornament is of the same type as those included in the harness of the Frankish army.*

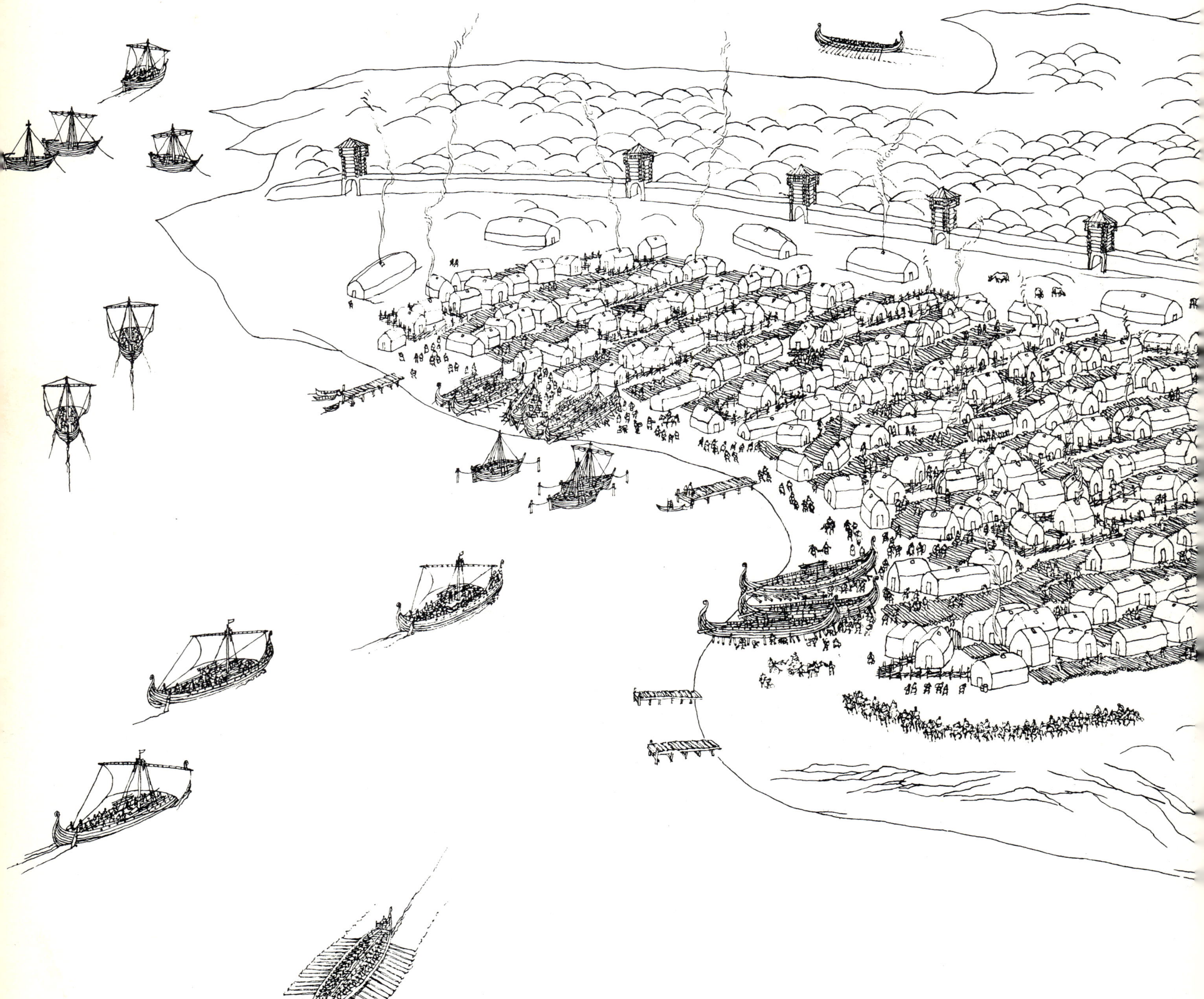

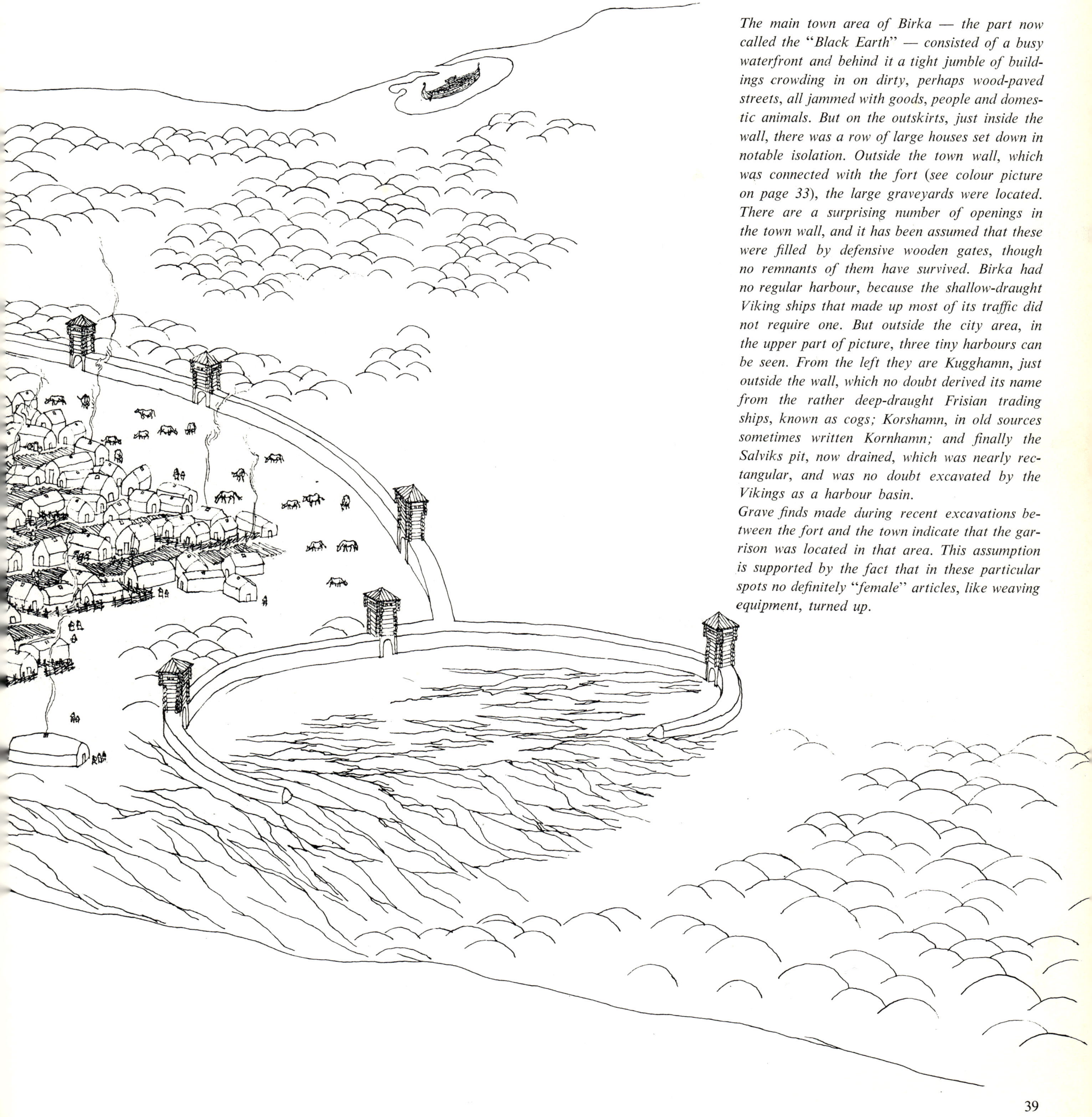

The main town area of Birka — the part now called the "Black Earth" — consisted of a busy waterfront and behind it a tight jumble of buildings crowding in on dirty, perhaps wood-paved streets, all jammed with goods, people and domestic animals. But on the outskirts, just inside the wall, there was a row of large houses set down in notable isolation. Outside the town wall, which was connected with the fort (see colour picture on page 33), the large graveyards were located. There are a surprising number of openings in the town wall, and it has been assumed that these were filled by defensive wooden gates, though no remnants of them have survived. Birka had no regular harbour, because the shallow-draught Viking ships that made up most of its traffic did not require one. But outside the city area, in the upper part of picture, three tiny harbours can be seen. From the left they are Kugghamn, just outside the wall, which no doubt derived its name from the rather deep-draught Frisian trading ships, known as cogs; Korshamn, in old sources sometimes written Kornhamn; and finally the Salviks pit, now drained, which was nearly rectangular, and was no doubt excavated by the Vikings as a harbour basin.

Grave finds made during recent excavations between the fort and the town indicate that the garrison was located in that area. This assumption is supported by the fact that in these particular spots no definitely "female" articles, like weaving equipment, turned up.

BIRKA'S OLDEST FORTIFICATION

Seen in summer and from the north-east, Birka's hill fort looks peaceful and unassuming. The town wall, built later, and connected with the fort wall, at one time extended over the field in the middle distance, but has now disappeared under cultivation. One of the 2000 grassy grave mounds around Birka can be seen in the foreground.

Birka was not forgotten. It was remembered in the Archbishopric of Bremen as the focus of its missionary endeavours in the north, and it was also remembered in Scandinavia in the so-called Law of Birka, *Björköarätt*. There can be little doubt that this was originally the law of a place called Birch Island (Björkö), and the wealth and importance of the Birka in Lake Mälar makes it hard to believe that it is named after any other place. The *Life of St. Anskar* makes it clear that in the ninth century Birka had already developed a characteristic form of urban organization and a code of law for a trading community. A new, special sort of law was particularly necessary in Sweden, where, on the basis of the oldest Swedish laws from Västergötland, men from the next province were cheap to kill — that is to say, the compensation which murderers, or those guilty of manslaughter, had to pay to the victim's relatives was low. As for complete strangers under the old law, they had no protection at all. Foreign merchants were therefore particularly vulnerable, so to prevent murder for profit, special protection had to be provided by the king and by the scales of compensation laid down in the new law of Birka. All this, of course, was essential to trade.

Such a town law could only have been introduced by a king in an area where he had complete control. This was certainly so in the case of Björkö, because that island was situated between two great estates of the king of the Svea people. Even so, the *Life of St. Anskar* shows that the townspeople as well as the king had considerable influence in questions of law. Even for the king, it must have been difficult to change the law, which existed as an age-old word-of-mouth tradition among the inhabitants.

When, therefore, it came to founding a town for the purpose of trade, for which one of the conditions was the radically new principle that even a foreigner from far afield would enjoy the full protection of the law, it must have been very important to look for a site where the current legal tradition was as vague as possible. From that point of view, Björkö was extremely suitable. It was a small island with very few inhabitants, located, not only between three different hundreds — that is, three different local courts (*thing*) — but also at the junction of two of the three districts (*folkland*) into which the central province of Sweden, Uppland, was divided. Each of these seems to have had its own law to begin with, and perhaps still had it at the time in question. In any case, Birka, centrally situated in Lake Mälar, lies so near the border between two provinces (Uppland to the north of Lake Mälar and Södermanland to the south) that there must often have been doubt as to which of the laws of these provinces

PLUNDER FROM IRELAND

This head from a bishop's crozier, of Irish workmanship, was found at Helgö near Birka.

A COSTLY FUNERAL

The grave of the woman found at Birka (right) contained a number of precious ornaments which suggest that the Vikings maintained a very high level of workmanship and design.
1. Delicately-carved gilt bronze ornament, found together with another in the neck region of the dead woman. The ornaments were sewn on the hem of a garment — probably the dress.
2. One of a pair of gilt bronze brooches, decorated with blue, red and green enamelling.
3, 4. Two silver ornaments — pendants worn as earrings, or worn on the necklace (see below).
5. A square-armed brooch of gilt bronze, ornamented in the typical Nordic animal style of the early Viking Age. The brooch probably fastened the dead woman's tunic at the neck.
6. Horse-shaped silver gilt ornament. This is also one of a pair, originally made as a pair of brooches, but sewn on the dead woman's dress.
7. A finely wrought necklace consisting of four silver rings and eight beads of rock-crystal and glass with gold and silver foil.

1

2

3

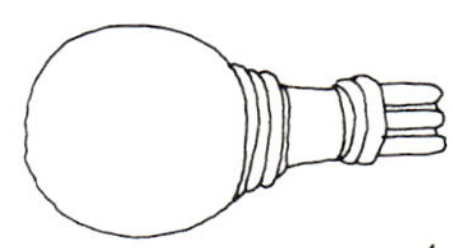

4

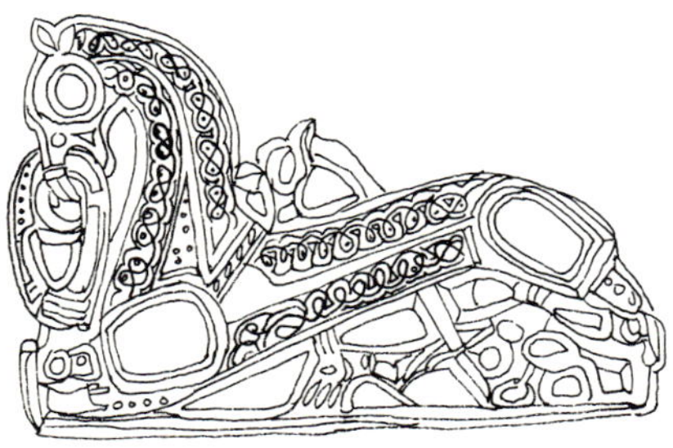

6

7

5

A BIRKA WOMAN'S GRAVE

Judging from the contents of the Birka graves, some women at least must have enjoyed a high position in the community. A reconstruction of one of the most important is seen here. It contained the well-preserved skeleton of a woman, placed in a wooden chamber built in a large burial pit: a so-called "chamber-grave". She must have been buried fully dressed, but only small pieces of silk, undoubtedly imported, have been preserved. This luxurious detail corresponds very well with the abundance of beautiful beads (eighty-one altogether) and silver and gilt bronze ornaments found near her neck. A Frisian-style jug, a glass beaker of Rhineland manufacture, a bronze cauldron of Anglo-Irish origin, all luxurious objects, were found in the grave. So were two wooden buckets and a small wooden box containing a comb of horn. The many imported articles suggest that the dead woman was a rich merchant's wife. She must have lived in the early or middle part of the ninth century.

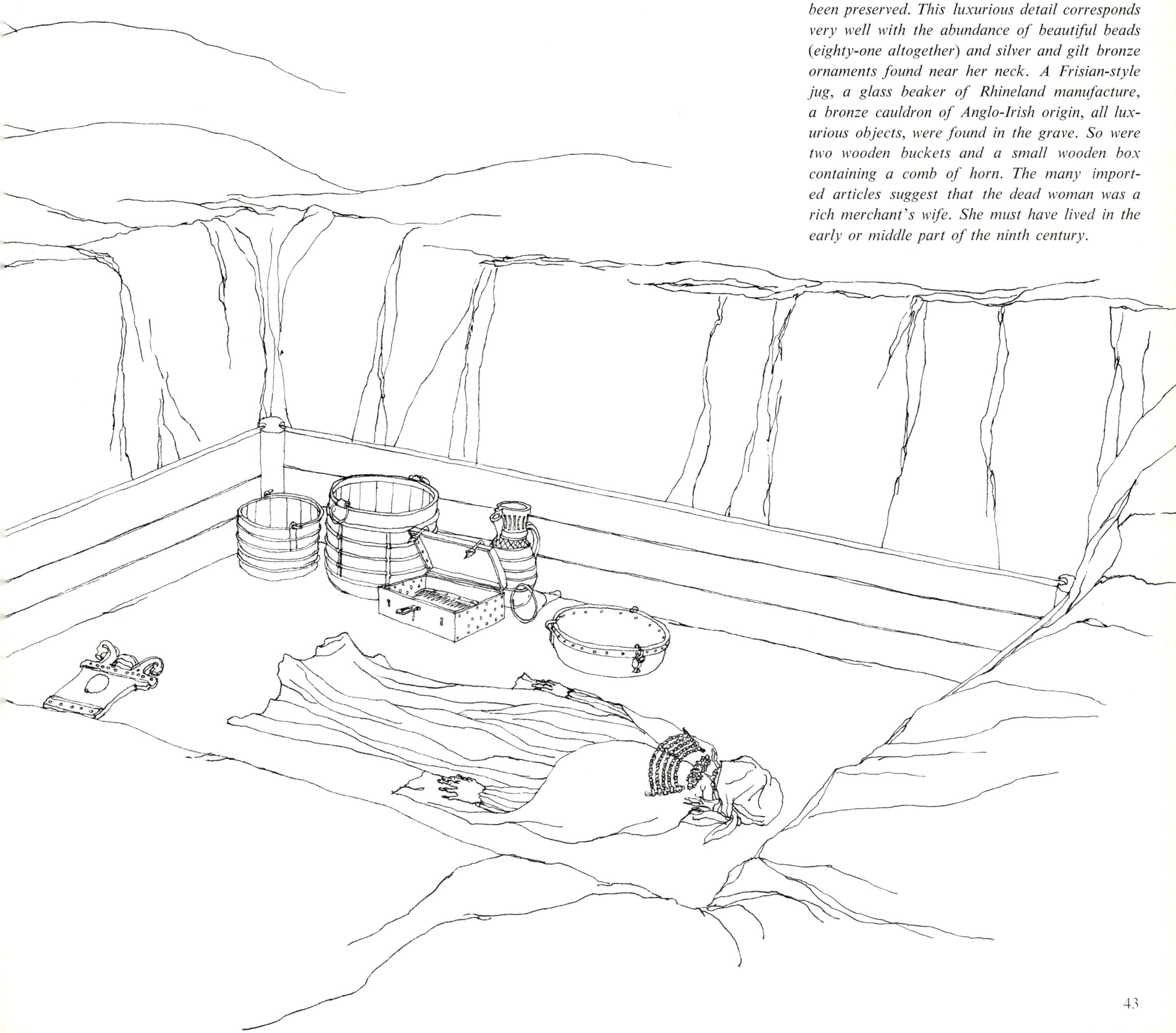

applied there. It was there, at what was, legally speaking, a virtual no-man's-land, that the king founded his trading town. As it was so near his own properties, he could guarantee military protection, and Birka was further safeguarded by being so far from the sea, behind a sheltering archipelago.
What did the king gain in return? The Birka law stated that the king, through his bailiff, had the right to purchase newly-imported goods three days in advance of everyone else. In other words, he controlled the market in quality products. The king of the Svea people in the Viking Age undoubtedly became such a rich man that he was able to gather power effectively into his own hands, whereas his immediate predecessors certainly had to share that power with their chieftains.
If the exact date of the rise of Birka is uncertain, recent excavations at a site nearer the outlet of Lake Mälar have, nevertheless, thrown new light on the town's origins. On this site, an important trading centre seems to to have existed long before Birka was founded.
On the small island of Helgö (Holy Island), the remnants of a settlement have recently been discovered which for centuries maintained an extensive trade with Europe and the British Isles. Inside and outside the remains of a series of buildings of various sizes, an enormous number and variety of articles have been found, ranging from unique objects like the figure of Buddha (page 35) and a bishop's crozier (page 34) to slag left over from local iron production. Of special interest are many fragments of glass vessels, testifying to stable contacts with glass-producing centres in Europe and Britain from the fourth to the ninth centuries.
There must have been a strong organizing power behind trade on the scale demonstrated in the Helgö finds. No Black Earth has so far been found on the site. Some authorities are inclined to think that the settlement was organized rather as a single commercial house than as a market town like Birka. But it seems quite clear that Birka was founded directly from Helgö. Taken together, the finds from Helgö cover a period of about 600 years from the fourth to the eleventh century, and most objects date from between 400 and 800 A.D. — that is, just up to the time when Birka first began to flourish as a trading centre. The archaeologists are still left with problems. If Helgö was really only a commercial house and not a town, how did it compete with its rich, well-protected neighbour Birka during its later centuries of existence? Such puzzles as this are commonplace difficulties for the scholar.

A BIRKA WARRIOR'S GRAVE

Though most of the graves at Birka were covered by mounds, many of the richest burials were found in the "chamber-graves" (see page 43). A reconstruction of one of the most famous is seen here. The chamber was found in the western part of the cavity. The position of the skeleton gave the impression that he had been sitting in the grave, rather than laid out. His two shields are at his head and his feet and a heavy two-bladed sword was found at his left-hand side. A beautifully decorated dagger, an axe, twenty-four arrows and a spear with silver and copper decoration on the socket were placed at the right-hand side of the body. The equipment indicates that this is a warrior's grave rather than that of a merchant. The skeletons of two horses found in the eastern side of the grave outside the actual "chamber", and the presence of stirrups, make clear that he was a horseman. The date of a silver coin, found underneath the skeleton of the dead man, provides a fairly good idea of the date of the grave: 913 - 980 A.D.

TOWN WALLS

It is a remarkable fact that only the two easternmost Viking towns, Birka and Hedeby, were protected by walls. Kaupang to the west, in Norway, never had a defensive wall; nor, it seems, did Dorestad on the Rhine. On the other hand, there is plenty of evidence of town walls of earth and timber all over eastern Europe, not only at Staraja Ladoga, which the Vikings visited, but also in Estonia and among the Slavs generally. These walled towns seem to have been at least contemporary with the Viking period, perhaps even earlier. In view of how late and scrappily towns and other population centres in Western Europe came to be fortified — quite frequently in the years around the turn of the tenth century in the case of the English "boroughs" — it is possible that the town fortifications of the Slavs influenced the evolution of the fortified Viking towns of Scandinavia. The oldest written record mentioning the subject, the Frankish Royal Annals, describes how in 808 A.D. the Danish king Godfred transplanted to Hedeby the inhabitants of a Slav town, Reric, which he had recently destroyed. The early medieval towns of Sweden dating from the twelfth century and after, which had a mostly immigrant German population, were developed in a similar way. In both cases Viking chiefs and traders seem to have found it necessary to use, exploit and even import people who had long experience in the organization of town life. The emergence of towns in Scandinavia in Viking times, therefore, though obviously the result of west European influence, owned a great deal to Viking initiative.

However, it may not have been only foreign influences that caused the fortification of Viking towns, and it may have come about later. One theory holds that at first Scandinavian trading centres had no need of such defences. In the early Viking Age and before it, Scandinavia was not so plagued by internal strife as it was later on. Town walls were less necessary than they were towards the end of the ninth century and the beginning of the tenth, when the Scandinavians took to fighting each other on a large scale. These internecine struggles might have helped to bring about the fortification of the towns.

AN ARAB DESCRIBES A SLAV FORT

The eleventh-century Arab geographer Al-Bekri describes a typical Slav fort, of the kind which the Vikings probably saw beyond the Baltic, and which may have influenced the building of their own town walls:

" In such a manner do the Slavs build most of their forts: they go to meadows, rich in water and undergrowth, and lay out a round or square place according to the form and extent of the fort, as they foresee it, dig around it and shovel the loose earth up, and this is secured with planks and posts in the manner of ramparts, until the wall reaches the intended height. The fort is given one gateway, on whatever side it pleases [the builders] . . . "

Kaupang in Vestfold, not far from Oslo, was Norway's only known trading town of the Viking Age. Looking at the site today, it is difficult to believe that it was ever an important harbour and centre of trade. The bay is shallow, the surrounding land is marshy, and the area suitable for habitation is severely limited, being squeezed in between craggy hills. In Viking times, however, the shoreline in the bay stood some six feet higher, while at the port of Kaupang at the head of the bay there was a broad and sheltered pool offering excellent harbour facilities for shallow-draught Viking ships. The innumerable islands and shoals of the archipelago which stretches across the mouth of the bay made it difficult for intruders to find their way through the channels without the assistance of a pilot. The hills flanking the bay provided not only shelter from storms and some protection from sudden attack, but also a vantage point from which to keep watch over the sea. Excavations have been carried out at Kaupang every summer since 1956. The burial places were examined first, then the area of the town and port. All the rich discoveries brought to light confirm and expand what was already known of the place from the sole surviving written source, the account given personally to King Alfred of Wessex at some time in the ninth century by the Norwegian merchant, Ottar (see page 50).

The settlement area along the edge of the bay occupies about five acres of the same sort of dark and greasy soil, known as Black Earth, that is found at Birka. Kaupang excavations have so far uncovered two piers. In construction both are the same, having a slightly rounded front facing the sea, and narrowing towards the settlement area. Near one of them, a heavy anchor of granite and oak was found. The shore opposite the larger pier has been faced with stones, giving the impression of a continuous pier. Behind these stone piers, just under plough depth, foundations of houses were found. The larger houses have slightly curved walls, the rest have straight walls. It is difficult to be sure whether these were the dwellings of a permanent population or whether they were occupied for short periods only, when markets were being held. Excavations at Kaupang have produced many finds which lend some colour to the rather monotone picture presented by the remains of the houses. Masses of animal and fish bones provide evidence of a farming and fishing economy. Slag, fragments of iron and waste from the working of lead, bronze and silver — and occasionally of gold too — show that a metal industry flourished in the town. Fragments of spinning and weaving implements prove that textiles were produced. The great quantity of soapstone waste and half-finished objects suggests

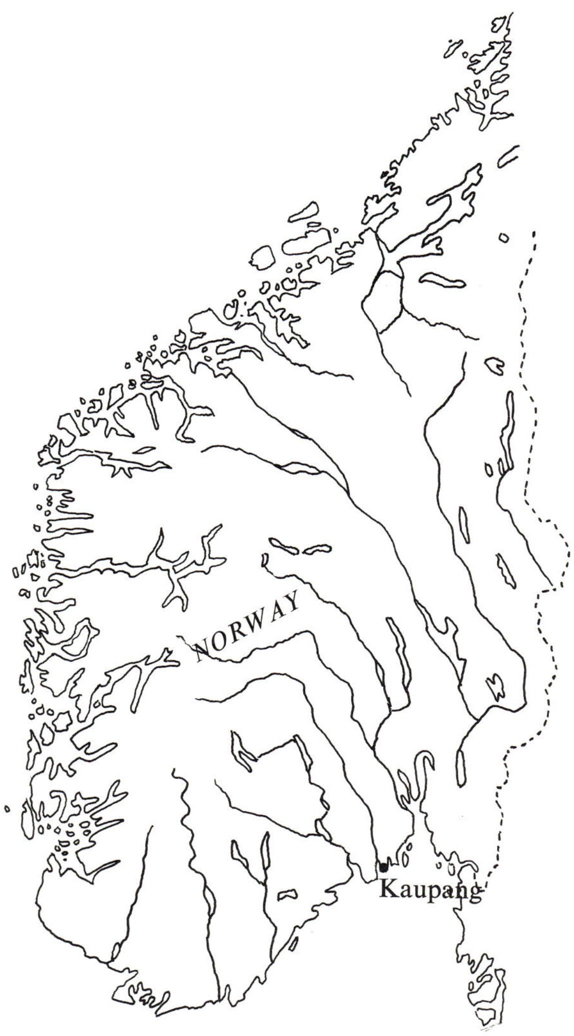

THE SAFE HARBOUR

The location of the Viking trading centre at Kaupang on the Norwegian coastline is shown on this map. The route of the merchant Ottar from the far north of Norway, so precisely described to King Alfred, hugged the coast. For some reason Ottar dared not make the short cut from the southernmost point of Norway (Lindesnes) to the top of Jutland, but preferred to follow the Norwegian coast as far as Kaupang. From Kaupang he must have crossed the Oslo Fjord to the Swedish (then Danish) coast, and sailed through Danish waters to Hedeby.

production of cooking-pots on a scale intended to meet more than purely local needs. Among imported objects, potsherds are the most numerous, mostly Rhenish ware. It is tempting to suppose that these big-bellied pots from the Rhineland were the wine casks of the day. If so, the wine must have been transferred subsequently to other containers, because shards of the Rhenish ware have not been found in any part of Norway except Kaupang. The great quantity of fragments of glass beakers that has turned up is something of a mystery to archaeologists. Most of the commerce at Kaupang was probably conducted on a barter basis, though a few fragments of coins have turned up there.

The relics emphasize a West European outlook, which even today is characteristic of the Vestfold area. Vestfold enjoys speedier sea routes to the Continent than any other part of Norway, and few Norwegians are as European in their attitude as the people hereabouts. Finds from the burial places also reflect an outlook directed seawards and westwards. In the twentieth century a thorough investigation of a burial ground was begun. One hundred and forty burial mounds or barrows were found, most of them in the marshy parts to the north of the settlement area. Most were cremation burials, and nothing notable was found other than shards of a very fine west European pottery. The burial ground situated beside the rocky hill known as Bikjholberg, which in Viking times projected like a ness or promontory into the sea opposite the settlement, was also excavated in the 1950s. The diggings revealed boats and coffins sunk into the sand, often not very deeply. They were covered not by mounds but by a heavy stone packing. Obviously these were the graves of rich people, for they contained objects showing workmanship of a high quality, probably of native and Anglo-Irish origin. The situation of these graves, their character and the quality of the grave-goods suggest that this burial ground was the last resting-place of big merchants and of their families. Perhaps it would be better to call them farmer-merchants, and assume that they worked their farms further inland in the fertile countryside, devoting themselves to trade as a seasonal occupation, at market times only. The layer of Black Earth at Kaupang is between one and two feet deep. This corresponds well with the theory that Kaupang flourished for only about a hundred years: from the beginning of the ninth to the beginning of the tenth century. The place was probably abandoned as a market town because the sea level dropped too much to permit larger vessels to enter the bay.

A NORWEGIAN MERCHANT GIVES SAILING DIRECTIONS

In part of the translation, ordered by King Alfred of Wessex, of Orosius' *Universal History*, Ottar (Ohthere), a Norwegian merchant, mentions Kaupang, which he calls Sciringesheal: "Ottar related that the district in which he lived is called Hålgoland. No one, he said, lived farther north than he. But there is a port in the southern end of the country. This port people called Sciringesheal, and to it, he said, one could not sail in less than a month if one camped by night and had favourable winds by day. And one must ever sail along by the land. And Ireland will be on the starboard side, and then the islands which are between Ireland and this country [England]. Then it is this country till one comes to Sciringesheal. And all the way on the port side is Norway. South of Sciringesheal a large sea runs up into the country. The sea is wider there than any man can see across."

THE BAY OF KAUPANG

This pleasant countryside, where rich fields slope gently to the shores of a shallow bay, was the site of Kaupang, the only known Viking trading centre in Norway. It was first discovered and excavated in 1956 when archaeologists noticed that the soil lying on either side of the road (foreground) near the bay was especially dark and greasy — just like the "Black Earth" at Birka. A pilot trench was dug, and continuing work (protected by the row of plastic tents) indicates that Viking traders worked and lived where farmers now grow potatoes. In Viking times, when the water level was six feet higher, the bay was larger and deeper — deep enough at best to receive Viking ships and serve as a busy trading port.

1 2 3 4 5 6 7 8 9

WESTERN EUROPEAN ORNAMENTS FROM KAUPANG

The material found at Kaupang includes the largest collection of western European metal ornaments found on a Scandinavian site. The majority of the ornaments are ecclesiastical, original mountings for shrines and holy books in the churches and monasteries of Great Britain and Ireland, probably brought to Kaupang as Viking loot. Many were transformed into brooches, like the magnificent rectangular ornament no. 7 found in the neck region in a rich woman's grave. This is a first class piece of metal-work, as are also nos. 5 and 8, while no. 9 is of inferior quality. Numbers 3 and 4 are beautifully enamelled ornaments — perhaps for bronze cauldrons. There are also pieces for secular use as, for example, a long pin, belonging to a pennanular brooch. (no. 6).
A unique object is the trefoil brooch (no. 2.) Its vegetable ornaments are completely alien to the nordic taste of the time. This brooch must have been imported from the continent.

GOTLAND THE TRADERS' ISLAND

During the whole of the Iron Age, before and during Viking times, the island of Gotland, situated in the middle of the Baltic, was a centre for trade from both east and west. Its world-wide commerce began early. A great many objects imported from Rome during the height of the Empire have been found there. By the late Viking Age, in the tenth century, Gotland enjoyed market conditions that must have made it, within a short while, a dangerous rival of Birka. In addition to richly-furnished burials of the tenth century discovered there, excavations in Gotland show a sharp increase in the quantities of silver coins from treasure hoards. Unlike Birka, Gotland seems to have enjoyed undiminishing richness of silver coins, Anglo-Saxon and German, until well into the eleventh century; so much so, in fact, that it must have been the true centre of Baltic commerce during this period. Out of the total number of 200,000 silver coins from the Viking Age found in Scandinavia, no less than half, that is 40,000 Arabic, 38,000 German and 21,000 Anglo-Saxon coins, were found on the little island of Gotland.

It is obvious that these coins, only recently unearthed, are only a fraction of what was, for one reason or another, buried on the island in the tenth or eleventh centuries. Moreover, buried coins do not, of course, represent anything like the entire amount of the silver that came to the island as the proceeds of trade. A total figure is hard even to guess at. But if one coin out of every thousand that constituted the proceeds of trade has been preserved — probably an optimistic estimate — the Gotlanders must have had an income of more than a hundred million silver coins during their century and a half of heaviest trade, possibly as much as a million a year. In spite of being called a penny, every Anglo-Saxon silver coin had a purchasing power of at least ten to twenty shillings (up to three dollars) in current values, so the proceeds of Gotlandic trade during the later part of the Viking Age were worth about one million pounds sterling (or nearly three million dollars) a year.

Judged even by the standards of Europe as a whole, this suggests trade on remarkably grand scale. This huge income may be explained in the same way as that of England's Honourable East India Company during the seventeenth and eighteenth centuries: the greater the risk from pirates and other enemies, the greater profits to be reaped on such goods as actually reached port. Perhaps the Gotlanders, because of exceptional sailing skill, possessed the fastest ships on the Baltic, enabling them to evade the Jomsvikings and other sea-going predators. Thus they would have been able to save their cargoes of furs from the north-east for the new-rich mine-owners of central Germany, and load

THE TRADING CENTRE WITHOUT A TOWN

The island of Gotland, shown on the map above, seems to have been an active trading centre both before and throughout the Viking era, but archaeologists have never found any town-like settlement. Gotland's rich farmers must have doubled as merchants. They had a turnover of the most amazing proportions, as the many finds of foreign money on the island show.

THE CLIFFS AND SHOALS OF GOTLAND

The harsh granite cliffs at Korpklint, on the west coast of Gotland, shown on the facing page, would have repelled the deep-draught trading ships of most nations, for the island has few natural harbours to accomodate them. But it does have shelving beaches, which were ideal landing-places for the shallow-draught Viking vessels. As a result Gotland became one of the richest of the Scandinavian trading centres.

their ships with ever-profitable woollen cloth on the return voyage. Despite certain archaeological evidence of Gotland's prosperity, contemporary records are strangely silent about her wealth. The historian Adam of Bremen, who did much of his reporting towards the end of the eleventh century, has not one word to say about Gotland. On the other hand, it was obviously this large-scale trading that provided the foundation for the prominent place which Gotland held, at the outset, among the new Hanseatic trading towns of the twelfth century. This position is particularly remarkable because the island has, and had, very few good harbours. The only exception was Visby (after the Viking Age), which was populated almost entirely by foreigners. But the rest of Gotland, too, continued to prosper up to the middle of the fourteenth century, in spite of having nothing but shelving shores. These, however, were easily negotiable for shallow-draught ships of the Viking type, which also could easily, without rehandling of cargo, penetrate long distances up all the rivers of the eastern Baltic, even as far as Novgorod in Russia. They possibly also reached the Slav lands on the southern coasts of the Baltic. From here the journey to the rich new silver mines of Harz in Germany was short. If the Gotlandic trade with Germany did go via the pagan, illiterate Slavs, that would explain the silence of the Christian commentators at least until the new town of Lübeck succeeded Slav cities as Gotland's trading partner.

The island of Gotland is also of particular interest for its wealth of monumental stones. These stones, which date from the 5th to the 11th century, may be simple limestone or sandstone slabs, rune stones or picture stones. Especial interest attaches to the last, which are adorned with pictures carved in low relief on the relatively soft stone. Their most characteristic shape is in the form of a keyhole with a slightly widened base and they may be as much as twice the height of a man. They are most frequently found in the vicinity of cemeteries and churchyards, although the latest of them date from earlier than the first known churches on the island. Their origin and purpose is not always clear, but many were probably tombstones, while others appear to have been wayside memorials and some have been found on the sites of ancient farmhouses. They most frequently depict boats and ships, men and women, the former frequently with weapons, particularly swords and axes, while other stones represent mythical subjects. The picture stone shown in the illustration comes from the parish of Lärbro in the north of the island. In the semicircular part at the top it depicts a battle scene, below which are two scenes probably representing a burial and the entry of a warrior into Valhalla. The use of the wider part near the base to depict a ship is typical.

A TYPICAL PICTURE STONE

This bas-relief was found in the northern part of Gotland. It is carved in limestone, now nearly nine feet high but originally about eleven feet, before the root stone was cut away.

In the Frankish Royal Annals for 804 A.D. a place called Sliesthorp, situated on a shallow bay at the head of a creek called the Schlei, on the site of the present town of Schleswig, is mentioned for the first time. It is often mentioned later in other written sources. Icelandic sagas, and the contemporary account of an Arab traveller, Ibrahim Al-Tartushi, testify that the town was known from Iceland to Baghdad. The names by which it is known, however, differ widely: Sliesthorp (the settlement on the Schlei), Slieswich, *aet haethum* (on the heath, at the heaths), Haithabu. All these names refer to the one place, Hedeby, which during the eighth century became of very great importance as a centre of trade between western Europe and the Orient, and as a junction for traffic between the Baltic and the North Sea.

The Norwegian merchant, Ottar, talking to king Alfred of England, described the voyage from Kaupang (Sciringesheal) southwards to Hedeby in these words:

"And from Sciringesheal he said that he sailed for five days to *æt hæthum*: mark [the Danish parts of Sweden] lay to port, while to starboard for three days was the open sea; and after that there was a further two days' sail to Hedeby during which Jutland, Sillende [south Jutland], and many islands lay to starboard; here the Angles had lived before they came to this country [England]. During those two days the islands belonging to Denmark lay to port."

The route eastwards from Hedeby into the Baltic is described to King Alfred by an Anglo-Saxon, Wulfstan: "Wulfstan said that he left Hedeby and came to Truso after seven days and nights and that the ship was under sail all the time. Vendland lay to starboard, while to port were Langeland, Loland, Falster, and Skåne, all of which belonged to Denmark. After that Burgundaland [Bornholm], which has its own king, was seen to port, and, after that, first the land called Blekinge, then Möre, Öland, and Gotland, all belonging to the Swedes. Right up to the mouth of the river Vistula, Vendland lay to starboard all the way."

THE STRATEGIC POSITION OF HEDEBY

At the southern extremity of the Jutland peninsula, now German territory, lies the narrowest neck of land between the water systems of the Baltic and the North Sea. Just here Hedeby was situated. It was easy to sail to the east through the long fjord of the Schlei. Today, just south of, and almost parallel to, the main Viking trade route which once ran from Hedeby to Hollingstedt on the North Sea is a modern trade route of great importance — the Kiel Canal.

Archaeological excavations have shown that the place must have been inhabited for about two generations before the earliest written reference to it. At first, there were three small villages situated close together, beside streams near the bay. Two of these villages, the northern and the southern, were abandoned towards the end of the eighth century. Their inhabitants may have joined forces with the people in the middle village to form a bigger community. In that way the place known as Sliesthorp in the year 804 and later as Hedeby came

into existence. In those early days the town was restricted to an area in the immediate vicinity of the shore.

A semicircular earthwork still remains as a prominent feature of the landscape. It is up to forty feet high, and encloses an area of sixty acres. The town could be entered only through two gates in the wall, on the south and north, or from the harbour. The side of the harbour that faced the inlet of the Schlei was protected by a strong palisade. The date of the Hedeby earthworks is not known. It includes two burial-grounds within its area. By the end of the tenth century, buildings covered the whole of the area enclosed by the earthwork. A third burial-ground lies outside the earthwork to the south, and a fourth, smaller one outside the northern gate. The most impressive of the burials is a chambered tomb, covered by a boat of which only the rivets remain. It is situated on the edge of the southern burial-ground, and dates from about 900. Hedeby's position, on the borders of Denmark and the Frankish kingdom, offered the best of prospects for the growth of trade. Because for two and a half centuries Hedeby controlled the traffic between the Frankish kingdom and Scandinavia, it was a place of great significance politically, too. Its strategic situation helped in this, because the town lay at the eastern end of a system of defensive earthworks called the Danevirke, which stretched right across the narrowest part of the Jutland peninsula. The Danevirke was begun by the Danish king Godfred early in the ninth century as a defence against attacks from the south. Its western end reached the marshy coastlands of the North Sea. Towards the east it branched off into what is known as the "Margareta-wall", which joined up with the semicircular earthwork of Hedeby. The Danevirke thus formed an effective barrier across the whole neck of the Jutland peninsula. In addition to the semicircular wall and the Danevirke, there is yet another defensive earthwork at Hedeby. It is immediately to the north of the settlement area on a stretch of steep hillside. The flat hilltop is surrounded by an embankment, and looks like a stronghold which may have served as a place of refuge for the inhabitants of Hedeby before they had built the larger semicircular wall. Small burial mounds have also been found here. As the town lay at the head of the very long and narrow Schlei creek, it was protected from sudden sea attack from the Baltic. The length of the Schlei made it possible for merchant ships to penetrate so far inland that the distance goods had to be transported overland to the North Sea was only ten miles (see map page 55). The corresponding port on the North Sea was Hollingstedt. In the harbour of Hedeby, it looks as if long rows of rammed-down piles formed piers which sheltered the ships tied up or at anchor. Larger ships must have been made fast at the pier, while smaller boats which could

THE HEDEBY AREA FROM THE AIR

In the aerial view of the Hedeby district on the facing page, the line of the great semicircular wall that protected the landward side of the town, now overgrown by trees, is visible in the centre middle distance. This formidable forty-foot barrier was probably built by the Swedes, who captured the town from the Danes in the middle of the Viking Age. The wide extent of the town area, which lay between the wall and the Schlei fjord (left), is clearly seen. The buildings erected at the archaeological diggings are just visible between the wall and the river, to the left of the lateral white road.

easily have been pulled up on land transported goods to and from them. The nature of the soil near the stream which flows eastwards through the town favoured the preservation of objects buried in it. This is also true of the area down by the shore, and from these two parts of the town one can gain a good idea of the ground plan and the constructional details of the wooden buildings, though their upper sections have long since decayed. Houses and storehouses, workshops, yards, washing places, wells, and roads have been all revealed. These give an accurate impression of how a commercial town of the Viking Age was built. The roofs of the houses nearly met across the narrow, wood-paved lanes. Some large buildings were set back behind fences, and had their own wells. Elsewhere, small workshops were packed closely together.

Although hardly any traces of trade goods made of organic materials like cloth have been found, those of imperishable material point to extensive commercial contacts: pottery from the Rhineland; basalt for grindstones from the Eifel area; soapstone from Norway; Frankish, Byzantine and Arabic coins; and ornaments from the Baltic and from Ireland. On the sites of the workshops raw materials and tools for making implements of various types were found, and also the actual implements, some finished, some half-finished. Workshops for many different products were situated side by side in the "craftsmen's quarter" of the town. In addition to pottery, iron, bronze, and gold were worked. The largest group among the craftsmen seems to have been the comb-makers. In addition to combs they carved spoons, needles, and spindle-whorls of antler. As glass slag has been found, it is even possible that glass was worked at Hedeby. It is conceivable that the so-called Haithabu half-bracteates (coins made from very thin plates) were struck there — which would make them the first money minted in Scandinavia.

Hedeby was the gateway through which Christianity was introduced into Scandinavia. The big commercial centres, Birka and Hedeby, which already had many Christian inhabitants, most of them foreign merchants of Frisian origin, were looked upon with eager eyes by the German Church as ripe for missionary endeavour. The first missionaries to come to Hedeby, in 823 A.D., had no success at all. In 826, the next, Anskar, who was at that time a monk and became a bishop, arrived. He made better progress, and it is known that he held services for foreign merchants. However, a few years after his arrival he proceeded to Birka, where he was well received by King Björn (see page 34) and by many of the inhabitants. He succeeded so well that when he returned to Hamburg, he was made a bishop. But he did not forget his failure in Hedeby. He returned, and by clever negotiation, obtained permission to build a church. This was in 832 A.D.; though it was not for some years that Anskar was

THE EARLIEST SCANDINAVIAN COINS?

These silver pieces, found at Hedeby and called "Hedeby half-bracteates", date from the beginning of the tenth century, and may be the first coins actually minted in Scandinavia. Until then, all coins were imported.

THE THRONGING WATERFRONT AT HEDEBY

Life in Hedeby, reconstructed in the drawing on pages 60-61, must have presented a lively, cosmopolitan and noisy scene. Women pound and rinse their laundry at the edge of the water (where the hairpins they dropped have been found by archaeologists). A cart-basket — the multi-purpose container of those days — filled with goods is being lifted from a boat onto its cart to be transported further along the Danevirke to Hollingstedt, for re-shipping there. Unmindful of the noise, two good neighbours play backgammon on the quay in the sunshine. A troop of horsemen in rig of Magyar cut, borrowed from the Hungarians via the Germans, come riding through the crowd. A pig has got loose and runs squealing among the cart-wheels and horses' hooves. According to the Arabian merchant Ibrahim Al-Tartushi, who visited Hedeby, the inhabitants made offerings of domestic animals to the gods by placing them on projections above the doors of houses. An offering of this kind has been made on one of the houses to the right. The permanent inhabitants all knew one another's names and trades, and the foreign merchants were easily recognized from their dress and behaviour. Many languages were bandied back and forth among the crowds milling in the narrow streets where they spent much of their daily life, but the peoples of the North Sea coasts probably understood one other easily enough at this time, before national boundaries grew up.

allowed to ring the church bell: it was thought that doing so would frighten the pagan gods.

Evidently everything went well as long as Anskar was still alive, but after his death in 867 A.D. no more is heard about a Christian mission in Scandinavia until 934, when the German king Henry I compelled the Danish king Gnupa, who may have been of Swedish origin, to accept the new religion. This event put new life into the missions. Unni, bishop of Bremen, went to Scandinavia, but in Birka he fell ill, and died there in 936. His trunk was buried at Birka, but his head was carried to the cathedral of Bremen and interred there.

A carved antler figurine of a child, with hands raised as if in adoration, may be the earliest representation of the Christ-child in Scandinavia. The discovery of moulds for the casting of such pagan objects as hammers of Thor as well as Christian crosses, shows that the pagan gods as well as Christ were worshipped at Hedeby. The co-existence of Christianity and paganism is unequivocally shown by other finds — among them several hammers of Thor, and a bronze representation, in relief, of a hero being greeted in Valhalla by a Valkyrie, one of the handmaids of the god Odin. Side by side with these were Christian objects such as a symbol of the Evangelist Luke dating from the tenth or eleventh century, a bronze crucifix, and a disc-shaped brooch with enamel bearing the representation of a saint. That two radically opposed religions should have overlapped in this way is not so surprising, when one recalls that merchants from the four corners of the then-known world came to Hedeby to do business. In fact the missionaries did not succeed in Christianizing the Scandinavians. If they wanted to do business with Christian merchants, some Scandinavian traders had to let themselves be signed with the Cross and declare themselves Christians, but they were not baptized, thereby avoiding offence to their own gods. Ibrahim Al-Tartushi, who visited Hedeby about 950 A.D., tells us that the people of the town "worship Sirius, except for a few who are Christians and have a church there. They hold a feast where all meet to honour their deity and to eat and drink. Each man who slaughters a sacrifical animal — an ox, ram, goat, or pig — fastens it up on poles outside the door of his house to show that he has made his sacrifice in honour of the god. The town is poorly provided with property or treasure. The inhabitants' principal food is fish, which is very plentiful. The people often throw a newborn child into the sea rather than maintain it. Furthermore women have the right to claim a divorce; they do this themselves whenever they wish. There is also an artificial make-up for the eyes: when they use it beauty never fades; on the contrary, it increases in men and women as well."

The evidence shows, therefore, that life in Hedeby at the turn of the millennium

was diverse and colourful, characterized by intensive commerce and industry, opposing religious beliefs, and political antagonism. The political history of the town is obscure in places. Hedeby lay on Danish territory and its rulers are described as Danish kings, but Adam of Bremen says that, earlier in the tenth century, a certain Olaf, coming from Sweden, conquered Denmark. He also tells us that Olaf's sons, Gurd and the Gnupa already mentioned, inherited the kingdom after their father's death. He mentions, too, a king named Sigerich, and still another called Hardegon. Adam himself was rather at sea. He adds: "It is very uncertain whether some of these kings (or rather tyrants) ruled the Danes at one and the same time, or whether one survived another for a short time." The inscriptions on two rune-stones found near Hedeby might help to solve the puzzle. One runs: "Asfrid created this memorial to Sigtrygg, her son and Gnupa's." The other stone says that "Asfrid, the daughter of Odinkar, set up this memorial to King Sigtrygg, her son and Gnupa's." Of these two written sources, the rune-stones, being contemporary with the events, should be the more reliable. At the same time, it can be assumed that the king called Sigerich by Adam is the same as the Sigtrygg of the rune-stones. But this merely gives us one of the names of the kings. We still do not know whether Denmark was divided into several parts, or whether Olaf conquered the whole of the country, or Hedeby alone. The archaeological finds at Hedeby do not help, for they are of a common Scandinavian type, without special Danish or Swedish character.

At all events, by the early decades of the eleventh century, the town was falling into decay, for reasons as yet unknown. In 1050 the Norwegian king Harald burnt Hedeby in the course of a battle against the Danish king Svein Estrithson. In 1066, the same year as the Battle of Hastings in England, a destructive attack was made on the town by the Slavs. This probably led to its abandonment. Its trading role was taken over by Schleswig, on the northern shore of the Schlei. Schleswig, in its turn, came to be superseded by the Hansa town of Lûbeck.

THE VIKINGS AT PLAY

Life for the Vikings was not always the serious business of fighting, trading, or wresting a living from the land and the sea. They threw dice, and played games with counters, as these finds from Hedeby show.

Vinlanda Insula
a Byarno repa
et leipho socijs
Mare Oceanum
Magnae
Insulae
Beati Brandani
Branziliae
dictae
Desiderate
insule
Mare Oceanum
Beate isule
fortune
Rex francorum
hispanorum rex
Tunesis
rex
Belo
rex

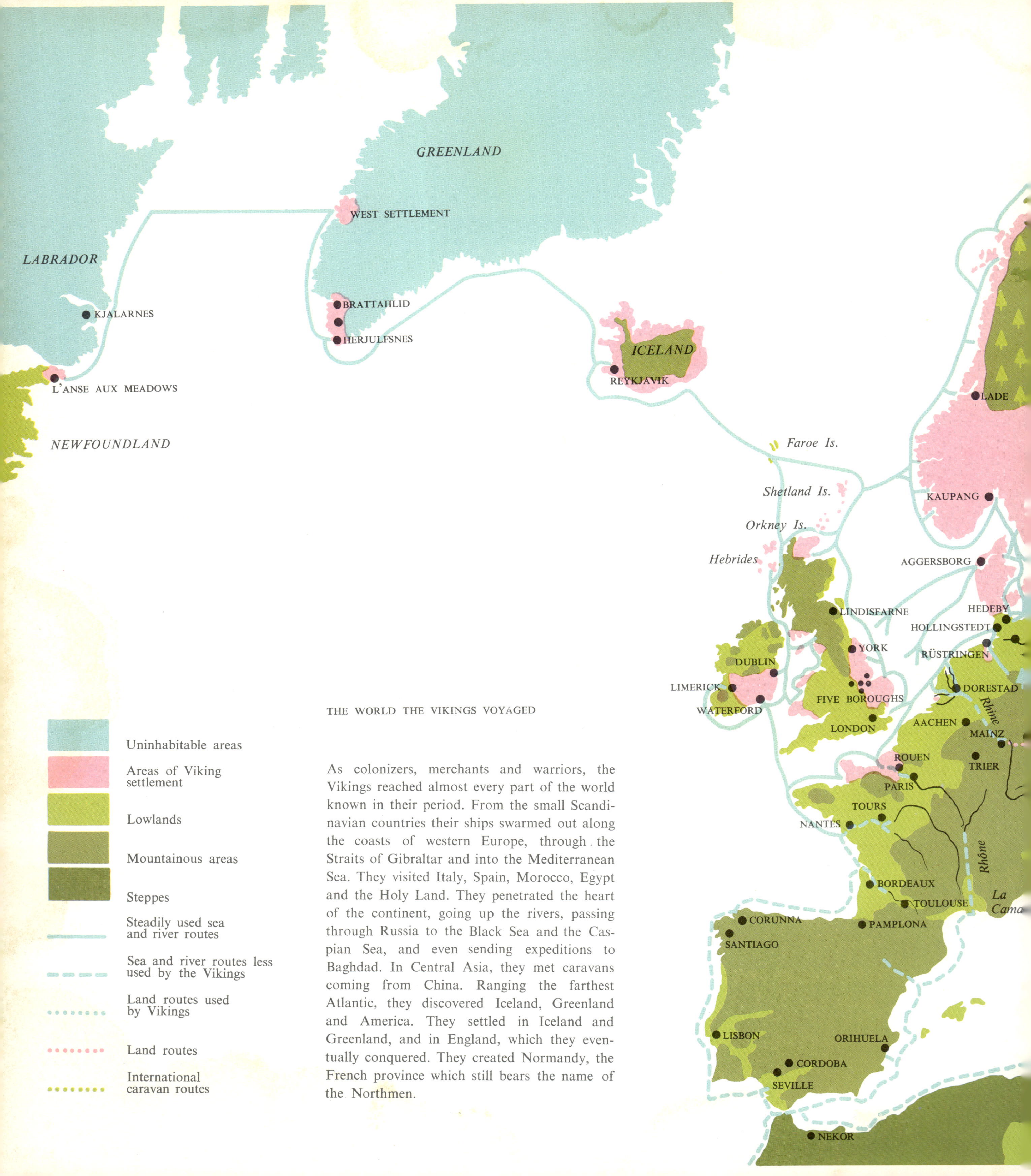

THE WORLD THE VIKINGS VOYAGED

As colonizers, merchants and warriors, the Vikings reached almost every part of the world known in their period. From the small Scandinavian countries their ships swarmed out along the coasts of western Europe, through the Straits of Gibraltar and into the Mediterranean Sea. They visited Italy, Spain, Morocco, Egypt and the Holy Land. They penetrated the heart of the continent, going up the rivers, passing through Russia to the Black Sea and the Caspian Sea, and even sending expeditions to Baghdad. In Central Asia, they met caravans coming from China. Ranging the farthest Atlantic, they discovered Iceland, Greenland and America. They settled in Iceland and Greenland, and in England, which they eventually conquered. They created Normandy, the French province which still bears the name of the Northmen.

L. Balkhash
To China
KASHGAR
To China
TASHKENT
Volga
BULGAR
STARAJA LADOGA
JAROSLAV
Aral Sea
SAMARKAND
NOVGOROD
Åland
BOKHARA
IZBORSK
CHOREZM
GNEZDOVO
Gotland
ATIL
MERV
WISKIAUTEN
Caspian Sea
TRUSO
KIEV
Dnieper
GURGAN
JUMNE-WOLLIN
BERDA
BEREZANJI
CRACOW
RAY
PRAGUE
Black Sea
MIKULCICE
MARAGHE
Danube
BYZANTIUM
BAGHDAD
ROME
SIDON
PIRAEUS
JERUSALEM
Viking pilgrims
Sicily
Crete
ALEXANDRIA

THE BRITISH ISLES IN THE VIKING AGE

This map shows the most important features and places relating to the Viking Age. The boundaries of the four English kingdoms (Wessex, Northumbria, Mercia and Kent), which existed separately at the beginning of the period, are not shown, because they shifted frequently and in some cases disappeared entirely over the 300 years in question.

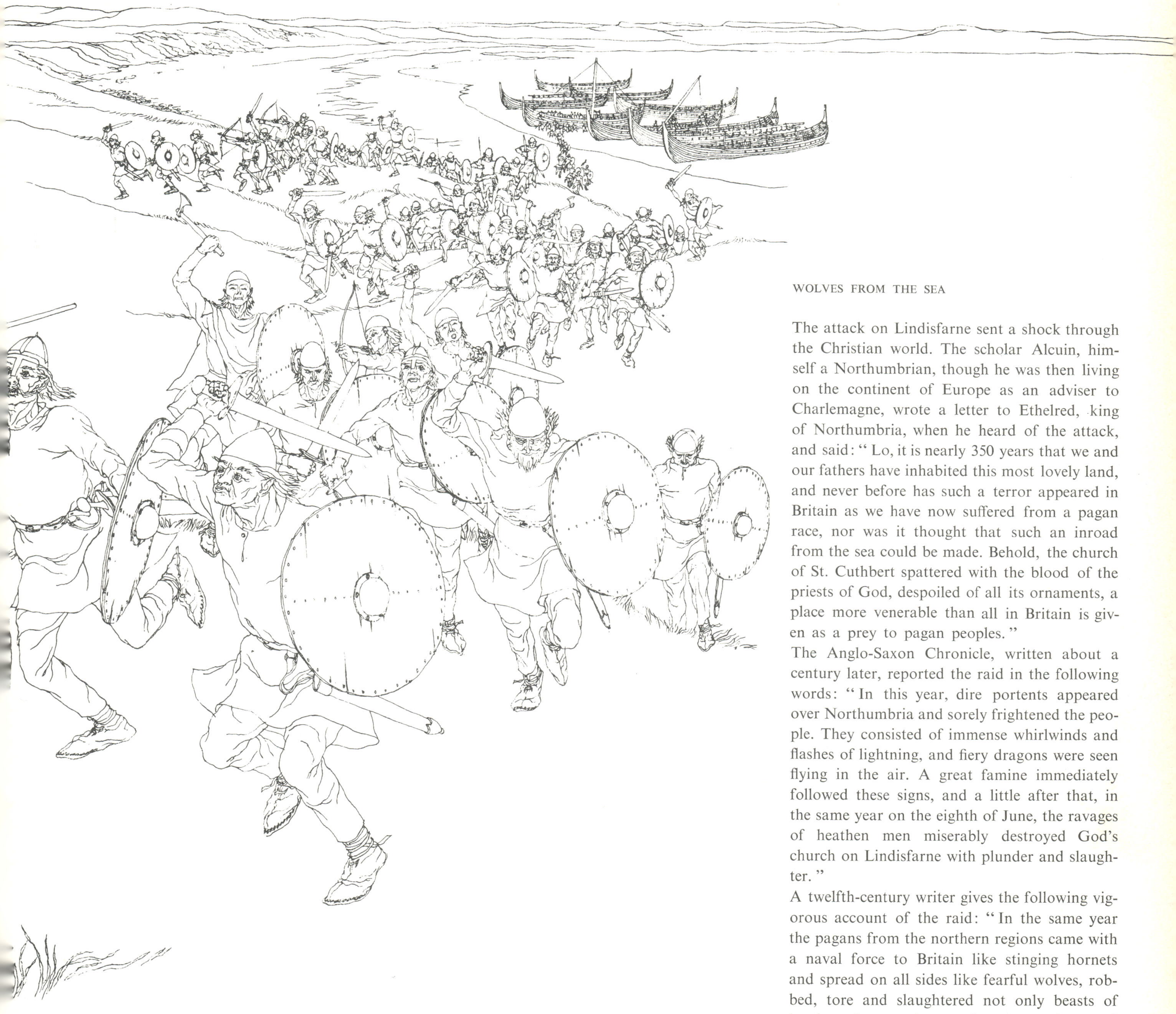

WOLVES FROM THE SEA

The attack on Lindisfarne sent a shock through the Christian world. The scholar Alcuin, himself a Northumbrian, though he was then living on the continent of Europe as an adviser to Charlemagne, wrote a letter to Ethelred, king of Northumbria, when he heard of the attack, and said: " Lo, it is nearly 350 years that we and our fathers have inhabited this most lovely land, and never before has such a terror appeared in Britain as we have now suffered from a pagan race, nor was it thought that such an inroad from the sea could be made. Behold, the church of St. Cuthbert spattered with the blood of the priests of God, despoiled of all its ornaments, a place more venerable than all in Britain is given as a prey to pagan peoples. "

The Anglo-Saxon Chronicle, written about a century later, reported the raid in the following words: " In this year, dire portents appeared over Northumbria and sorely frightened the people. They consisted of immense whirlwinds and flashes of lightning, and fiery dragons were seen flying in the air. A great famine immediately followed these signs, and a little after that, in the same year on the eighth of June, the ravages of heathen men miserably destroyed God's church on Lindisfarne with plunder and slaughter. "

A twelfth-century writer gives the following vigorous account of the raid: " In the same year the pagans from the northern regions came with a naval force to Britain like stinging hornets and spread on all sides like fearful wolves, robbed, tore and slaughtered not only beasts of burden, sheep and oxen, but even priests and deacons, and companies of monks and nuns. And they came to the church of Lindisfarne, laid everything waste with grievous plundering, trampled the holy places with polluted steps, dug up the altars and seized all the treasures of the holy church. They killed some of the brothers, took some away with them in fetters, many they drove out, naked and loaded with insults, some they drowned in the sea. "

+ mid uncre clænan feo ðæt ðonne wæs mid clæne golde. Ond ðæt wit deodan for godes lufan ond for uncre saule ðear

Aelfr

XPI AUTEM GENERATIO SIC ERAT CUM ESSET DESPONSATA MATER EIUS MARIA IOSEPH ANTEQUAM CONVENIRENT INVENTA EST IN UTERO HABENS

Pbil

Alhdr eou

Ond forðon ðe wit noldan ðæt ðas halgan bec lencg in ðære hæðenesse wunaden, ond nu willað heo gesellan inn to Cristes circan gode to lofe ond to wuldre ond to weorðunga ond his ðrowunga to ðoncunga, ond ðæm godcundan geferscipe to bruc ðe in Cristes circan dæghwæmlice godes lof rærað, to ðæm gerade ðæt heo mon arede eghwelce monaðe for Aelfred ond for Werburge ond for Alhðryðe heora saulum to ecum lecedome. Ða hwile ðe god gesegen hæbbe ðæt fulwiht æt ðeosse stowe beon mote... Ec swelce ic Aelfred dux ond Werburg biddað ond halsiað on godes almaehtiges noman ond on allra

Throughout the early years of the tenth century, Alfred's son Edward the Elder strove mightily to contain the Viking threat from the north and east, and to reassert the authority of his dynasty over Danish-occupied territories. The English began to build fortifications in a determined way, and with great success. The south of England was straddled by a series of at least thirty boroughs, as these fortresses were called, and from 910 onwards they were used as bases for the reconquest of Danish-occupied England. Such camps were certainly on a much larger scale than those of the ninth century. For example, the borough of Witham in Essex, built by King Edward in 912, consisted of an elaborate maze of embankments and ditches covering a total area of twenty-seven acres. Witham is an exception, not in the scale of its defences, but in the fact that it was never developed into anything more than a camp. Some of these fortifications were constructed around existing towns, like those at Worcester and Winchester. In other cases the fortification quickly became a local centre of economic and administrative importance, and many, like Warwick, grew into the chief town of the shire. These boroughs were constructed, maintained and manned by local forces drawn from the countryside around. The arrangements for this are well known because of a tenth century text known as the Burghal Hidage, in which many boroughs are named and the assessed area to support them is given. At Winchester, arrangements were made to defend 3,300 yards of wall, which is so close to the 3,280-yard length of the old Roman walls that it is clear the defences were based on those of the Roman town. Before Edward's death, he was accepted as king by all men living south of the river Humber, English and Danes alike. North of the Humber, the Scandinavian settlers seemed more secure. The native Northumbrians had little love for their southern neighbours, and may even have welcomed the Vikings for the help they could provide in resisting the pretensions of the kings of Wessex. The original Danish settlers in the north were soon joined by Vikings from the west, men of Norwegian descent who had at first settled in Ireland, and then been driven out. Early in the tenth century, in any case, Norwegian adventurers from Ireland established themselves as kings of York. But the Northumbrian attempt to assert independence finally failed in 954 when the last Scandinavian king of York, Eric Bloodaxe, was expelled and killed. England was then, at last, united. But it was not for long to be left in peace.

In 978 King Edward the Martyr was murdered and his place was taken by his half-brother Ethelred. Within two years a fresh series of Viking attacks

A HOLY BOOK RANSOMED

The picture on the facing page is taken from the Codex Aureus in Stockholm, a gospel book made in England in the eighth century. At some time in the ninth century, it was taken as loot by Viking raiders, and bought back by one Earl Alfred, whose recovery of the book is recorded in the English text written at the top and bottom of the page. This begins: "In nomine domini nostri Jesu Christi. *I, Earl Alfred, and Werberg my wife, have acquired this book from a heathen army with our true money, that is, with pure gold, and this we have done for the love of God and for the good of our souls, and because we were not willing that this holy book should remain any longer in heathen hands. And we now desire to give it to Christ Church [Canterbury] for the praise and glory and worship of God and as a thank-offering for His Passion and for the use of the religious community which daily celebrates God's praise in Christ Church.*"

A KING'S REEVE DIES

At almost the same time as the attack on Lindisfarne, another raid (reconstructed at left) was reported from the south coast of England. For the West Saxon chronicler who told of it, "those were the first ships of the Danish men which came to the land of the English." The chronicler calls them Danes, but he also says that they came from Horthaland, that is, from Norway. The account preserved in another version of the Chronicle is precise and extraordinarily effective: "When the very pious king Brihtric was ruling over the domains of the West Saxons, the people spread over their fields were then making furrows in the grimy earth in serene tranquillity, and the burden-bearing frames (i.e. *sides) of the oxen placed their necks under the yoke in nearest love. Suddenly a not very large fleet of the Danes arrived, speedy vessels to the number of three; that was their first arrival. At the report, the king's reeve (a royal official with duties like a steward) who was then in the town called Dorchester, leapt on his horse, sped to the harbour with a few men (for he thought they were merchants rather than marauders) and admonishing them in an authoritative manner gave orders that they should be driven to the royal town. And he and his companions were killed by them on the spot. The name of the reeve was Beaduheard."*

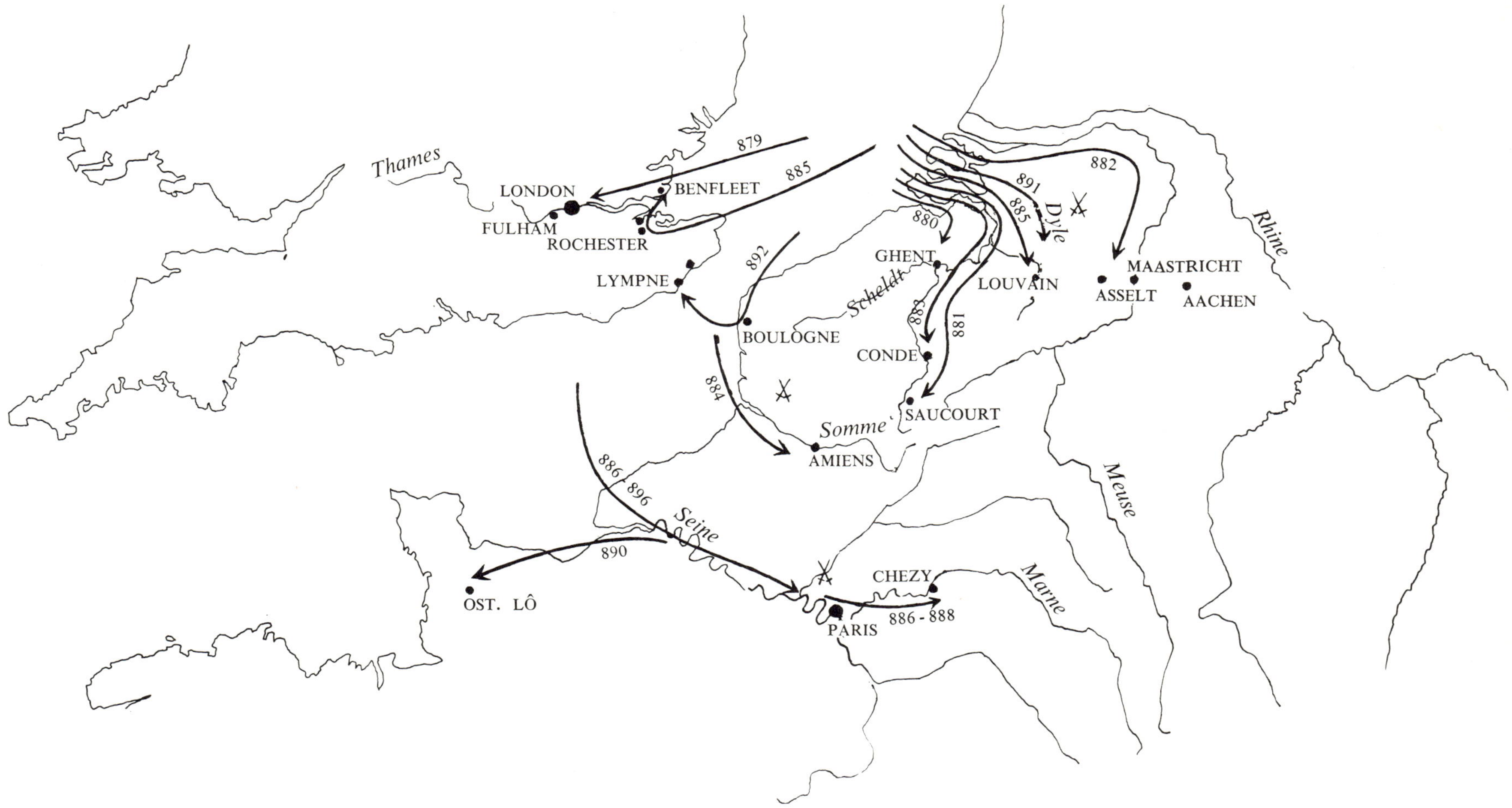

MOBILITY: THE MAIN VIKING WEAPON

For four years, beginning in 892, King Alfred was engaged in a bitter struggle against the second great Danish army to land in England. The chronicler who told of his efforts was careful to describe the movements of this army before it attacked England, and the map above tracing their progress back and forth across the Channel is based on his account. It shows the extreme mobility of the raiders, and the difficulty of maintaining an effective defence against them in an age when regular standing armies and navies were rare.

began, soon developing into large-scale raids. This new generation of Vikings came not for land, like their predecessors in the ninth century, but for booty, which they found in huge quantities, for England was then rich.

Among the leaders of these renewed attacks were such men as Olaf Tryggvason of Norway, who in 991 won a famous victory (celebrated in one of the greatest Anglo-Saxon poems) over the English forces at Maldon in Essex. Leaders like Olaf, or the Dane Svein Forkbeard, soon overcame the defensive system that had been so effective against the earlier settlers. In 1009, for example, a Viking army, in the words of a contemporary, "journeyed as it pleased" and burned the borough of Oxford; an act of destruction that is confirmed by numismatic evidence, for the Oxford mint ceased to produce coins from that year until the end of Ethelred's reign. In the following year the boroughs of Thetford, Cambridge and Northampton were burned. The essence of the English problem was that they were facing a mobile enemy interested not in land, but in tribute. The English could have coped with a settled enemy with the boroughs — they had shown how to do that a century before — but the latter were less successful against the raiders of Ethelred's reign, not just because many of the defences had by then fallen into disrepair, but because the raiders bypassed them if they were well-held. The popular idea of Ethelred as being "Unready" is not therefore, entirely deserved; and in any case this adjective is a

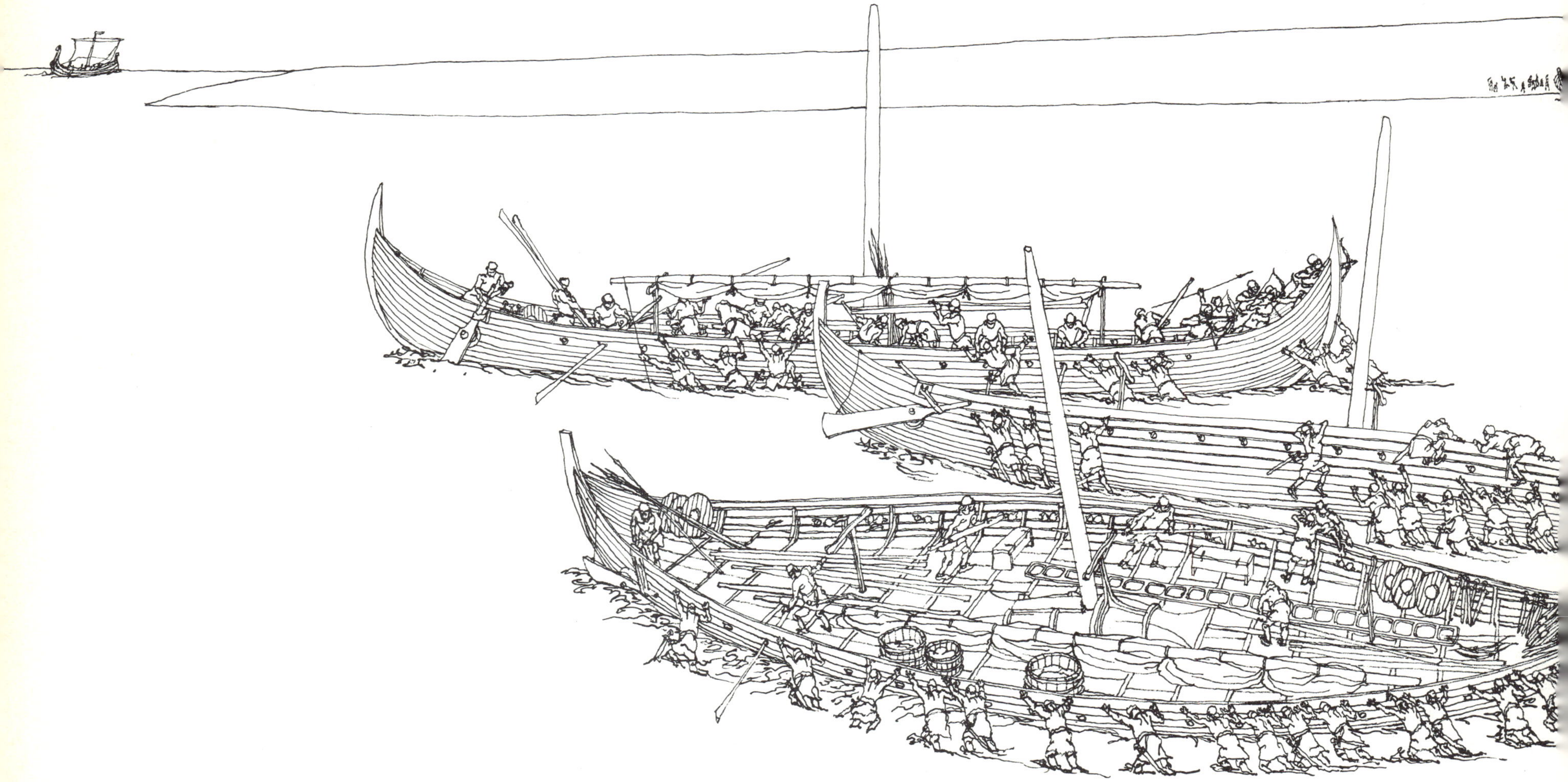

mistranslation of the Anglo-Saxon word "redeless" which meant "ill-advised". The continued usefulness of defences at key points was shown by Olaf of Norway's unsuccessful attack on London, also in 1009.

The renewed onslaught from the Northmen reawakened interest in sea defences. Early in the eleventh century King Ethelred "ordered that ships should be built unremittingly over all England." Towards the end of his reign, he began to employ Scandinavian mercenaries, and in 1012 some forty-two longships "came over to the king and they promised to defend this country." The problem of naval defence was to maintain a fleet in a constant state of readiness, and there was the additional difficulty that a wind favouring an attacking fleet would tend to blow the defenders away. The advantage always lay heavily with the invaders.

In the end the Danes conquered England, and in 1016 A.D. Cnut the Great, Svein Forkbeard's son, was accepted by the English as their king. The pagan warrior became a Christian, a benefactor of churches and a pilgrim to Rome. He, or one of his advisers, wrote: "I humbly render thanks to Almighty God who has permitted me in my lifetime to visit his holy apostles, Peter and Paul, and all the sacred places of which I could learn, either within or without the city of Rome, and to worship and adore them in person there in accordance

ALFRED'S NEW SHIPS IN ACTION

The best description of a naval battle against the Vikings is found in the Anglo-Saxon Chronicle under the year 896 A.D. An episode is reconstructed in the drawing above. "Six ships came to the Isle of Wight and did great harm there, both in Devon and everywhere along the coast. Then the king ordered [a force] to go thither with nine of the new ships, and they blocked the estuary from the seaward end. Then the Danes went out against them with three ships, and three were on dry land further up the estuary; the men from them had gone up on land. Then the English captured two of those three ships at the entrance to the estuary, and killed the men, and the one ship escaped. On it also the men were killed except five. These got away because the ships of their opponents ran aground. Moreover, they had run aground very awkwardly: three were aground on that side of the channel on which the Danish ships were aground, and all [the others] on the

other side, so that none of them could get to the others. But when the water had ebbed many furlongs from the ships, the Danes from the remaining three ships went to the other three which were stranded on their side, and they then fought there. And there were killed the king's reeve Lucuman, Wulfheard the Frisian, Aebba the Frisian, Aethelhere the Frisian, Aethelfrith the king's geneat*, and in all sixty-two Frisians and English and 120 of the Danes. Then, however, the tide reached the Danish ships before the Christian could launch theirs, and therefore they rowed away out. They were then so wounded that they could not row past Sussex, but the sea cast two of them onto the land, and the men were brought to Winchester to the king, and he ordered them to be hanged. And the men who were on the one ship reached East Anglia greatly wounded."

* Companion

with my desire." Cnut may have been transformed, but England was not. There was no great wave of land-grabbing such as followed the Norman Conquest fifty years later, and Cnut ruled in all respects just like an English king, except that he maintained a force of Scandinavian mercenaries who were paid by a tax levied on the English. His sons who succeeded him continued the practice, and one of them, Harthacnut, was well-hated for his extortion. Eventually the kingship passed back to Alfred's heirs, to Ethelred's son, Edward, known as the Confessor. The threats from Scandinavia continued. Magnus of Norway and Svein Estrithson of Denmark both thought they had claims on the English throne, and the threat of Scandinavian invasion was only eliminated by the defeat of King Harold Hardrada of Norway by Harold of England at Stamford Bridge in 1066, about two weeks before the battle of Hastings, and, later, by the failure of a plan by the Danish king Cnut the Saint to invade England in 1085. The Norman Conquest meant that for centuries England was to be ruled by men with important and extensive interests in France. Except for the fact that William the Conqueror had in his veins the blood of the Viking conquerors of Normandy, the links between England and Scandinavia in this period were economic and religious, not political or dynastic.

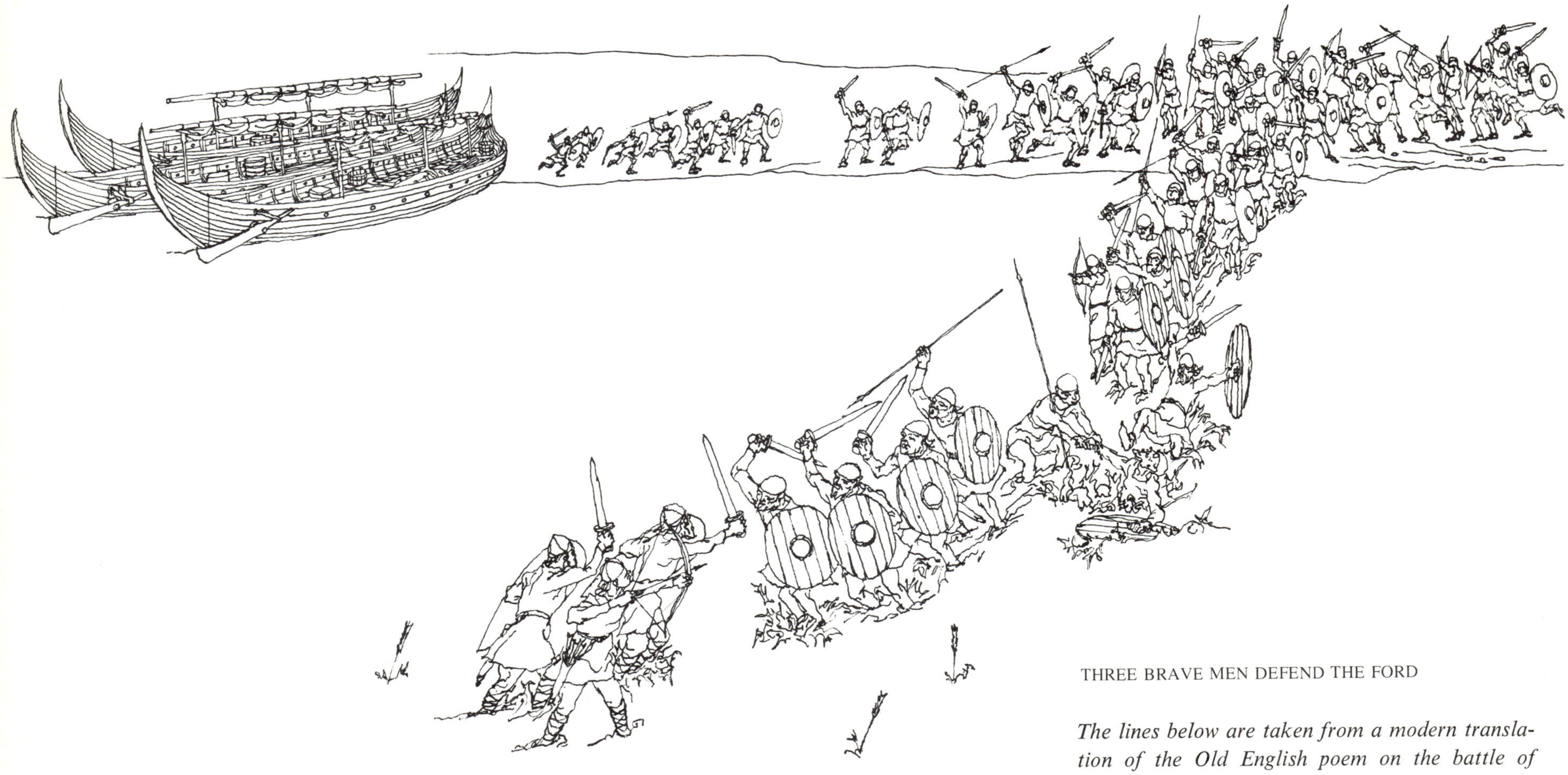

THREE BRAVE MEN DEFEND THE FORD

The lines below are taken from a modern translation of the Old English poem on the battle of Maldon. This famous battle, which ended in an English defeat, was fought in 991 between an English force led by Brihtnoth (Byrhtnoth in the poem) and a Viking army. The latter had landed on the isle of Northey in the estuary of the river Blackwater, which was connected with the mainland at low tide by a ford. The two sides could not come to grips with each other. But as the water ebbed the Vikings crossed. They were held up for a time by three Englishmen, Wulfstan, Aelfhere and Maccus:

Then Byrhtnoth, brave protector of his men, ordered
A warrior, Wulfstan by name, to defend the ford.
He was Ceola's son, outstanding for his courage
amongst courageous men.
He struck the first seafarer with his spear
Who stepped intrepidly into the ford.
Two experienced warriors stood with Wulfstan,
Aelfhere and Maccus, both brave men.
Nothing could have made them take flight at the ford.
They would have defended it
For as long as they could wield their weapons.
But as it was, the Danes found the dauntless guardians
Of the ford too fierce for their liking . . .

KING CNUT AS A CHRISTIAN CONVERT

This pen drawing was made early in the reign of Cnut, and comes from the Liber Vitæ *of New Minster, Winchester. It shows Cnut, now a Christian king, with his wife Aelfgifu, placing a cross on the altar of New Minster.*

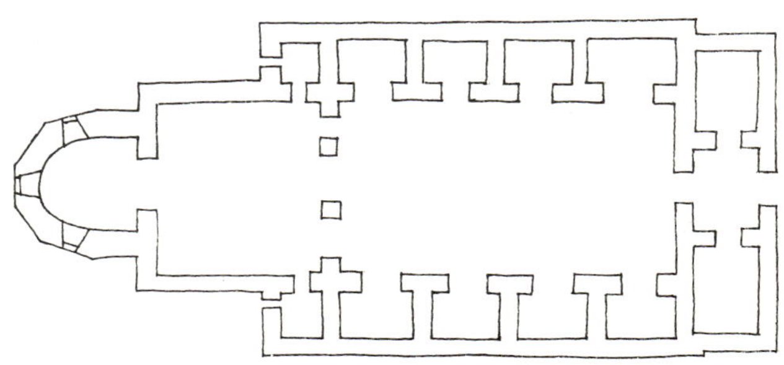

A CHURCH 1300 YEARS OLD

Brixworth Church (right), near Northampton, built in Roman brick and tile in the late seventh century, is one of the most remarkable monuments from the Europe of the Dark Ages. The tower was enlarged in the tenth century by the addition of a spiral straircase, and originally the central body of the church was surrounded by small chapels. But even in its present altered state it provides an idea of the kind of building encountered by the Vikings when they plundered the Christian west. It is shown without its later spire.

No one knows how many Scandinavians settled in England in the ninth and early tenth centuries. Contemporary writers, all of them Christian churchmen, naturally dwelt more on Vikings as raiders and plunderers than as settlers. The Anglo-Saxon Chronicle's account of the settlement in England is consequently very slight. In fact the only useful sources of information are linguistic evidence, and names. The language spoken by the Norse newcomers was closely related to the language of the English. But there were many differences of vocabulary and pronunciation, and the dialect of the areas in which the Scandinavians settled was greatly affected by them. Some important and useful English words, such as "them", "they", and "take" are of Scandinavian origin. The Scandinavian influence on placenames is even more obvious. The Vikings brought with them a fairly distinctive stock of personal names and words, which they used to describe farms and villages, hills, streams, woods and fields. Where the English would call a farm or a village a *tun*, from which we get the modern "town", the Scandinavians used their own word *by*, which means the same thing and is commonly used nowadays in the word by-law, meaning, literally, the law of the village. The English placenames Stanton and Stainby mean the same thing, but one is English and the other Scandinavian. When the Scandinavians used their own personal names, the contrast is sometimes even more marked: Aismunderby in Yorkshire and Osmondeston in Norfolk are basically the same name, but one, "Aismund's by", is Scandinavian, while the other, "Osmond's tun", is English. In the north and east of England a large number of such names are still in use; over 700, for example, end in *by*, and many others have the element *thorp*, meaning a lesser settlement. The study of these names can reveal a great deal about the extent of Viking settlements, about the main areas of colonization, and about the intermixture of the English and Scandinavian populations. It is also possible to distinguish Norwegians from Danes. If there is still disagreement about the number of colonists, there is no doubt that in most parts of the country the Scandinavian settlers and conquerors did not so much displace the English homesteaders as establish new homes on land that was as yet unoccupied. This was clearly the case in the north-west of England, where men of Norwegian descent settled in the late ninth century on land that was very thinly populated, or may, indeed, have been entirely free of human settlements. The areas of intense Scandinavian settlement were probably very limited in extent, and many of them were outside the main centres of population and wealth.

The Scandinavians were, however, conquerors as well as settlers, and in

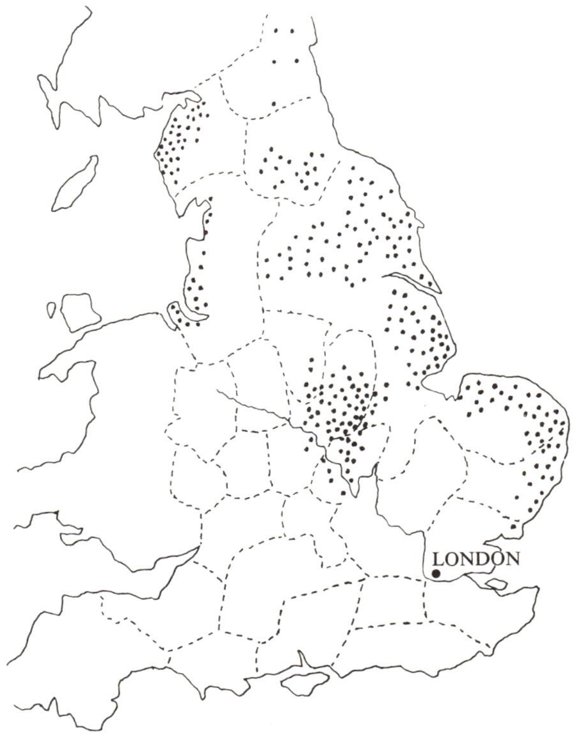

VIKING ENGLAND

The map above shows English parishes which still have Scandinavian names. It also shows the line of the boundary agreed between King Alfred and the Danish leader Guthrum, probably soon after Alfred's capture of London in 886. According to their treaty the border was said to run "up the Thames, and then up the Lea, and along the Lea to its source, then in a straight line to Bedford, then up the Ouse to the Watling Street."

many parts of England, Scandinavian warriors replaced English lords. One such place was probably Middleton in the Vale of Pickering in Yorkshire, a village with an unmistakably English name but where, in the church, there are a number of crosses with distinctive Scandinavian ornament, two of them bearing representations of an easily recognizable Scandinavian burial. These must have been erected by the descendants of some Scandinavian chieftain who made his home in the village. Even so, the newcomers, particularly the relatively wealthy ones who settled in such villages as Middleton, soon became indistinguishable from the English, and acknowledged an English king. The Scandinavian conquests of English settlements were short-lived and had little effect on the main development of English history. Scandinavian settlements on new land, however, were far more significant, because their efforts at making a living in the north and east contributed greatly to the economic improvement that, in the eleventh century, made England such a rich and tempting prize to later Viking raiders.

THE VIKINGS CONVERTED

One of the remarkable Scandinavian-Christian crosses from the church at Middleton in Yorkshire. The panel shown here depicts a typical pagan Viking burial.

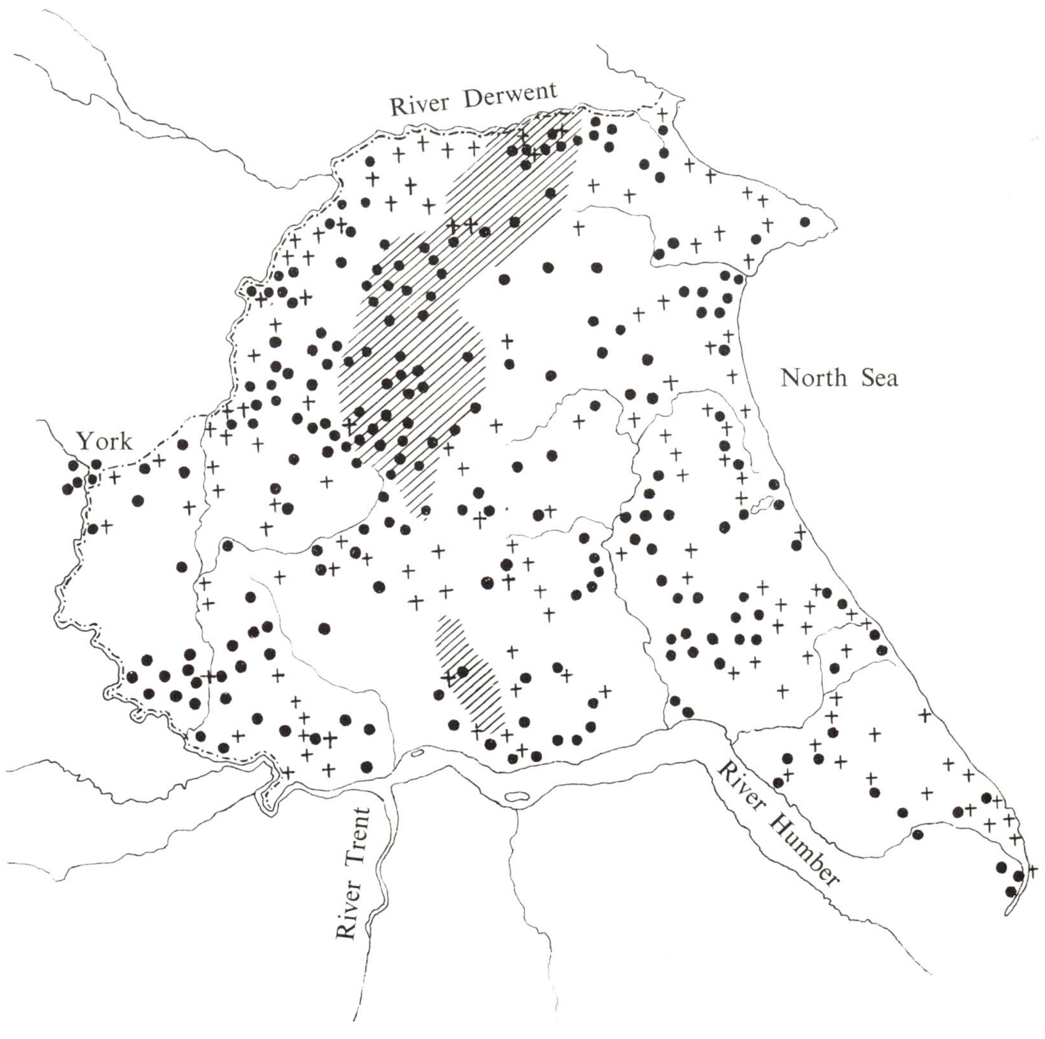

THE NEIGHBOURS

The map on the right shows part of the East Riding of Yorkshire with the large number of Scandinavian placenames that are found there. The best sites, with convenient access to the hills above and to the low-lying ground, generally have English names. There is a concentration of Scandinavian names, shown as dots, on the waterless Wolds (shaded areas). Others are less important settlements below the line of English settlements (the crosses).

On September 26th, 1066, Harold, king of England, won one of the most significant victories in the history of medieval warfare. At Stamford Bridge the English showed that they had the answer to precisely the kind of mobile threat that had been posed by recent generations of Viking raiders. These marauders depended for their success on the speedy movement of relatively large bodies of well-armed men, and the psychological effect of their sudden appearance where they were least expected was as important an element in their success as their military skill. The real answer lay in being able quickly to mobilize a force adequate to counter the invaders wherever they popped up. That is exactly what the English Harold did at Stamford Bridge. His predecessor as king, Edward the Confessor, had left no heirs with strong direct claims. Harold, as Earl of Wessex, was the most powerful man in England, and being on the spot, was able to get himself crowned as soon as Edward was buried. However, in 1038 or 1039 Magnus king of Norway and Harthacnut, the last Danish king of England, had agreed that if either died without an heir, his kingdom should pass to the survivor. Harthacnut died without an heir, and Harald Hardrada, who succeeded Magnus as king of Norway, considered that the latter's rights had passed on to him. Allied to Harold of England's disaffected brother Tostig, he landed in the north of England, and on Thursday, September 20th, 1066 fought and won a battle against the local forces. When he then began proceeding the traditional way, demanding hostages and preparing to move south, he found himself forestalled by the unexpected arrival of the English king. The latter had made a forced march, probably from the south of England, and with the minimum of delay the Norwegians were brought to battle and defeated. Meanwhile, a second threat was developing to the south. William, Duke of Normandy, also considered that he had a strong claim to the English throne. It seems likely that Edward the Confessor had recognized William as his heir, probably during William's visit to England in 1051-52. Furthermore, when Harold had fallen into William's hands after being shipwrecked on the French coast in about 1064, he had solemnly acknowledged William as his lord and promised to help him to the English throne, or so William claimed. Harold can only have done this in order to escape from William's clutches, and regarded the oath as an empty one extracted under duress. When Harold gained the English crown, William proclaimed him an oath-breaker and prepared to make good his claim by force. Three days after Harold's victory in the north, William of Normandy made his long-awaited landing at Pevensey Bay, near Hastings. He knew what was

A CONFRONTATION OF COINS

The silver penny on top, showing King Ethelred, was struck about 1009. Below it is a coin of King Cnut, his Danish rival, with a portrait of the king in profile. Many coins like these found their way to Scandinavia in the purses of mercenaries employed by Cnut.

HOW THEY FOUGHT AT STAMFORD BRIDGE

From *Heimskringla*:
Now the battle began. The Englishmen made a hot assault upon the Northmen, who sustained it bravely. And the fight at first was but loose and light, as long as the Northmen kept their order of battle; the English could do nothing against them. But when the Northmen thought they perceived that the enemy were making but weak assaults, they set after them, meaning to drive them into flight; but, when they had broken their shield-rampart, the Englishmen rode up from all sides, and threw arrows and spears on them. Now when King Harald Sigurdsson saw this, he went into the fray where the greatest clash of weapons was. There was a sharp conflict, and many people fell on both sides. King Harald then was in such a rage that he ran out in front of his men, and hewed down with both hands; neither helmet nor armour could withstand him, and all who were nearest gave way before him. It was then very near with the English that they had taken to flight.
King Harald Sigurdsson was hit by an arrow in the throat, and that was his death-wound; he fell, and all who had advanced with him, except those who retired with the banner. There was afterwards the warmest conflict, and Earl Tosti had taken over the king's banner. They began on both sides to form their array again, and for a long time there was a pause in the fighting. But before the battle began again, Harold Godwinesson offered his brother Earl Tosti peace, and also quarter to the Northmen who were still alive; but the Northmen called out all of them together that they would rather fall, one across the other, than accept of quarter from the Englishmen. They set up a war-shout, and the battle began again. Eystein Orri came up at this moment from the ships, with the men who followed him, and all were clad in armour. Then Eystein got King Harald's banner Land-Ravager. And now was, for the third time, one of the sharpest of conflicts; many of the Englishmen fell, and they were near to taking flight. This conflict is called Orri's storm. Eystein and his men had hastened so fast from the ships that they were quite exhausted, and scarcely fit to fight before they came into the battle; but afterwards they became so furious, that they did not guard themselves with their shields as long as they could stand upright. At last they threw off their coats of ring-mail, and then the Englishmen could easily lay their blows at them; and many fell from weariness, and died without a wound. Almost all the leaders of the Northmen fell.

needed, and had carefully prepared his fleet for the invasion. These preparations are well depicted in the Bayeux Tapestry, which also shows the landing itself with the horses stepping out of William's low, shallow-draught Viking ships. Harold was almost certainly still at York when he heard of the landing. He made a dramatic march south, covering the 250 miles in thirteen days. This achievement was the more remarkable when it is remembered that he had only shortly before made a similar rapid march north. He clearly recognized the need for speed, and his main mistake may well have been his over-confidence, which he paid for with his life at the battle of Hastings on October 14th.
William's landing proved the last successful operation of its kind to be mounted on a large scale in English history. The changes in the techniques of ship construction, which the needs of developing European commerce demanded, would in any case have made it difficult to stage an amphibious operation of this kind in the twelfth or thirteenth centuries. The traditional type of Viking ship continued to be used in Scandinavia, but generally for fighting in home waters, not for crossing the open sea. And even in Scandinavia there were changes leading to the development of larger fighting ships. The new need there was not so much for landing craft as for fighting platforms, and the advantage naturally lay with the larger ship that could command a battle. This was recognized and demonstrated by the Norwegian king Sverrir with his great *Mariasuden*, which, although unseaworthy, won its critical fight.
William himself was threatened by Scandinavian invasions. The most serious attack was that planned by Cnut of Denmark for the year 1085. The contemporary English chronicler describes how, when William found out about this, "he went to England with a larger force of mounted men and infantry from France and Brittany than had ever come to this country, so that people wondered how this country could maintain all that army. And the king had all the army dispersed all over the country among his vassals, and they provisioned the army each in proportion to his land." The real key in such operations lay, once again, in rapid mobilization and maintenance of an effective force. William found the answer in mercenaries, whose services could only be commanded by cash, which would also be needed to equip and keep them. The fact that England was rich had made it a prize worth attacking. But eventually, once the nature of the attacks and how to counteract them had been recognized, it was the richness of England that enabled her to insure herself militarily against invasion.

Ireland was much set upon by Vikings in the ninth and tenth centuries. The first attackers were Norwegians, whose landings seem to have been extensions of their settlement of Orkney, Shetland and the Hebrides. Already before the end of the eighth century the Annals of Ulster report: "Patrick's Island was burned by the Gentiles; and they took away tribute from the provinces, and Dochonna's shrine was broken by them, and other great incursions were made by them, both in Ireland and in Scotland." In the following years such attacks were common, and the Irish chronicles are full of tales of destruction and pillage by these pagan strangers from the north. Many such tales were exaggerated. One chronicler wrote: "The entire town of Munster, without distinction, was plundered by them, on all sides, and devastated. And they spread themselves over Munster; and they build duns,* camps and fortresses, and landing-ports all over Erinn, so that there was no place in Erinn without numerous fleets of Danes and pirates; so that they made spoil-land and sword-land and conquered-land of her, throughout her breadth and generally; and they ravaged her chieftainries and her privileged churches and her sanctuaries and they rent her shrines and her reliquaries and her books. They demolished her beautiful ornamented temples; for neither veneration, nor honour, nor mercy for Termonn [sanctuaries] nor protection for Church or for sanctuary, for God or for man was felt by this furious, ferocious, pagan, ruthless, wrathful people. In short, until the sand of the sea or the grass of the field or the stars of heaven are counted, it will not be easy to recount or to enumerate or to relate what the Irish all, without distinction, suffered from them; whether men or women, boys or girls, lay or clerks, free men or serfs, old or young; indignity, outrage, injury and oppression." The purpose of the raiders seems to have been the search for plunder rather than land; neither archaeology nor place-names suggest that the Scandinavian settlements in Ireland were dense or extensive. Their main holdings were along the coast where, in such centres as Dublin and Waterford, they established trading towns that later grew in importance. The monasteries of Ireland may well have attracted raiders because of their riches of gold and silver, and the hoard of silver objects recently found in the Shetlands on St. Ninian's Isle may well be the profits of such raids. The plundering expeditions of the Vikings were made easier by the complex and accessible system of rivers that reach far into the island. None of the holy places of Ireland was far from the coast or such inland waterways,

* hilltop camps

THE ISLE OF MAN

For the Scandinavian chieftains and traders who sailed the Irish Sea, the Isle of Man must have been a prominent landmark. The Scandinavians did not, however, simply use the islands as a landmark, they settled there. Scandinavian influence is revealed in such placenames as Ramsey or Laxey and in the Viking graves and ornate memorial stones that are found there, often in Christian burial grounds. It is significant that the unity once created by these Scandinavian seamen who pillaged Iona and other churches should be commemorated in a Christian diocese. The see of Sodor and Man unites the Isle of Man with the Sudreys, the Southern Isles, the name the Scandinavians gave to the Hebrides.

ODIN IS EATEN, CHRIST IS VICTORIOUS

The Thorwald cross at Andreas, in the northern part of the Isle of Man, is on a stone slab. Beside it is depicted a scene from the legendary Norse poem Ragnarök, "*Doomsday of the Gods*", *in which the great god Odin is eaten by the wolf Fenris. Another side of the same slab depicts the coming of Christianity, represented by a figure bearing a cross and a Bible.*

IRELAND AND THE IRISH SEA IN THE VIKING AGE

This map shows the principal places and main rivers, and towns in Britain that had trade connections with Ireland. The Irish kingdoms and their boundaries are not included, as they did not remain permanent throughout the Viking Age.

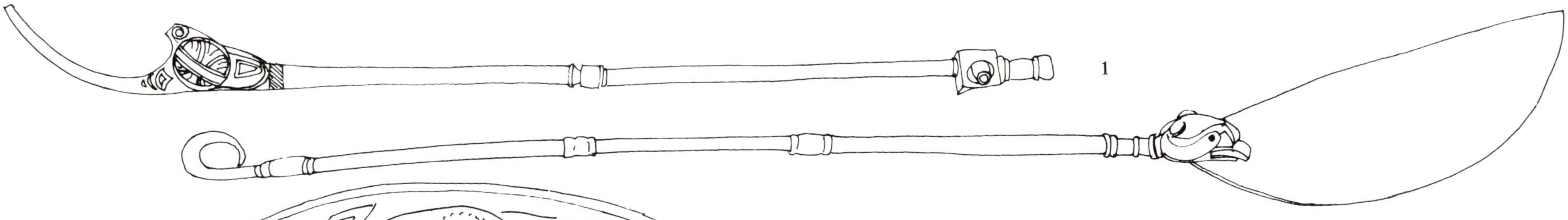

1

2

3

4

5

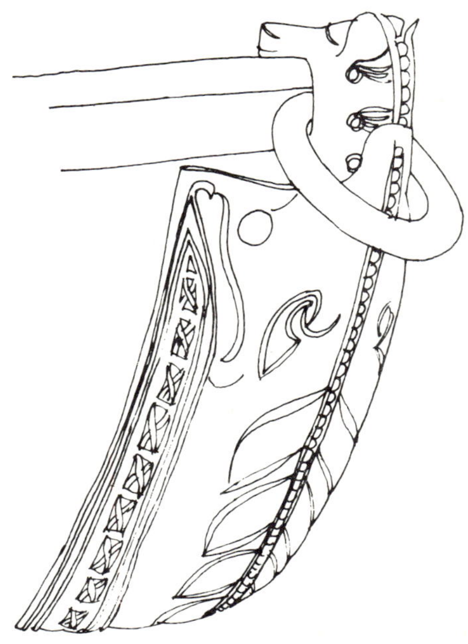

6

and they all suffered in consequence. The raiders were also aided by the bitter internal rivalry between warring Irish clans and chiefs and by the fact that some Irish hoped to use the Vikings as useful allies.

A number of Irish went into exile to escape the ravages of the heathens, some of them finding refuge in the Carolingian lands, in places like Liège, Laon and Rheims. These men brought books and drawings which had some influence on the thought and art of the time. The most famous of all these Irish emigrés was John Scottus, the great philosopher who was one of the few men in his time to master Greek. In the margins of a book brought from Ireland at this period is a little verse which reflects the fear of the Vikings that drove some men from their native land:

Bitter is the wind tonight
In tosses the ocean's white hair.
Tonight I fear not the fierce warriors of Norway
Coursing the Irish Sea.

The Irish were not the only emigrants from Ireland in the ninth century. Within a century of their first attacks, men of Norwegian descent were leaving Ireland to search for new homes westward toward Iceland or eastwards in England. The reasons for this are not clear. The Scandinavians who stayed on in Ireland were those interested in war or in trade, but for both, the key area was the Irish Sea. There were several attempts in the first half of the tenth century to join Dublin and York together under the rule of one chieftain, and after these had failed, the men of Dublin, the Ost men, so called because of their Scandinavian or eastern origin, were active in a trade that joined the west of France, Bristol, Chester and the Scandinavian north. The commercial importance of the towns, and of Dublin in particular, survived the great military defeat of the Scandinavian intruders at the famous battle of Clontarf, outside Dublin, in 1014. In this battle, the great men on both sides, Brian, king of the Irish, and Sigurth from Orkney, both fell. But the king of Dublin, Sigtrygg Silkbeard, took no part, and watched the battle from the security of Dublin, which he continued to rule profitably for another twenty years.

BURIED TREASURE, PERHAPS FROM IRELAND

For ten centuries, a treasure which may be loot from a Viking raid on Ireland lay buried in the remains of a tiny, pre-Viking church on St. Ninian's Isle, a lonely dot of land in the southern Shetlands not far north of Jarlshof. Some of the articles are bowls, brooches and sword furniture, but others are of ecclesiastical origin.

1. *Communion spoon, with dog's head lapping from the bowl, and a one-pronged edged implement possibly used for cutting and picking up the Host.*
2. *Bowl with design of four pairs of animals.*
3. *Sword-pommel, once gilded. It has a silver pin inside, possibly for using the pommel as a brooch.*
4. *Inscribed hooped mounting with animal heads. It may have been a protective tip for a sword scabbard, or else a weight for a stole.*
5. *Silver bowl with loop attachments for hanging up.*
6. *Detail of underside of the hanging bowl, showing a spreadeagled dog or boar.*

Among the most northward Atlantic islands are the Faroes, or "islands of sheep." They are difficult to approach, with steep jagged cliffs rising from rough seas. But above are green fields, and a climate so mild that the sheep which have given the islands their name can stay out all the year round. For some reason, however, there have never been any trees on the Faroes. There were no true "aboriginal" people there. But when the first Norwegians came to the Faroe Islands they nevertheless found some inhabitants. About 825 A.D. the Irish monk Dicuil said in his book *De Mensura Orbis Terra* (Concerning the Distances of the Earth) that: "For a century the hermit's life has brought large numbers of Irish monks to the many islands in the northern part of the British Sea, which one could reach from the north British islands in two days and nights when the wind was favourable. Those islands, uninhabited and unnamed since the world began, have now been abandoned by the hermits in consequence of the arrival of Scandinavian pirates. There are countless sheep and a lot of different seabirds to be found . . ." The islands alluded to may include Iceland, but at any rate they certainly include the Faroes, because the rest of the Atlantic island groups, even the most distant of the Shetlands, could be reached in half of the stated sailing time. The reasons for the Viking settlement appear to have been the search for new land to cultivate, due to a shortage of land in the homeland, and emigration in protest against King Harald Fairhair's régime, which also characterized the emigration to Iceland. The Faroes have their own saga, *Färoeinga Saga*, which was written down in Iceland about 1200 A.D.: "There was a man called Grim Kamban," runs the saga, "He was the first one who settled in the Faroe Islands in Harald Fairhair's time. At the time many left the country because of the king's lust for power. Some settled down on the Faroe Islands and cultivated new land there." The Icelandic historian Snorre Sturluson says that in the summer the colonists cruised back to their former homes in Norway to ravage there.

At Tjörnuvik on the island of Streymöy, a small graveyard from the tenth century has been found. The only object which could be dated is a ring-headed pin of bronze, of Scottish type. At Kvivik, also on Streymöy, two house-sites have been excavated, both of a well-known oval shape with a "long-fire" in the middle of the floor, which have these and other features in common with the Lindholm Höje site in Denmark. However, they cannot be dated more accurately than around the year 1000. A similar house-site is known in Fuglafjördur on the island of Eysturoy.

THE FAROES

These bleak islands are situated in the North Atlantic, about midway between Scotland and Iceland, and 415 miles from Norway. Traces of Viking settlement have been found at Tjörnuvik and Kvívík on Streymöy, and at Fuglafjordur on Eysturöy.
The total area of the twenty-one islands is approximately 540 square miles. Narrow waters and dangerous currents separate them.

THE ISLANDS OF SHEEP

The Faroese landscape, seen at right at the village of Kirkeby, is bleak and windswept, consisting of bare rock and grass lashed by the wind and the sea. It must have reminded the Viking settlers of the islands off the Atlantic coast of Norway.

Iceland is the third largest island in the North Atlantic, after Greenland and England, Scotland and Wales. Lying across the Arctic Circle, it is made habitable for human beings only by the warm currents of the Gulf Stream. The history of Iceland shows how the Vikings took a previously uninhabited country and made it their own, and how they set up an organized community after their own tastes without any external pressures. Iceland was destined to become a chosen sanctuary for Norse culture, a place where the memories and history of the North Germanic race were more diligently preserved than anywhere else, and recorded in books which are today the richest source of knowledge of the Viking Age.

Who were the people who colonized Iceland? Imagine that we are in one of the deep, winding fjords of Western Norway, some time in the last decades of the ninth century A.D. Along the shoreline, drawn up on the beach, are some long, narrow boats, set with shields from stem to stern, easily recognizable as the war galleys or longships of the Viking voyages. Beside them are other ships, shorter, wider and with a higher gunwale; not so lithe and deadly-looking as the warships, but solid, sea-going vessels. A small one is being loaded. People are carrying all kinds of baggage and stores aboard — household articles of every sort, and livestock: sheep, cattle, horses, pigs, even squawking chickens. Finally the people themselves embark — rugged, bearded men, young and old, girt with swords, carrying spears, axes and shields; women in full-length gowns of homespun, youngsters and babies. They say goodbye to a group of friends; then the boat is pushed off and rowed out into the fjord. When a fair wind begins to blow, a square sail is hoisted and the vessel moves slowly out of the fjord to sea. The course is northwest. Gradually the sail grows smaller and smaller to the lingering watchers left behind, and it finally disappears. Such scenes were common. The captain and owner of the boat was on his way to colonize Iceland with his family and attendants.

The story of the "Landtaking" or Time of Settlements and of the earliest history of Iceland is recorded mainly in the priest Ari Thorgilsson's *Book of the Icelanders*, written about 1100 A.D. But other elements also appear in the various versions of the *Book of the Settlements*, a large work by many writers, as well as in the great Family Sagas, like *Egil's Saga*, dealing with events in the tenth century.

The basic elements of the ancient records are undoubtedly based on sound tradition. Although the discovery and the earliest settlement of Iceland were not reported in any written sources, it can be inferred from archaeological

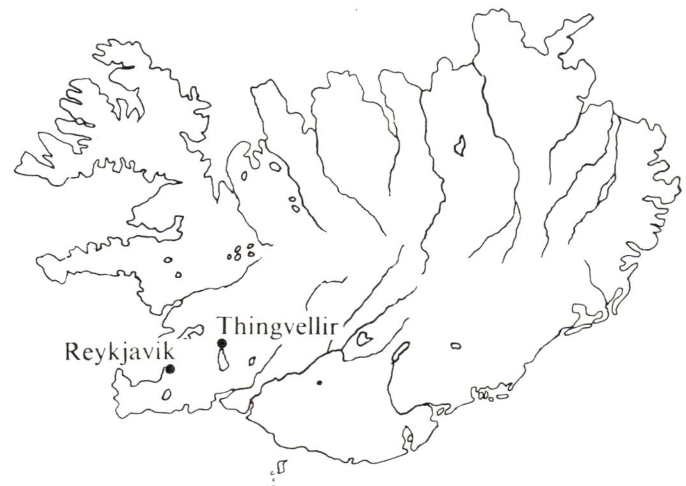

A NEW LAND GETS A COLD NAME

The Book of the Settlements *relates how an early Viking voyager, Floki, and his followers reached the east coast of an island in the North Atlantic: "They sailed then to the south of the land. But when they sailed west of Reykjanes, and the fjord opened so that they saw Snaefellsnes, Faxi said: 'It must be a big land which we have found; here are large rivers.' That is since called Faxaós. Floki and his men sailed westward over Breidafjord. The fjord was full of fish, and because of the fishing they neglected to provide themselves with hay, and their cattle all died in the winter. The spring was rather cold. Floki went north on the mountain and saw a fjord full of ice; and they called the land Iceland, as it has since been called. In the summer they returned to Norway." The latitude of the southernmost point of the island is 63° 24' North, and that of the northernmost, 66° 32' North. The coastline is indented with firths and inlets, and the interior of the country is mountainous, with glaciers, stretches of sand and lava fields.*

THE FIRST SETTLER'S PILLARS ARE FOUND

From the Book of the Settlements
As soon as Ingolf sighted Iceland, he cast his high-seat pillars overboard for an omen, vowing he would settle where the pillars came ashore. Vifil and Karli found his high-seat pillars by Arnarhval, west of the heath. In the spring Ingolf came down over the heath, to site his home where his pillars had come ashore, and lived at Reykjavik. Ingolf was the most celebrated of all the settlers, for he came here to an unlived-in country and was the first to settle down in it: the other settlers did so by his example.*

* *part of his house furniture*

THE ISLANDS OF MURDER

The Westman Islands, seen on the next page, rise majestically out of turbulent seas off the south coast of Iceland. Grim and forbidding, they are an appropriate setting for the story told in the Book of the Settlements, *which says that the islands got their name from some Irish slaves (Westmen) killed there by Ingolf the settler.*

finds that Iceland was first populated very near the middle of the Viking Age. And yet, according to Ari Thorgilsson, the settlers found a few Irish hermits, whom the Norsemen called *papar*, *i.e.* priests. These people must have managed to get to Iceland from Ireland in their frail currachs; tiny oared boats of skin and wicker. They are reported to have fled when the Norsemen came because they hated the heathen ways of the new arrivals.

Iceland was separated from the nearest inhabited land, Scotland and Norway, respectively by 431 and 529 miles of open sea. The North Atlantic is not a gentle ocean, so such distances as these presented an almost insurmountable barrier prior to the remarkable advances made in ship-building and navigation

in Norway in the Viking Age. The Norwegians had their eyes turned to the west, looking for land no less than for fame and booty. Once discovered, Iceland was bound to become populated, since in many ways it offered farming conditions similar to, and in some respects better than, those in Norway. Norway was almost certainly an overpopulated country in the Viking Age, exhausted from long exploitation of its agricultural resources — a fact which in part explains the Viking voyages in general.

From the *Book of the Settlements* we know the names and families of all the leaders among the settlers, and where they came from, back home. The great majority were of Norwegian descent, and a few were probably Swedish or Danish. Some settlers were of mixed stock, and did not come to Iceland direct from Norway. They belonged to families who had lived for some time in the

INGOLF OF ICELAND

From the *Book of the Settlements*
Iceland was first settled from Norway in the days of Harald Fairhair, son of Halfdan the Black, at the time (according to the belief and account of Teit my tutor, son of Bishop Isleif, and the wisest man I have known) when Ivar, Ragnar Lodbrok's son, had the English king Saint Edmund put to death, and that was 870 years after the birth of Christ, according to what is written in his, Edmund's saga. A Norwegian named Ingolf is the man of whom it is reliably reported that he was the first to leave there for Iceland, when Harald Fairhair was sixteen years old, and a second time a few years later. He settled south in Reykjavik.

NORSE EMIGRANTS LEAVING FOR ICELAND

Though Iceland was a Viking settlement, a great many of the settlers had never taken part in the famous and infamous Viking raids. They were simply people looking for land, more interested in cattle and sheep and good pastureland than in warfare, loot and glory. The drawing above is an attempt at reconstructing a scene in a Norwegian fjord towards the end of the ninth century, based on archaeological finds and contemporary chronicles. An emigrant family are taking leave of their friends, bringing their livestock and household articles on board ship for a three-week trip which will take them to their new home on the distant island in the ocean.

Viking colonies in the British Isles. Not a few of the settlers had Celtic blood in their veins, other had Celtic wives, and they certainly brought with them many followers of Celtic stock. Even so, the prevailing culture — material, spiritual and social — was Viking.

In Iceland Viking settlers established themselves as farmers. Although great tracts of this land of glaciers and volcanoes are uninhabitable, especially in the interior, everywhere near the coast there are plains and valleys with wide sweeps of grassland, excellent for raising sheep and cattle. Among the cereals, only barley could be grown successfully in these cold northern latitudes. Fish abounded in the seas, lakes and rivers, and from the very beginning formed an important part of the people's livelihood. The island harboured many kinds of birds. In many parts of the country there were extensive birch-woods, which

provided fuel for heating the houses and making charcoal. Great quantities of bog ore allowed the settlers to pursue the ancient art of iron-working. The ocean protected the islanders against external enemies, yet it was not too wide to prevent Icelandic and foreign merchants from keeping up a lively trade between Iceland and several other countries. Above all, there was plenty of room for everybody — at least in the beginning.

Then, there were about 400 *landsnámsmenn* or leading colonizers. The total number of the people who migrated to Iceland is, of course, much higher. Some scholars think that the population totalled about 30,000 by 930. Until that time there was no universal system of law and justice in Iceland. Naturally the settlers brought their own codes from their homelands. The main characteristics of the Viking were individualism and personal pride, and these found fertile soil in the new country. As time passed, however, the need for a more organized political system was more and more keenly felt. It was an ancient custom of the Teutonic peoples to settle their disputes at meetings called *things*, where every free man could come and defend his rights. In the year 930 the first great event in the history of Iceland occurred — the establishment of the general assembly or parliament of the whole nation (Althing). This was the first step in the foundation of the old Icelandic republic. "*Apud illos non est rex, nisi tantum lex*", wrote the historian Adam of Bremen, discussing the Icelanders about 1076 A.D. "They have no king; only law." The republic was a democracy, or, as it is sometimes called, an aristo-democracy, in which the chiefs divided the power between them and formed the Althing. As a meeting-place they chose the magnificent lava plain of Thingvellir in the south-west of Iceland.

What appeared to be a republic was a kind of interlocked family dynasty. Most of the chiefs who were given the greatest power at the foundation of the Althing are thought to have been either members of the same family or connected with it through marriage, descendants of a certain Björn buna, a chief of Sogn in Norway. According to this theory, the members of the family joined hands and divided the power between them throughout the country. This explains how a tricky operation such as the foundation of the Althing and the republic could take place peacefully. The country was divided into twelve, later thirteen, lesser *things* (a word which also meant jurisdictions), and there were three chiefs in each *thing*. These thirty-six (later thirty-nine) chiefs formed the legislative body of the Althing, where the laws were made, and so shared the supreme power between them.

In the course of time the Icelanders compiled extensive codes of law, which in later times were known as the Grágás, the laws of the ancient republic. During

IRISH HERMITS IN ICELAND

From the *Book of the Icelanders*:
There were Christian men here then whom the Norsemen call "papar". But later they went away because they were not prepared to live here in company with heathen men. They left behind Irish books, bells and croziers, from which it could be seen that they were Irishmen.

From the writings of Dicuil, an Irish monk, about A.D. 825:
It is now thirty years since priests who lived in that island from the first day of February to the first day of August told me that not only at the summer solstice, but in the days on either side of it, the setting sun hides itself at the evening hour as if behind a little hill, so that no darkness occurs during that very brief period of time, but whatever task a man wishes to perform, even to picking the lice out of his shirt, he can manage it precisely as if in broad daylight. And had they been on a high mountain, the sun would at no time have been hidden from them.

RUNIC INFLUENCE IN ICELANDIC ART

The carved panel on the opposite page was discovered on Flatatunga farm in the north of Iceland. No rune-stones have been found in Iceland, but this panel shows foliage of rune-stone type in full bloom, as well as haloed human figures which show how Christian saints were represented in Northern art.

the first couple of centuries, these laws were not written down. The Lawspeaker or *lögsögumaör* presided over the legislature (*logrétta*) and in a way was the president of the Althing. He had to know all the laws by heart and proclaim them at the Althing during his three years in office, reciting one-third of them each year. Eventually the ancient laws were put into writing in the year 1118.

The parliament was also a judicial assembly with four courts, one for each quarter of the country, and later a fifth court was set up, the supreme court or court of appeal. But strangely enough, the Icelandic parliament had no executive power. When sentence had been passed, it lay in the hands of individuals to enforce it. In the long run this primitive feature proved dangerous to the stability of society. During the fourteen days every midsummer that it lasted, the Althing was a national meeting-place, a festival in which everybody was entitled to take part. Chieftains from all parts of the country brought large groups of followers with them. Young people liked to go to the Althing, men and women, craftsmen of many kinds, traders, tramps and adventurers. At Thingvellir people met in friendship and in hostility, sentences were passed and fates were sealed.

More than anything else, the Althing helped to form a nation from the more or less unorganized masses of people who kept pouring into the new country for various directions during the last years of the ninth century.

The free republic of ancient Iceland survived in its original form until 1262, when the king of Norway succeeded in his long-cherished plan of bringing the Icelanders under his rule. The old governmental system of the Viking Age had had its day. But the memory of it lived on, and for the Icelanders of today, the descendants of the Viking settlers, Thingvellir symbolizes the golden age of freedom. For them, it is a challenge to preserve an inheritance that can be traced back over a thousand years.

Half way through the eleventh century, the population of Iceland had probably almost doubled, to about 60,000. That, roughly speaking, was the greatest number of people Iceland could support at this stage of agricultural development (although the *Book of the Icelanders* says that all land had been " occupied " — " possessed " is more likely — a century earlier). Farms had been built wherever it was possible to live, from the outermost coastal headlands to the deepest valleys that reached inland towards the barren and uninhabitable parts of the highlands. Many farms built hopefully in the no-man's-land between habitable and uninhabitable country quickly fell into disuse. Some of them have not been rebuilt or lived in since.

Places of this kind offer a fine opportunity for investigating the kind of house

THE LAWSPEAKERS

From the *Book of the Icelanders:*
Wise men have said that in the space of fifty years Iceland was fully occupied, so that after that there was no further taking of land. About then Hrafn, son of Haeng the Settler, took the lawspeakership next after Ulfljot and held it for twenty summers [A.D. 930-49]. He was from Rangarhverfi. This was sixty years after the slaughter of King Edmund, and a winter or two before King Harald Fairhair died, according to the reckoning of well-informed men. Thorarin, brother of Ragi and son of Oleif Hjalti, took the lawspeakership next after Hrafn and held it a further twenty summers [950-69]. He was a Borgarfjord man.

FAIR SHARES FOR ALL

From the *Book of the Settlements:*
Some of those who came out earliest lived close up to the mountains, remarking the quality of the land there, and how the livestock was keen to get away from the sea up to the high ground. Those who came out later thought that these first-comers had made over-extensive settlements; but King Harald Fairhair made peace between them on these terms, that no one should settle land more widely than he and his crew could carry fire round in one day. They must light further smoke-fires, so that each might be observed from the other, and those fires which were lighted when the sun showed in the east must burn till nightfall. Afterwards they must walk until the sun was in the west, and at that point light other fires.
. . . It was the law that a woman should not take land in settlement more widely than a two-year-old heifer, a half-stalled beast in good condition, might be led round on a spring day between the rising and setting of the sun.

THE VIKINGS BRING LAWS WITH THEM

From the *Book of the Icelanders:*
And when Iceland had become settled far and wide a Norwegian named Ulfljot first brought law out here from Norway (so Teit told us); this was called Ulfljot's law. He was the father of that Gunnar from whom the Djupadalers are descended in Eyjafjord. For the most part these laws were modelled upon the then Gulathing Law, on the advice of Thorleif the Wise, Horda-Kari's son, as to what should be added, taken away or be differently set out. Ulfljot lived east in Lon. It is said that Grim Geitskor was his fosterbrother, he who at Ulfljot's direction explored the whole of Iceland before the Althing was established. For this every man in the land gave him a penny, which he later donated to the temples.

A STRANGE SITE FOR A PARLIAMENT

The lava plain of Thingvellir (shown on the following page), where the Icelandic parliament met each summer is not merely a landmark in Scandinavian history; it is also famous for its strange and bright-hued geological formations.

the Vikings built in their new-found country. Ari the historian, in the *Book of the Icelanders*, states that at the time of the settlements the country was covered with forest between mountains and seashore. This must not be taken too literally. The " forest " must have been the same kind of birch-wood that is still found in Iceland. It does not yield timber suitable for building. Probably an abundance of driftwood made up for this lack. The Viking settlers built their houses with thick walls of turf and rough stones. The houses were basically oblong, but slightly oval in shape, and consisted of a large hall with a *langeldr* or long fire burning in the middle of the floor, and sleeping-benches along the walls. These houses were quite impressive, and followed more or less perfectly the building customs that the settlers had known in their own countries. This type of house proved ill-suited, however, to the cold and wet climate of Iceland. Before long came the development of the feature that particularly characterizes Icelandic house design: the large hall was divided into a number of smaller apartments, which did not need such large timbers for their construction, and were far easier to heat.

The other major group of archaeological finds in Iceland, the grave finds, yield much information on the religion of the Vikings. The settlers of Iceland were for the most part heathen, though some of them knew a little of the Christian faith, and others were actually Christian. Some were mixed in their beliefs. Helgi the Lean, for instance, believed in Christ, and called his farm Kristnes in His honour. But he made vows to Thor before sea voyages, when in a tight corner, or in fact whenever circumstances of real importance arose. All over Iceland there are farms with the name *hof*, *i.e.* temple, and it may be assumed that on all such sites heathen places of worship once stood. But it has proved as difficult in Iceland as elsewhere to decide what these edifices were like, and the same is true of many other details in the Icelanders' religion. The most important sources of information on this subject are the Poetic Edda, a collection of poems about gods and heroes of ancient times composed in Iceland, and the Prose Edda, the mythological treatise compiled in 1220 by the Icelandic chieftain, poet and historian Snorre Sturluson. This was two centuries after heathendom had come to an end in Iceland, and parts of the Edda may, therefore, be unreliable.

Graves from the Viking Age have been found in most parts of Iceland. It is surprising that cremation seems to have been quite unknown there, even though the settlers came from countries where cremation was as frequent as burial. The dead were buried in low mounds of earth and rough stones. They were fully dressed, the men with their weapons — which in some cases are of the finest quality — the women with their jewellery. Sometimes the deceased was buried

THE ALTHING IN SESSION

A reconstruction (left) of a part of the scene at Thingvellir during a session of the Althing, the Icelandic parliamentary session held once a year at about the end of June and the beginning of July. To the right is the so-called Law Rock, which was the centre of parliamentary activites and the place where the president of the Althing, the Lawspeaker, took his stand. A group of men are gathered at the Law Rock, and more are on their way to it. A lawsuit is about to be cited, or some public announcement made. The Law Rock is an excellent place from where to speak, for voices reverberate from the perpendicular wall behind, known as Almannagjá. On the plain below and in front of the Law Rock, the attendants of the chieftains are going about their everyday duties, cooking food and carrying water, and looking after the horses and the booths or huts, of which there were many hundreds. The walls were of turf and stones but the roofs were homespun woollen cloth, and put up for the occasion only.

From the *Book of the Icelanders*:
The Althing was established where it is now at the instance of Ulfljot and all the people of Iceland; but before this there had been a thing at Kalarnes, which Thorstein, son of Ingolf the Settler, and father of Thorkel Mani the Lawspeaker, held there together with those chieftains who allied themselves with it. But a man who owned the land at Blaskogar had been outlawed for the murder of a thrall or freedman. His name is given as Thorir Cropbeard, and his daughter's son was called Thorvald Cropbeard, the one who later went to the Eastfirths and there burnt his own brother Gunnar to death (so Hall Oraekjuson told us). The name of the murdered man was Kol, from whom the ravine gets its name, which has ever since been called Kolsgja, where the corpse was discovered. The land thereafter became public domain, and the Icelandic people set it apart for the use of the Althing, for which reason wood can be cut free for the Althing in the forests there, and on the heaths there are common pastures for the use of the horses. This Ulfhedin told us.

in a boat, as in Scandinavia, but the custom was rare. It was, on the other hand, usual — more so than elsewhere in Viking areas — to bury a horse with the body. Strong and hardy Icelandic ponies had become numerous early on. They had found excellent living conditions, and it cost little to provide the dead man with a mount for his last journey.

When, by the consent of the Althing, the Icelanders officially adopted Christianity in the year 1000, heathen burial customs ceased. Odin, Thor, Freyr and other heathen gods were gradually replaced by Christ and the saints. The Icelandic church was not, however, fully organized until the first Icelandic bishop, Isleif, was consecrated in 1056. The establishment of an episcopal see in Iceland marks the end of the real Viking Age there, since from that time onwards the country is just one of the many strongholds of the Church of Rome. But in spite of this, much of the spirit of the Viking Age lived on with remarkable tenacity in this remote island in the Atlantic. Even today, the Icelanders speak a language which is only slightly different from that spoken by their Viking ancestors who claimed the country for human habitation nearly 1100 years ago.

THE CONVERSION OF THE ICELANDERS

From the *Book of the Icelanders*:
The next day Gizur and Hjalti (who were trying to get Christianity adopted in Iceland) went to the Law Rock and made known their message, and report says that it was remarkable how well they spoke. And what followed from this was that one man after another, Christian and heathen, called witnesses, each swearing that he would not live under the same laws as the other, after which they left the Law Rock.

Then the Christians requested Hall of Sida that he should proclaim that law which was right and proper for Christians; but he got out of this in that he made payment to Thorgeir the Lawspeaker that he should proclaim the law — even though he was still a heathen. And later when men had returned to their booths, Thorgeir lay down and spread his cloak over him, and lay quiet all that day and the night following, and spoke never a word. But the next morning he sat up and announced that men should proceed to the Law Rock, and once men had made their way there he began his speech . . . "I think it policy that we do not let those prevail who are most anxious to be at each other's throats, but reach such a compromise in these matters that each shall win part of his case, and let all have one law and one faith. It will prove true if we break the law in pieces, that we break the peace in pieces too." And he so concluded his speech that both sides agreed that all should have that one law which he would proclaim.

Then it was made law that all men should be Christians, and be baptized, those who so far were unbaptized here in Iceland. But as for the exposure of infants, the old laws should stand, and for the eating of horseflesh too. Men might sacrifice in secret if they so wished, but it would be a case for lesser outlawry should witnesses come forward. But a few years later this heathendom was abolished like the rest. This was the way, Teit told us, that Christianity came to Iceland.

THE FLATEYJARBOK, THE MOST MAGNIFICENT OF THE MEDIAEVAL ICELANDIC MANUSCRIPTS

A detail from a page in the Flateyjarbók, which contains among other things the lives of the kings of Norway. The miniature shows the Viking and missionary king, Olaf Haraldsson, being killed in the famous battle of Stiklarstad 1030 A.D.

GREENLAND

Greenland is the largest island in the world, having an area of 840,000 square miles, a length of 1650 miles and a breadth of 760 miles, but nearly all of it lies inside the Arctic Circle, and about five-sixths is permanently under ice. From Viking times onwards, European settlers have been confined mainly to the south-west, where grass, bushes and a few small trees grow.

"GREENLAND": A STRANGE EXPLANATION

From the writings of Adam of Bremen, about 1076 A.D:
In the ocean there are very many islands, of which not the least is Greenland, situated far out in the ocean opposite the mountains of Sweden . . . To this island, they say, it is from five to seven days' sail from the coast of Norway, the same as to Iceland. The people there are greenish from the salt water, whence, too, that region gets its name. The people live in the same manner as the Icelanders, except that they are fiercer and trouble seafarers by their piratical attacks. Report has it that Christianity of late has also winged its way to them.

GREENLAND: A STRUGGLE FOR LIFE

Around the year 960 a boy named Erik, later called Erik the Red, and his father Thorval were forced to leave their home in Jären in southern Norway, after Thorval had been concerned in a murder. Erik and Thorval found a new home in Iceland, like many others before them. Erik had inherited his father's quarrelsome temper. History repeated itself. After committing two murders, in about 985, he was outlawed for three years. Erik had heard about a man, Gunbjörn, whose ship, early in the same century, had been driven off course, far to the west. Here he had seen a hitherto unknown land. Erik decided to try to find " Gunbjörn's Rock ", as the land had been called. It was as good a way as any other of staying away from Iceland for a while. He eventually reached " Gunbjörn's Rock " at its most inhospitable point, the east coast, where nothing tempted him to go ashore. The drift-ice threatened his ship every hour of the day and night. Nevertheless he set course south, and worked down to Cape Farewell, then turned north again. Here he found fertile valleys with green grass suitable for cattle and sheep, rivers full of fish, and walrus and seal in the sea. After exploring for two more summers as far north as Disko Island, Erik went home to Iceland. He had sailed about 2800 miles, not counting detours into the fjords. On Iceland land was short, so it was easy for Erik to find people who were interested in moving with him to Greenland. Erik had named the new country thus because, he said, people like to go to a new land only if it has an attractive name. In the following summer Erik led a fleet of twenty-five ships, each fully loaded with eager emigrants and their goods. There must have been about 500 people in all. But only fourteen of the ships got through. Some were wrecked in the high seas, currents, fogs and ice off Greenland. Others drifted back to Iceland. In the succeeding years, several more ships went off to Greenland. The East Settlement, in its prime, included about 200 homesteads. The West Settlement, which lay about 300 miles further north, comprised about a hundred homesteads. In all, the Viking population of Greenland might have totalled about 3000 inhabitants. Erik seems to have chosen the place for his own home on his first voyages. It was called Brattahlid, and was situated at the inner end of Erik's Fjord, which today is called Tunigdliarfik. Its ruins have been excavated, together with those of other village farmhouses, monasteries and churches. Christianity inevitably reached Greenland. It was Leif, the son of Erik the Red, who first brought the Faith with him, after he had been christened by King Olaf Tryggvason of Norway in 999. He took a priest back with him to undertake missionary work in Greenland.

The saga has this to say about the homeward voyage, which became historic: "Now Leif went off on his homeward journey. He drifted around on the sea for a long time, and he found countries of which he had earlier known nothing. Here [Vinland] there were self-sown wheat fields, and trees so big that they could be used as timber for house-building. Leif also found some people who had been shipwrecked on a rock, and brought them back with him. Leif landed in Erik's Fjord, and later went home to Brattahlid, to a warm welcome. Soon he started to preach the Christian faith, and delivered King Olaf Tryggvason's message to the people, that explained how much holiness and glory there was in the new religion. His father Erik was slow to become a convert, but his wife Thjodhilde was soon persuaded, and she had a church built at some distance from the houses. There she and the others who had accepted Christianity said their prayers. From the time Thjodhilde adopted the faith, she refused to have intercourse with Erik, and this he disliked very much . . ."

So began the hard struggle for existence of a little society which stood fast for nearly 500 years before being extinguished. It was a poor life, ruled by the shortage of raw materials, among other things wood for building ships and houses. The settlers lacked iron too, but in most cases they understood how to make do with existing materials: driftwood, whalebone and stone.

They did not succeed in growing corn. Sheep and cattle, together with fishing and hunting, kept them alive. But these provided a bare existence, on the borderline of starvation. Just one hard winter could be disastrous. Cairns have been found on the island of Kingigtorssuag, 900 miles north of Cape Farewell, with a runic inscription commemorating the men who ventured thus far in the fourteenth century. It was the yield of such hunting trips that provided the Greenlanders with their main exports, the furs and skins, the walrus ivory, Greenland falcons and even Polar bears, which were in great demand in medieval Europe. The teeth of the narwhal should not be forgotten. In medieval Europe, they were thought of as the horns of unicorns. They were regarded as being full of potent magic, and therefore commanded enormous sums. By selling all these goods the Greenlanders were able to buy from Europe the goods, especially the tools, on which their life literally depended. By the fifteenth century these Norse settlements in Greenland had disappeared, possibly because the climate, already bad enough, got worse. After the union of Iceland with Norway in the middle of the thirteenth century, Greenlanders were forbidden to have ships of their own. They were in no position to defy such a ban, and total dependence on the ships of others to bring timber, iron and tools must have made their life still more precarious.

SIGNS OF LIFE AT THE EDGE OF THE ICE

The photograph above proves that now, as in Viking times, wheat crops can be raised along the sheltered edges of Greenland's south-western fjords and islands. On the shores of Erik's Fjord, shown on the left, now called Tunigdliarfik, stood Brattahlid, which was Erik the Red's home. The grass and moss is green, but the white of snow on the mountains and ice in the fjord dominate the scene.

It was inevitable that some traveller to Greenland sooner or later would be driven off course towards the west — and towards the North American coast. It was a much shorter distance from the villages of Greenland to Labrador than to Iceland. Some sagas mention a man called Bjarni as the first to have seen land to the westward, but whether it was he or Leif, the latter's narrative prompted many to seek out "Vinland", as he called it. The name Vinland had nothing to do with drinking. "Vin" is an old Norse word for "pastures" or "meadows". The saga certainly tells of vines, but this is a later addition intended to explain the name Vinland, whose original meaning had been forgotten by the time the saga was written down. Besides, the saga writer probably wanted to demonstrate his knowledge of the Bible, and of the story of Joshua who sent scouts into "the promised land", from where they came back with big clusters of grapes. His information about "corn sowing itself", and about timber so big that one could build houses of it, must have been particularly attractive. It was not long before a new expedition was equipped. This time, Leif's brother Torstein was the leader, and old Erik the Red also joined in. But they were not in luck. Storms and currents carried the ships to Iceland and to Ireland, and they had to return to Brattahlid without having reached their objective. The following autumn a couple of merchant ships came to Brattahlid, each with a crew of forty men. They stayed with Erik during the winter. As Christmas drew nearer, he gradually became more and more depressed. There was not enough corn to make the traditional Christmas beer. However, one of the skippers, Torfinn Karlsevne, provided Erik with the goods he had brought with him, so that, in the end, this became a Christmas so festive that "they had never seen such magnificence in such a poor country". Everyone being together during the long winter, Vinland was of course discussed again. They decided to risk another voyage of discovery, and even planned a new colony; a new emigration. In the spring of 1001, two Icelandic ships and a third from Greenland started on an expedition with Torfinn Karlsevne as leader. It included several women, and the Vikings' personal belongings and domestic animals. The little fleet first went north to the West Settlement, from where the distance to the coast of Vinland was shorter. Arriving in Vinland safely, they followed the coast southwards until they came to the neighbourhood of the places which Leif had described after his first visit. Here the expedition settled down for the winter. The Icelandic skippers, however, disagreed, and one of them returned northwards with nine men. After this, there were only two ships left to carry the Vikings and their cattle. These sailed further towards

"VINLAND" — NEWFOUNDLAND?

Recent research suggests that Vinland is to be found around L'Anse aux Meadows at the northern tip of the island of Newfoundland, which lies at the mouth of the Gulf of St. Lawrence, off the north-east coast of Canada. The rocky north-eastern shore of the island is cut up by fjords and studded with islands. "Markland" was probably located on the American mainland to the north-west, on the coast of Labrador. This, too, is deeply indented and fringed with islands.

the south until they reached a place which suited the settlers much better. Here they decided to stay. Then the unexpected happened — the expedition met other people. The natives rapidly turned hostile, after at first trading peacefully. The "Skraelinger", as the Scandinavians called the natives, came back at the beginning of the winter, and began to attack in such great numbers that the emigrants did not dare to stay. They sailed back to the original Vinland, further to the north, where they spent a third winter. Though they had not suffered heavy losses in the fighting against the "Skraelinger", they had been so frightened and depressed that they gradually became convinced of the hopelessness of the whole enterprise. Here are the words of the saga: "They now realized that even if the country was very rich, there would be danger of conflict with the original inhabitants of the country. They therefore made themselves ready to leave the country, and set out on the way to their home village." On the northward voyage, they searched for the Icelandic captain and his men who had left them in the beginning, but without result. In another fight with the natives, Erik the Red's son, Torstein, was killed by an arrow. It can easily be seen how the Vikings became nervous and edgy, and when the men also started to fight over the few women, it was clearly time to go home. One of the ships was stranded on the coast of Ireland, but Torfinn Karlsevne's ship reached Brattahlid safely. A heroic enterprise had come to a sad end. This was an expedition which was doomed to failure from the beginning, if only for the reason that the distance from Greenland was so great that no help against the hostile natives could be counted upon.

Several sagas tell of the Vinland expedition, and even if they did not quite agree concerning events and their order, they still describe the same places, which were given names such as Vinland, Helluland ("flat-stone land"), Markland ("forest-land"), Furdustrandi and so forth.

How can these be identified? According to the saga texts, these localities are situated near to each other. Markland may be Labrador, and everything suggests that the original Vinland is Cape Bauld at the northern tip of Newfoundland. It is in this area, too, that there have been found what are said to be the remains of a Scandinavian settlement, at L'Anse aux Meadows. But it is still enormously difficult to date the ruins, which appear to be of an Iron Age site of Norse type. Excavations revealed traces of houses, the turf walls of which had all but disappeared. The hearths uncovered resemble those in the houses of Iceland and Greenland. In addition to the topographical justification for seeking Vinland and the other "lands" in this area, there are also ethnographical reasons — the descriptions in the sagas of the weapons of the natives. A kind of throwing weapon is mentioned, and suggests the harpoons

THE "ISLAND" TO THE WEST

From the writings of Adam of Bremen, about 1076 A.D:
Another island of the many found in that ocean is called Vinland because vines producing excellent wine grow wild there. That unsown crops also abound on that island we have ascertained not from fabulous reports, but from the trustworthy relation of the Danes. Beyond that island, no habitable land is found in that ocean, but every place beyond it is full of impenetrable ice and intense darkness.

THE " WONDERFUL BEACHES "

The thirty miles of sand beach at Cape Purcupine, south of Hamilton Inlet, Labrador, may have been the " Furdustrandi" (" wonderful beaches") of the sagas. For the Vikings on their voyage south to Vinland such beaches would have been a landmark visible far out to sea.

of the Dorset Eskimos. These Eskimos did not know anything about the bow and arrow, which, however, was the weapon preferred by the Indians. But in just these regions were found both the harpoon-throwing Eskimos and the archer-Indians mentioned in the sagas. During archaeological excavations near Sandnäs farm in the West Settlement of Greenland, an arrow-head of American origin was also discovered. It was made of a sort of quartz which is only found in Labrador. It seems likely, therefore, that it was an unpleasant souvenir of a journey to America made by one of the inhabitants of Sandnäs.

No more narratives about colonization experiments in Vinland are known, but nevertheless a later colony of Scandinavians may have existed. In 1121 a Greenlandic bishop, Erik Gnupsson, went to Vinland, and might have done so in order to visit a congregation in need of pastoral care. Anyhow, it is logical that the Greenlandic Scandinavians visited Vinland and Markland to find their vital timber, for the distance to Norway was much greater. Some investigators believe that the Vikings penetrated as far south as Cape Cod, in the neighbourhood of present-day Boston. This will not be proved until relics of their presence are found.

THE VIKINGS FIND HELLULAND AND MARKLAND

From the *Saga of Torfinn Karlsevne*
There they approached the coast, and when they had let fall the anchor they lowered a small boat, rowed to land and saw no grass there. Farther away there were only huge glaciers, and the nearest strip of land between the glaciers and the sea was like one enormous slab of stone and the land seemed deprived of anything that could be useful. Then Leif said, " We have not failed to land, as Brani did. Now I will give this land a name, and call it Helluland" [*Hellu* — a flat stone]. Then they re-entered the boats and took to the sea, and then they found the next land in order. Once more they went to the coast, put down a small boat and went to the land. This coast was flat and full of trees, and here they found long stretches of white sand, and the shore was not steep. Then said Leif: "This land should be named after what is in it, and be called Markland" [forestland]. Then they went back to the ships as fast as possible. Then they went out on the sea with a wind from the north-east and they sailed on the open sea for two days before seeing land.

SOUTH TO THE MEDITERRANEAN AND EAST TO ASIA — THE VIKINGS CARRY WAR, COMMERCE, AND NEW PEOPLE INTO OLD EMPIRES

Whatever the Vikings came for, trade, land, or plunder, the people on the continent of Europe first saw and fought them as they are shown in the symbol from a picture-stone at the head of the page.

From the very beginning of the Viking Age, lively contacts existed between Scandinavia and the Frankish Empire. They took four forms: political and military conflicts, trade, religious and cultural connections, and settlement, the last mainly confined to Normandy. At first, violence overshadowed all the rest, and remained as a bloody thread running through Viking history even after more peaceful relations had generally been established.

In 799 A.D. the first Vikings landed in Aquitaine. Around the year 800, the increasing threat of Viking raids forced Charlemagne, king of the Franks, to raise a number of forts, like Esesfelth near Neumünster, along the north-western borders of the Frankish Empire. In spite of this, the North Sea coast remained as wide open to Viking attacks as before, and later Frankish rulers relied more on diplomacy. In the year 826 the Danish king Harald — driven out of his own country — was given Rüstringen in Frisia. In 841 the island of Walcheren was presented to Harald by the German emperors, who in this way hoped to afford themselves and their empire some degree of protection. But even such notable concessions as these failed to produce permanent peace. On the contrary, only two years later new Danish hordes began forcing their way up the Frankish rivers, and in 845 Vikings sacked and burned the city of Hamburg. By 850 the Swedish Viking Rurik had no trouble in conquering the whole of Frisia on the North Sea coast, and in 882 bands of Vikings plundered all along the Rhine and burned a number of towns to the ground. The raiders, moving by ship and on horseback though fighting on foot, had the advantage of mobility. They could strike and escape. The traditional, slow methods of defence — assembly of local forces by the king's regional representatives — were useless against such a flexible enemy. Also, the local levies were mostly ill-armed, undisciplined peasants who could not stand against the

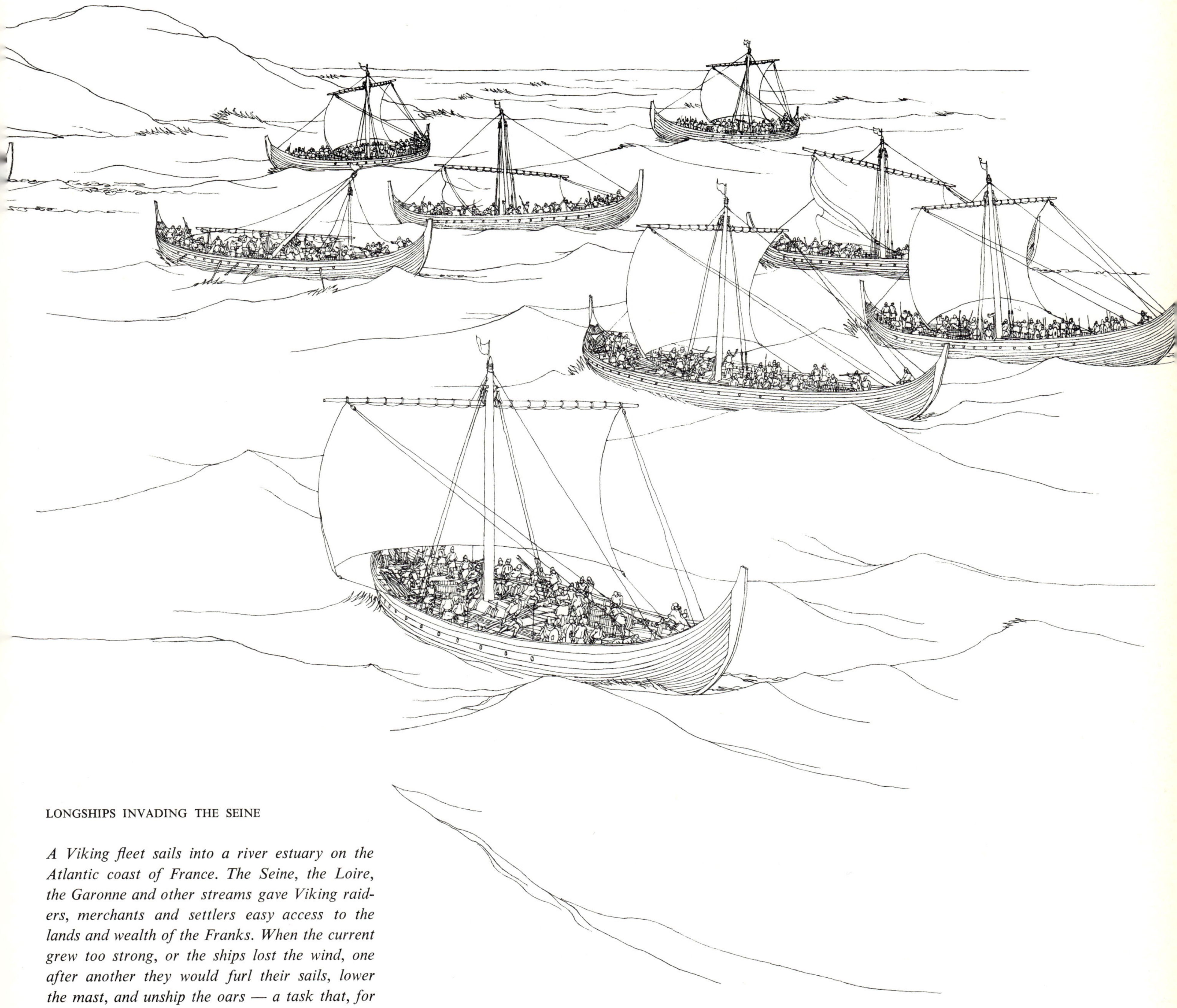

LONGSHIPS INVADING THE SEINE

A Viking fleet sails into a river estuary on the Atlantic coast of France. The Seine, the Loire, the Garonne and other streams gave Viking raiders, merchants and settlers easy access to the lands and wealth of the Franks. When the current grew too strong, or the ships lost the wind, one after another they would furl their sails, lower the mast, and unship the oars — a task that, for a trained crew, should not have taken more than a few minutes. With their combination of sails, oars, and shallow draught, Viking ships could adapt themselves to all waters.

formidable Viking warriors, even if they did bring them to battle. The failure of the Frankish kings to provide protection from Viking raiders both caused and reflected the decline of their power, and the rise of the power of local chieftains who could more successfully protect their own areas and peoples. The only effective defence against Viking attacks in France was the development of mobile, heavy cavalry to catch and break the Viking foot-soldiers, along with the construction of fortified centres: the beginnings of medieval castles. These strongpoints could resist attack, and in their turn could serve as the bases for counter-attack. The Franks were extraordinarily reluctant to recognize the inevitability of Viking raids, and it was only in the second half of the ninth century that they made efforts to create such strongpoints. When they did, and when heavy cavalry came into general use among the Franks, Viking raids quickly became much less profitable and more risky.

In the tenth century, Scandinavians were rarely found operating on the Continent. The success of these new techniques, and the beginning of the end of the Viking menace in France, was symbolized by the successful defence of Paris in the great siege of 885 - 886, when the defenders were led by Odo, count of Paris, who was shortly afterwards himself chosen as king. However, it was only after a peace treaty had been made in 927 between the Franks and the Vikings who had settled in Normandy, and after Gnupa, the Swedish ruler of Hedeby, had been defeated in 934 by the German king Henry the Fowler, that the way was prepared for more peaceful times. Even so, the tranquillity of the Frankish Empire continued to be disturbed for decades by border clashes and minor Viking plundering expeditions.

It is surprising that despite, and indeed during, these political troubles, commercial exchanges grew on a scale unheard-of earlier. A number of trading towns were established on Frankish and Scandinavian soil. They were necessary to the trade, and grew with it. The most important were Dorestad near the mouth of the Rhine, Hedeby on the southern boundary of Denmark, Kaupang in Norway and Birka in Sweden. The Scandinavian towns have already been described between pages 32 and 62. The commercial importance and wealth of Dorestad, which lay within the Frankish domains, is shown by texts like the ninth-century *Life of St. Anskar* (page 32), so it is not surprising that Viking raiders should have paid this town so much attention in the ninth century. The town's trade does not, however, seem to have been concerned with imports destined for the Franks so much as with goods that eventually found their way through Frankish territory to Islamic Spain. The relative importance of south-western France and therefore, probably, of Spain across the Pyrenees, is shown by coins from that area of France found at Dorestad.

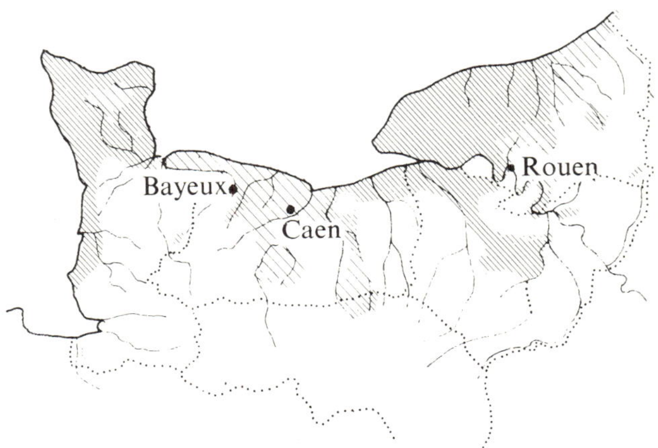

THE NORSE SETTLEMENT IN NORMANDY

On this map the darker shading shows where placenames of Scandinavian origin which still exist today are thickest, and the lighter shading where they are less thick, thus suggesting the extent of Viking settlement in Normandy. Some Norman placenames are of wholly Scandinavian type, like Yvetôt (compare with Ivetofta in southern Sweden), or contain a Scandinavian man's name.

A VIKING WORD - AND HOW IT TRAVELLED

When the Vikings came to France and settled down in Normandy, they put their stamp on the language. An notable example is the Scandinavian word *skipa* — pronounced with a short *i* — which meant to equip, especially a ship. This word is still used in French in the form *équiper*. (The Frankish tongue could not possibly manage the *sk* sound combination at the beginning of a word.) The English language has borrowed the word from the French in *equip* and *equipment*, and after seven or eight centuries the Swedish language has re-adopted the old word *skipa* in words like *ekipera* and *herr-* and *dam-ekipering*, now meaning "equipping" with clothes.

THE WATERWAY THAT LED TO PLUNDER

The Seine, shown on the following pages, was one of the rivers which Vikings used to penetrate the heart of France. This view is dominated by the ruins of the Château Gaillard, a post-Viking medieval castle at Les Andelys. Further upstream lay Paris, a rich prize which the Vikings besieged but never took.

Commercial relations did exist between Franks and Moslems, but what the Moslems really wanted, and could afford to buy, were furs and slaves, which came not from France but beyond.

Dorestad was also significant in another way. Not only was it the chief Frankish trading-port for Scandinavia, but it also furnished the main supply of coins for Frisia and the north. Silver pennies (or deniers) from Dorestad have been found in large numbers in Scandinavia. Finds at Dorestad also show trading connections with England. Dorestad did not survive into the tenth century. A disastrous change in the course of the Rhine took away its traffic. When Dorestad and similar towns like Domburg on the island of Walcheren declined, their trade was taken over by such places as Stavoren on the Zuider Zee and Tiel on the river Waal in present-day Holland.

The spread of Christianity promoted ecclesiastical contacts between the Frankish Empire and the North. In 834, the archiepiscopal see of Bremen was given responsibility for the whole of Scandinavia. Thirty years later the headquarters were moved to Bremen. About 950, thanks to the rising power of the German kings, who were Christian, it was possible to establish episcopal sees in Denmark, at Hedeby, Århus and Ribe. The majority of the missionaries working in Scandinavia were Frankish, although a number of Scandinavians were educated in Frankish monasteries, who later returned to their native land to spread the Gospel. There was also some Frankish influence on Scandinavian handicrafts. Highly-developed zoomorphic (animal) ornamentation had been part of the native Scandinavian tradition since pre-Viking times, but another style, plant ornamentation, ultimately derived from classical art, was imported from the Franks of Germany about the year 800, though it was not fully accepted by Scandinavian craftsmen for another 200 years.

As a result of all these contacts, the Scandinavian north gradually freed itself from its age-long isolation, and thereafter became part of Christendom. This development, however, marked the end of the Vikings' own, individual civilization, and of their characteristic political influence. Scandinavian heathendom was lacking in deep religious feeling. When, therefore, Christianity was established in Scandinavia about the year 1000 and western culture came with it, an independent culture capable of measuring up the rest of the world artistically was destroyed.

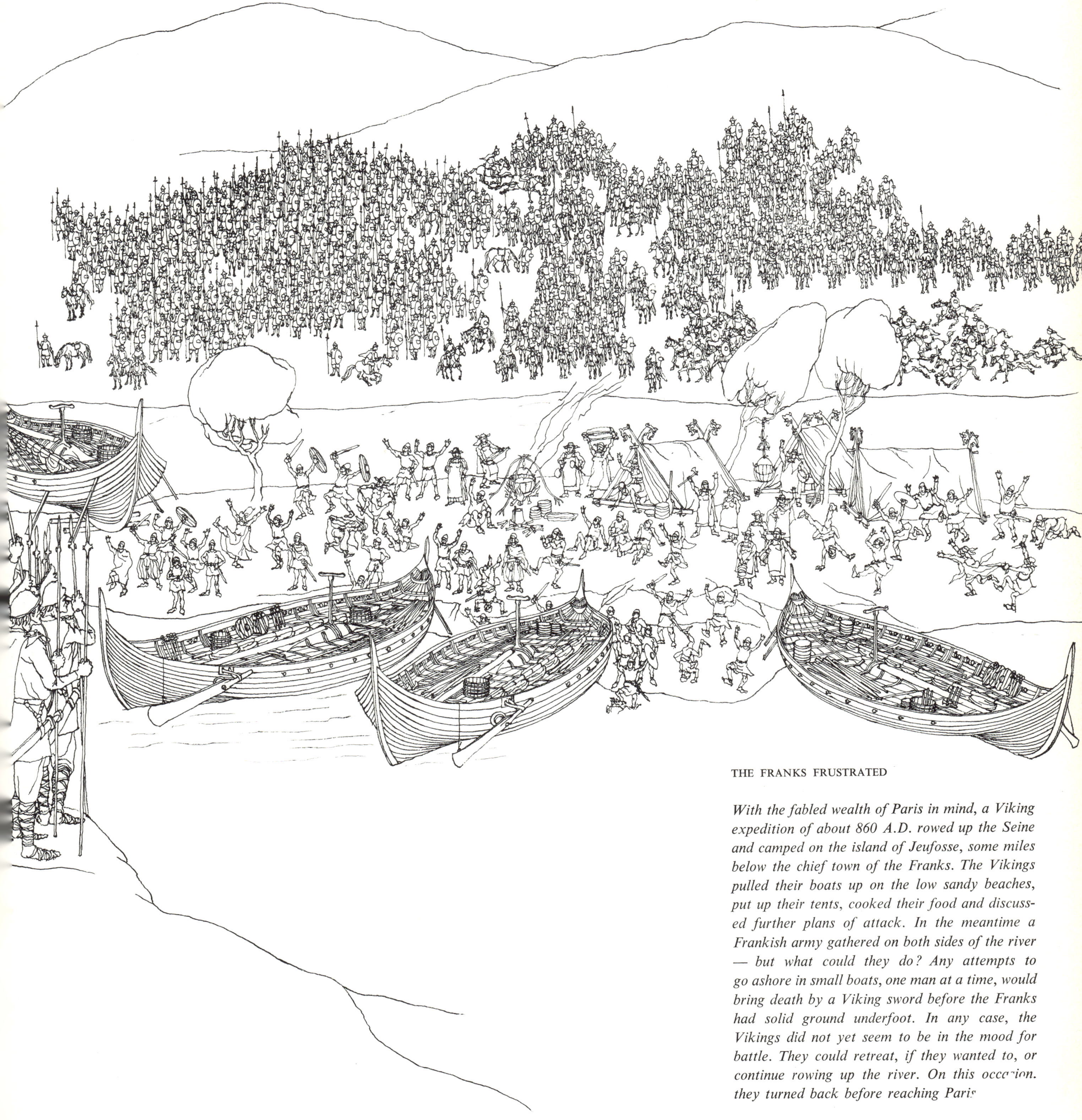

THE FRANKS FRUSTRATED

With the fabled wealth of Paris in mind, a Viking expedition of about 860 A.D. rowed up the Seine and camped on the island of Jeufosse, some miles below the chief town of the Franks. The Vikings pulled their boats up on the low sandy beaches, put up their tents, cooked their food and discussed further plans of attack. In the meantime a Frankish army gathered on both sides of the river — but what could they do? Any attempts to go ashore in small boats, one man at a time, would bring death by a Viking sword before the Franks had solid ground underfoot. In any case, the Vikings did not yet seem to be in the mood for battle. They could retreat, if they wanted to, or continue rowing up the river. On this occasion, they turned back before reaching Paris.

The Scandinavians did not settle as extensively in France as they did in England. But they achieved a remarkable success in France, symbolized by the grant to their leader Rolf, or Rollo, in 911, of the area of north-western France that was the nucleus of the duchy of Normandy. Around the time when Rollo and his forces, consisting mostly of Danes, were established by King Charles the Simple in the region of the Lower Seine, other Vikings were also settling, on their own initiative, in western Normandy. In the course of the tenth century, a slow infiltration of Scandinavians reinforced these first arrivals. Studies of language have shown that many latecomers were Danes who had immigrated from England, or, less frequently, Norwegians from the western parts of the British Isles.

It is generally agreed that this colonization was mainly aristocratic in character. Above all, it provided reinforcements for a rural society which the native Frankish lords had, to all appearances, largely deserted. Most notably, the family of Rollo, the first duke, despite conversion to Christianity, preserved certain customs that were typically Scandinavian. The most celebrated example was a marriage custom called *more danico* by contemporaries, and plain polygamy by us. If the Scandinavian settlers brought women with them, they cannot have been many: an examination of texts dealing with Normandy in the period from 911 to 1066 shows only six women, as opposed to 300 men, having Scandinavian names. On various occasions during the tenth century, the dukes of Normandy, though technically Christians, appealed to the pagan Vikings for aid in opposing their Frankish adversaries.

The great changes seen in the placenames of Normandy between the end of the tenth century and the beginning of the eleventh show that many estates came into the hands of new rulers. These changes are particularly impressive in eastern Normandy, where, of the many placenames found in pre-Viking documents, only a very small number remain by the eleventh century. It is possible that in certain areas, particularly along the coasts, the Scandinavian immigration was still heavier. The fishing and boat-building terminology in the speech of coastal dwellers was very rich in Scandinavian elements in medieval times. Even today Norse terms are often used by fishermen and seamen on the northern coast of the Cotentin peninsula. On the other hand, the revolt of the Norman peasants (described by the chroniclers William of Jumièges and Wace), which disrupted the duchy in the closing years of the tenth century, has been offered as proof of a massive influx of Scandinavian peasants. These peasants, accustomed in their countries of origin to personal and

THE RIVER RAIDERS

The swords and black circles on the map opposite indicate places plundered or at least attacked by the Vikings. The map reveals how closely the Vikings stuck to their ships. They went up rivers such as the Garonne and the Rhône as far as Toulouse and Lyon, normally in search of booty or trade rather than land, ravaging monasteries and towns wherever resistance was weak.

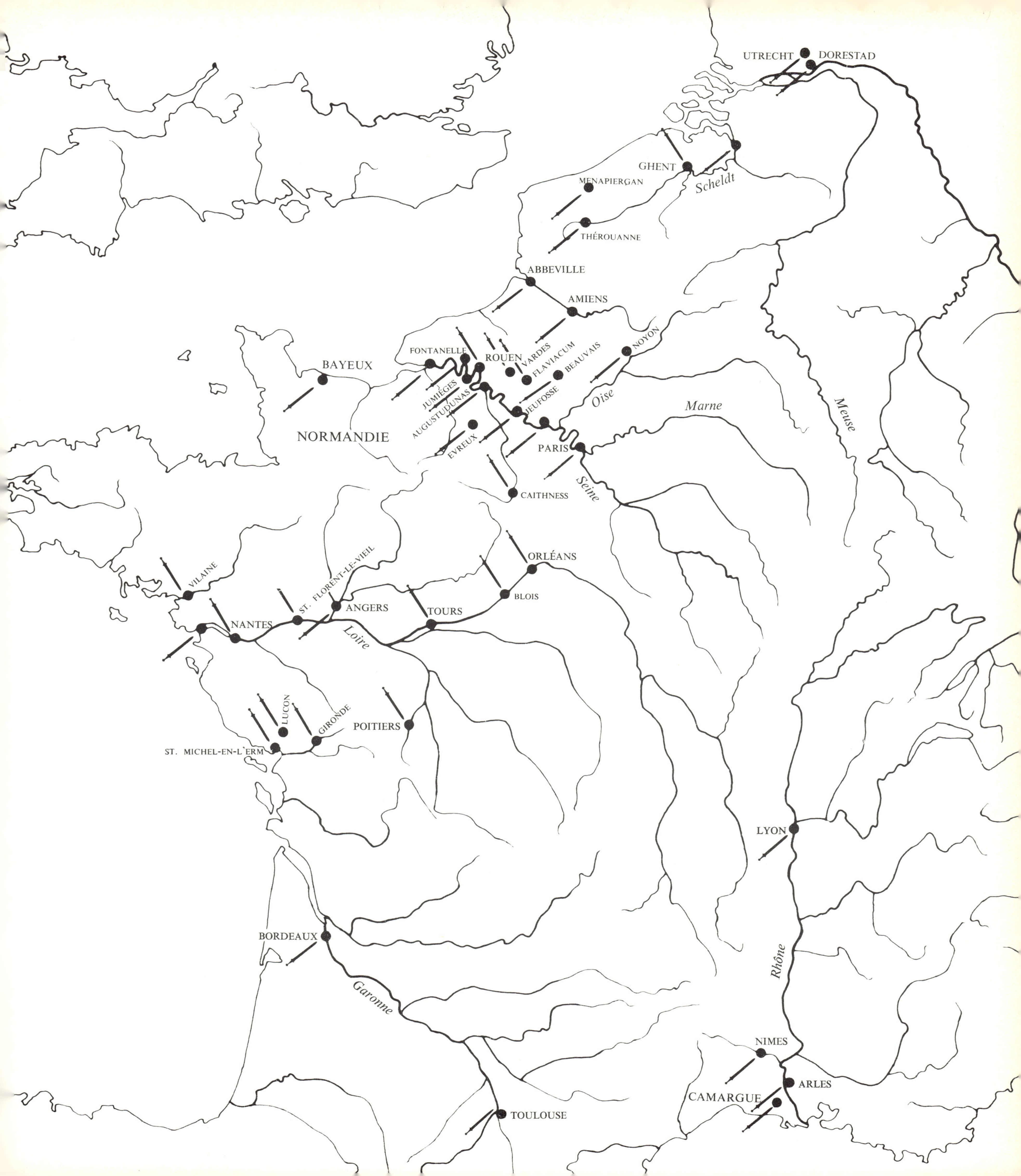
UTRECHT
DORESTAD
GHENT
Scheldt
MENAPIERGAN
THÉROUANNE
ABBEVILLE
AMIENS
NOYON
FONTANELLE
ROUEN
VARDES
FLAVIACUM
BEAUVAIS
BAYEUX
JUMIÈGES
AUGUSTUDUNAS
JEUFOSSE
Oise
Marne
Meuse
NORMANDIE
EVREUX
PARIS
Seine
CAITHNESS
ORLÉANS
VILAINE
ST. FLORENT-LE-VIEIL
ANGERS
TOURS
BLOIS
NANTES
Loire
LUCON
GIRONDE
POITIERS
ST. MICHEL-EN-L'ERM
LYON
BORDEAUX
Rhône
Garonne
NIMES
ARLES
CAMARGUE
TOULOUSE

Town unfortified
Town with new fortifications
Royal palace
Important church
Cathedral
Cathedral town with Roman fortifications still in use
Viking incursions
HEDEBY
HOLLINGSTEDT
HAMBURG
LEEUWARDEN
BREMEN
STAVOREN
UTRECHT
DORESTAD
HILDESHEIM
MÜNSTER
CORVEY
WALCHEREN
GHENT
MAASTRICHT
KÖLN
AACHEN
LIÈGE
FULDA
MAINZ
MAIN
TRIER
BAMBERG
WORMS

The Baltic
Ladoga
Swir
St. Ladoga
Volchov
NOVGOROD
Lovat
Volga
Duna
Gnezdovo
Smolensk
Oka
Volga
Kama
Bulgar
Chernigov
Kiev
Don
Don
Dnieper
rapids
Dnieper
Don
Don
Sarkel
Volga
Berezanji
Atil
Caspian Sea
Black Sea
Forest areas
Highlands
Steppe
River trade routes
Caravan routes
Finds of Byzantine coins
Grave-finds with Scandinavian objects
Finds of West European coins (Anglo-Saxon, German)
Finds of Arabic coins

BOATS OVERLAND

In the Viking Age, and for centuries afterwards, waterways were the most natural travel routes. The Vikings' ships were not only well adapted for all kinds of sailing. Their shallow draught and relatively light weight made them remarkably manoeuverable when it became necessary to haul them overland. Short stretches of dry land, like those by-passing difficult falls and rapids or dividing one river system from another were, therefore, only minor obstacles.
Reloading cargo was a long and troublesome business, so the simplest thing was to move the entire ship. The easiest way was by rolling it on logs, a method which is sometimes used even today. On the Russian river systems forests were never far away. The Vikings had only to take what they needed when they needed it. The oars were shipped, the steering-oar was hung from the gunwale on a hawser so as to be out of the way, and then the entire crew helped push, removing the logs at the stern when the ship had rolled over them and replacing them at the bows.

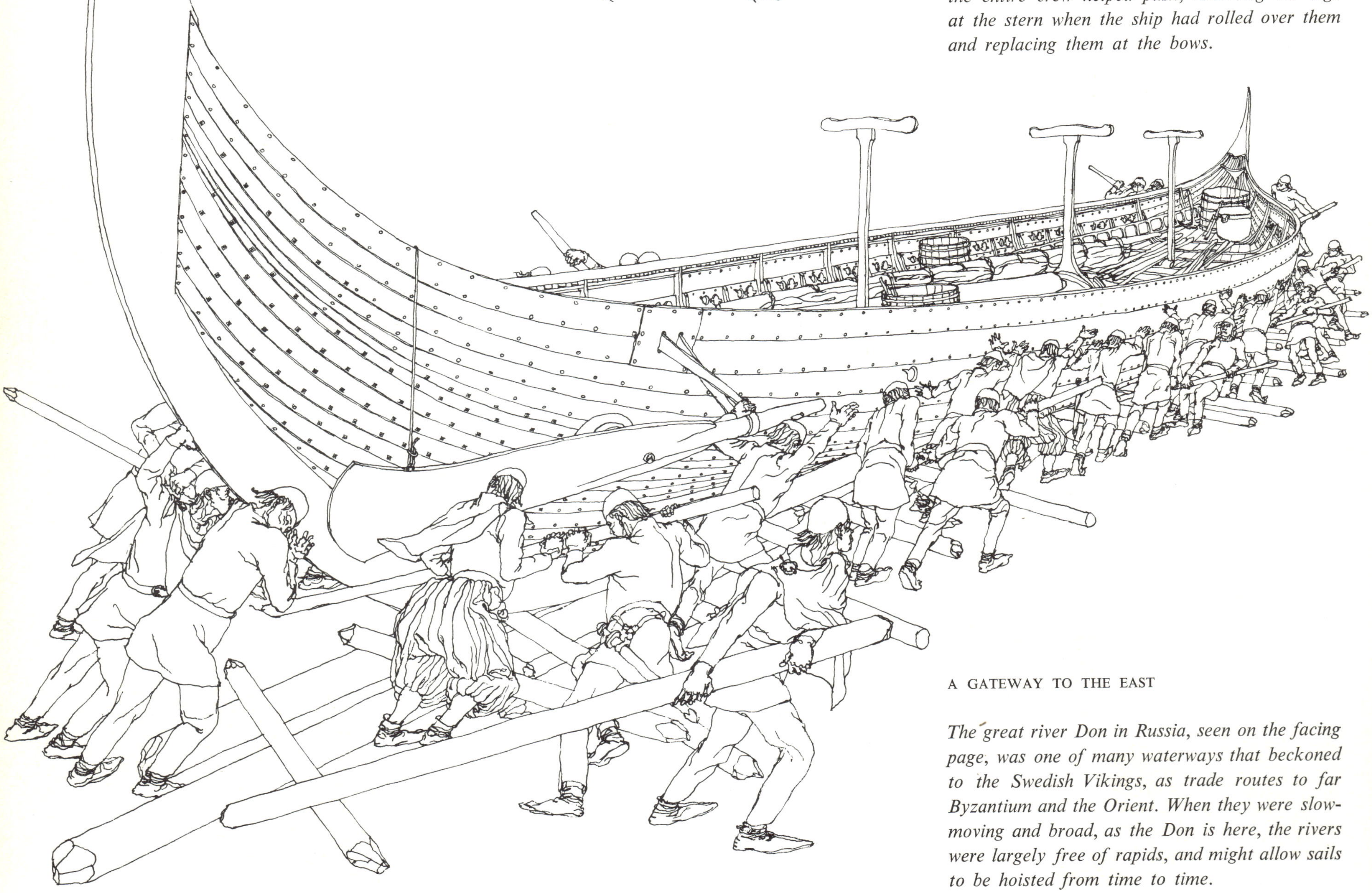

A GATEWAY TO THE EAST

The great river Don in Russia, seen on the facing page, was one of many waterways that beckoned to the Swedish Vikings, as trade routes to far Byzantium and the Orient. When they were slow-moving and broad, as the Don is here, the rivers were largely free of rapids, and might allow sails to be hoisted from time to time.

VIKING MERCHANTS PRAYING TO THEIR GODS FOR PROFIT

The drawing above is a reconstruction of a scene described by an Arab trader, Ahmad ibn Fadhlan, who met Norse merchants on the Volga in the year 921. He wrote a description of the merchants' combination of business and religion, which was typical of Viking opportunism:
" When they [the merchants] came to this anchorage all of them left the boats with bread, meat, onions, milk and 'nabid' [a sort of alcohol]. They went to a high wooden pillar which had a human face. Round about it were small figures, and behind them tall posts were placed... He [the merchant] approaches the tall figure, prostrates himself before it, and says: 'Oh my Lord, I have come a long way with so many slave-girls and so many sable furs [and then he mentions all the goods he has with him]. Now I come to you with these offerings.' He places what he has with him before the tall figure, and says:

the Oka and ultimately to Bulgar, has been mentioned already. The second runs along the Dvina and into the Baltic. These facts suggest that in Viking times Gnezdovo was not merely a burial place, but a central station for Russian trade.

In 969 A.D., an attack on the east-west route from Bulgar to the Baltic was made by Prince Swiatoslav of Kiev, who controlled the north-south route from Novgorod to the Dnieper. His aim may have been to destroy the silk trade along the Volga, for Kiev was also on the edge of the steppe commanding another east-west caravan route, and he might naturally wish to discourage rival trade. The rulers of Kiev might once have been Swedish, but the ruler here involved was by this time not even a Scandinavian. A Byzantine source describes his dress and his hair-style, which are obviously Slav or even Tartar. Moreover, the results of his attack on the Volga route were anything but advantageous for Scandinavia. Trade with Bulgar seems to have been given up,

'I want you to send me a merchant who has lots of dinars and dirhems and will buy on my terms without being difficult.' If the bargaining slows down, he returns with an offering or two. If everything is going wrong, he will bring offerings to all of the small figures too, and asks for their intercession, saying: 'These are the wife, the daughters and the sons of my Lord'. Sometimes business goes well, and he sells without difficulty. Then he returns to the tall figure and says: 'My Lord has covered my needs. Now it is my duty to repay him.' Then he takes a certain number of sheep or cattle and kills them. Part of the meat is given away to the poor. The rest is thrown to the tall figure and the smaller figures standing around it. The heads of the cattle and the sheep are hung on the posts. When night falls the dogs will come and eat all the meat. He who has made the offering will say: 'Assuredly, my Lord is pleased with me and has eaten my offerings.''*

* *Arabic currency*

and the flow of Arab silver into the north was stopped. It is possible that the sudden disappearance of Birka and the decline of Hedeby as trading centres were the direct result of Swiatoslav's attack.

There was quite a strong connection between the north and Byzantium, the capital of the East Roman empire, even though only a tiny proportion — about 500 — of the coins found in Scandinavia are Byzantine. Miklagárd —"the Great City",the Norsemen called Byzantium, and so it appears again and again in the sagas. These tell of how the Byzantine Emperor's bodyguard included a proportion of Scandinavians who had entered the imperial service. "Väringer", they were called, and they called themselves after their Greek nickname, which means "the hoarse ones". The best-known of all "Väringer" is the Norwegian Harald Hardrada, who became commander of the entire imperial bodyguard and also the Emperor's tax-collector in the Kiev district. A century at least before Harald, there were "Väringer" in the bodyguard. This appears in a book of Emperor Constantine Porphyrogenitus: *De Ceremoniis Aulae Byzantinae* — Concerning the Ceremonies of the Byzantine Household. On the ninth of the Twelve Days of Christmas, according to Constantine's account, people waited at both entrances of the Emperor's large dining-hall ready to perform the "Gothic game". At the left-hand door is the Admiral of the Fleet with a few men and flute-players from his ships. Behind him are two "Goths" (Väringer) dressed in fur coats with the hair-side turned outwards, and wearing masks. At the right-hand entrance, the commander of the bodyguard is waiting with a detachment of his men. As soon as the Emperor arrives, he orders the Master of Ceremonies to lead in the performers, and "they then hurry into the room, and at the same time they hit the shields which they carry with their spears, and thereby produce a big noise, and they cry *jul, jul**: and they do not stop until they reach the holy table. There, the two units run together from both sides so that they form a double circle. After having run three times around the holy table in this way, both units withdraw to their places, the navy at the right and the army at the left, and those out of the two units who are called Goths then read out the so-called Gothic song". Then follows a long song in praise of the Emperor. It is perfectly true that the text says "Goths", but the real Goths or Germans had disappeared from the imperial mercenaries by about 500 A.D. In the tenth century it was the Scandinavians who formed the most important element in the bodyguard. This, incidentally, is the oldest known description of a Nordic Christmas celebration.

Byzantine monks or missionaries came to Scandinavia, but Byzantium was too far away to exert serious religious influence. The Roman Church prevailed in Scandinavia, because the bishopric of Hamburg was close by. However, very strong evidence of powerful Byzantine cultural influence can be seen in some of the coins which the eleventh-century Danish king, Svein Estrithson, struck. They are in a sharp contrast to the coins of his predecessors, which were of Anglo-Saxon design. One minted in Lund depicts Christ sitting enthroned with a Gospel book on one side, and on the other an angel presents a holy banner to the king, who appears dressed in Byzantine costume.

* Yuletide, the pagan Christmas.

HOW SWEDES CAME TO RULE RUSSIA
According to the Primary Nestor Chronicle

The tributaries of the Varangians* drove them back beyond the sea and, refusing them further tribute, set out to govern themselves. There was no law among them, but tribe rose against tribe . . . They said to themselves, " Let us seek a prince who may rule over us and judge us according to the law. " They accordingly went overseas to the Varangian Russes . . . [they] said to the people of Rus, " our land is great and rich, but there is no order in it. Come to rule and reign over us. " They thus selected three brothers, with their kinsfolk, who took with them all the Russes and migrated.

* A word applied to the inhabitants of all lands round the Baltic sea. According to the story, they had extorted tribute from the Slavs of Russia before the latter invited the Swedes, one of the Varangian peoples, to rule over them.

Who exactly were the Vikings, these seafaring Scandinavians who suddenly appeared on the scene of history? Ethnically they were Teutons, and their language was Germanic. It was called "the Danish tongue", and it was common to all Scandinavians up to the end of the Viking period. The common language in the whole Scandinavian area created a feeling of solidarity, which should not be underestimated. Close contact with the sea, too, gave rise to a sense of shared experience between the three Scandinavian countries. There were no separate national states like those of today, so that it is perfectly justifiable to treat Scandinavia as a whole when speaking of the Viking Age. The differences in customs and trade routes were due mainly to the geographical position of the countries and to their physical make-up. Anyone will understand how it is that the Norwegians came to operate in the North Atlantic area, the Swedes in the Baltic Sea and via the Russian rivers towards the Orient, and that the Danes went in a south-eastern direction along the coasts to France, Spain and the Mediterranean. But these are only generalizations: none of the three countries ever had a monopoly of any of the routes mentioned. It is, moreover, obvious that people who lived in the rough skerries on the west coast of Norway would have a way of life different from that of the inhabitants of Denmark with its flat fields and cosy, sheltered fjords.

There were plenty of small wars inside Scandinavia during the Viking Age, but at least as far as the first half of the period is concerned, such wars were mostly attempts by rival local magnates to subjugate as many as possible of the neighbouring areas, rather than struggles between nations. It did not take much to call oneself king at that time, and it was not until towards the end of the Viking Age, that is about 1000 A.D., that the real national states arose. The peasants or carls formed the nucleus of society. They made up a large, broad "middle" class. They were free, and had the right to carry arms and to appear before the *thing* (local assembly) in their capacity as landowners. Thus far, there were no differences of rank, but it can be assumed that — as today — a man who owned a hundred acres of land was held in higher esteem than one who had only ten. Over the peasants was ranged a very small upper class, the earls or greatest chieftains, and the kings. They were leaders chosen by the people, and it was they who conducted the great campaigns of conquest. Their lofty descent and their wealth made them natural standard-bearers, but these attributes were not always enough. If a leader was unsuccessful, or if he was unjust, he was discarded, and his people joined someone else. The same was true of the king. He, incidentally, could not become the legitimate ruler unless the people

Although Viking marriages were usually arranged between heads of families, sagas and poetry sometimes suggest that the Vikings were far from strangers to romantic love. In the poem *För Skirnis* (Skirnir's Journey) the god Freyr describes to his servant Skirnir his passion for the giantess Gerd, daughter of the giant Gymir:

" From on high I beheld in the halls of Gymir
a maiden to my mind;
her arms did gleam, their glamour filled
all the sea and the air.
This maiden is to me more dear
than maiden to any man;
but aesir and alfs* all will have it
that strangers aye we stay. "

Skirnir journeys to Gerd's home, and persuades her to become Freyr's bride, but she insists on delaying the meeting for nine nights. When he hears this, Freyr is beside himself:

" Long is a night, longer are two,
how shall I thole† three?
Shorter to me a month oft seemed,
than half this hovering time. "

* gods and elves
† bear

(that is, those who were free) had sworn allegiance to him at the *thing* — in spite of the fact that, in principle, the son of a king was heir to the throne. The everyday life of the peasants has been copiously described in the sagas, and in general it does not seem to have differed much from the life of Scandinavian peasants as late as the beginning of the age of mechanization. All farms were self-sufficient. Only for rare, specialized tasks was a professional craftsman sent for. The latter made up a separate class, though they sometimes farmed as well as practised their craft. The most important was probably the village blacksmith, who was also often reputed to "know a thing or two" about darker arts. Other things which they could not produce themselves, especially luxury articles, the peasants had to buy from tradesmen. Merchants constituted another separate class, although they, too, might be landowners.

The greatest difference between the society of the Vikings and that of Scandinavia in more recent times is that they included still another class, the lowest of them all: the thralls. To the thralls was assigned all the hard, unspecified work, which required nothing but physical strength. They virtually belonged to their masters from birth. They had no legal rights and, of course, were not allowed to carry arms. A free woman who had a child by a thrall thereby degraded herself to the father's level. However, for a master to have children by his bondswomen was regarded as a useful increase in the manpower of the farm. It should be noticed, however, that in all other respects women were on an equal footing with men. It was significant that the insignia of the housewife was the bunch of the keys, which she carried at her belt. She was the ruler within the four walls of the home, and often she had to manage the whole farm when her husband and sons had gone out on a Viking or business expedition. All these things have been extablished by archaeological finds. There exist many examples of women having rune-stones raised to commemorate their husbands or sons. The arrangement of the graves also shows that women were regarded as the equals of men: there is no difference in the value of the grave-goods. Marriages were often contracted by agreement of the families, and love would have to come later as best it could. But this had always been a common practice among farming populations. In some cases, however, love might defy all economic considerations, as some of the sagas show.

Children, of course, were the pride and wealth of the family. The family as a whole was of greater significance than the individual, and without children the family could not go on. It is true that some ancient Scandinavian laws permitted the exposure of unwanted children in order that they might perish, but this was not a common practice: only deformed children might suffer this fate. Healthy babies were not exposed except in periods of severe famine.

THE UNFORGIVABLE CRIME

In King Olaf Tryggvason's saga we are told that Earl Hakon ruled over sixteen counties in Norway, and began using his power to possess not only the daughters of powerful men but also their wives. This, of course, made him a lot of enemies. When Olaf came back to Norway from an expedition to England, many put their trust in him, and the people rose against Hakon. Followed only by his bondsman Kark, Earl Hakon fled to one of his mistresses, Thora at Rimul, and asked her to hide him. Kark dug a trench in her pigsty, into which both men climbed. Thora then covered it up. Olaf and his army came to Rimul to look for Hakon: "Olaf summoned the people together out in the yard, and standing on the rock which was beside the swine-sty spoke unto them, and the words that he uttered were that he would reward with riches and honour the man who would work mischief to Earl Hakon. This speech was heard both by the Earl and Kark. Now by them in the sty had they a light there with them, and the Earl said: 'Why art thou so pale, yet withal as black as earth? Is it in thy heart, Kark, that thou shouldst betray me?' 'Nay,' said Kark, 'we two were born on the self-same night, and long space will there not be twixt the hour of our deaths.' Towards evening went King Olaf away, and when it was night Kark slept, and the Earl kept watch, but Kark was troubled in his sleep. Then the Earl awakened him and asked him whereof he dreamt, and he said: 'I was now even at Ladir*, and Olaf Tryggvason placed a gold ornament about my neck.' The Earl answered: 'A blood-red ring will it be that Olaf Tryggvason will lay about thy neck,

* Olaf's home

intensifies: the sky reddens with fire, the firmament is cloven in two. The powers of evil, led by traitors, fire-demons and giants, converge on the home of the gods. Freyr slays the giant Beli but falls to the fire-demon Surt. Odin is swallowed by the Fenris-Wolf; his son avenges him. But when Thor and the World-Serpent slay each other, the end has come: "the sky blackens, the stars are gone, the earth sinks into the sea. Steam there is, smoke and fire: the flames play against heaven itself." The destruction is complete.

Here the sibyl stops for a moment, and when she continues, it is in a calmer strain. In a quiet epilogue she foresees how even after this last holocaust, a new green earth will rise out of the sea, how gods and men will return to their old homes, and how all ills will be repaired:

She sees a hall
lovelier than the sun,
roofed with gold in Gimle.
The noble warriors
there shall dwell,
enjoy eternal pleasure.

Just as the seeress speaks in *Völuspá*, so in the longest poem of the *Codex Regius*, the *Havamal*, the god Odin tells of his personal experiences. He tells how he seduced Gunnlöd and so won the mead of poetry from her father, the giant Suttung (Odin is the god of poetry), and how he was crossed in love by "Billing's maid". Most of the poem, however, consists of a series of precepts for behaviour in what seems to have been a lawless, suspicious and cynical society: "He who wishes to rob another of his property or to take his life should get up early; the lazy wolf will get no meat nor the sleeping man victory". The audience is particularly advised to avoid over-drinking: "There is a bird called the heron of forgetfulness which hovers over the ale-bout. It robs a man of his wits. With the feathers of this bird I was fettered at the house of Gunnlöd." Most dangerous of all, however, is the deceitfulness of womankind: "To have the love of a deceitfully-thinking woman is like driving a frisky two-year-old stallion over slippery ice when it has not been broken in; or like steering a boat without rudder in a wild wind; or like trying to catch a reindeer on thawing fells when one is lame".

In contrast, scaldic poetry was deliberately elaborate, elliptical and complex. Tradition tells that before the battle of Stamford Bridge in 1066, the Norwegian invader of England, King Harold Hardrada, declaimed two verses to his waiting troops. The first was as follows:

We stride forward,
fighting bravely,

Hear now how the scion of heroes
harried on the Wendish homelands,
in this burden; fortune-favoured
fared his ships from shipyard rollers;
hardly ever had a ruler
highborn launched more ships — 'twas ruled
rued by Wends — the foaming main to furrow,
frosty-prowed — against the folk-land.

Skylding king! With fire then fell you
furiously upon the heathen,
made great carnage, keen-eyed rapine —
queller, bloody, south by Jomsborg;
heathen hosts durst nowise shield their
halls within the ample breastworks:
fire and hurtling flame, high-blazing,
frightened townsmen, king, awe-stricken.

though byrnie*-less,
'gainst blue-steel swords.
Helmets do shine —
I have not mine:
our armour lies
below in the ships.

After this, he said: " This is crudely composed poetry. I shall now make a second, better verse. " He then recited the following: " In battle, we cringe not from the clashing of weapons in the shelter of shields — the valkyrie of the hawk's ground, true of word, exhorted me thus long ago. The necklace-bearer, in days gone by, bade me bear my helmet-support high in the din of metal, where the ice of battle and skulls meet. " The distinction Harold was making was between the relatively simple, Eddic style of the first verse and the so-called " scaldic " style of the second verse. It provides some relatively simple examples of kennings, or metaphors. " The helmet-support " is the head and " the ice of battle " is the gleaming sword. " The hawk's ground " is the arm, a term taken from falconry. The kenning can be considerably more complicated and abstruse. For example, in the poetry of an eleventh-century Icelandic scald, the following paraphrase for a warrior appears: " the slinger of the fire of the storm of the troll of the protecting moon of the boat-house's steed ". " The steed of the boat-house " is a ship. " The protecting-moon of the ship " is a shield, a reference to the fixing of shields along the gunwales of Viking ships. " The troll of the shield " is the sword, " the storm of the sword " is battle and " the fire of battle " is again the sword. Finally, " the slinger of the sword " is a warrior.

The ornate effect produced by the kenning is increased by the intricate scaldic verse forms. The so-called "Court Measure" cultivated by most scaldic poets is one of the most complicated metres ever used. Like the Eddic metres, alliteration is part of the structure, but in addition it demands set internal rimes and assonances, a six-syllable line and an eight-line strophe. Composing scaldic verse according to the rules must have been very much like constructing a crossword puzzle.

The poems were sometimes misunderstood even by the saga writers. A famous example of this is in Snorre's Saga of St. Olaf. He quotes a poem of the scald Sighvat Thordarson which described Olaf's sixth battle, in which he attacked London Bridge and " offered Ygg's strife to the English ". The meaning is clearly that Olaf was fighting against the English, but Snorre believed and wrote

* Byrnie: a coat of mail

KING HELGI SAILS FOR THE LAND OF HUNDING

From *The First Lay of Helgi the Hunding-Slayer*

Rose the din of oars, of iron clashing,
crashed shield 'gainst shield with shock of rowing,
as dashed through the waves the warrior's fleet;

the staunch wave-steeds† stood out to sea.
It burst on the ears when, buffeting,
the long ship keels met Kolga's sister°,
as if surf with cliff did clash in storm.

Then higher Helgi bade hoist the topsails —
the crews shunned not the shock of billows —
when the dreadful daughter of Aegir
would overwhelm the hawser-steeds.†

But Sigrun‡ on high hovering above
did shield them stoutly, and their ships also;
the king's brine-hogs† out of Ran's§ clutches
glided safely at Gnipa Grove.

† Kennings, or poetic metaphors, for ships.
° A daughter of Aegir, the sea-god, *i.e.* "the wave".
‡ A valkyrie.
§ Aegir's wife.

in his history that Olaf was always on the side of the English king Ethelred. He therefore has Olaf and Ethelred as allies jointly attacking London Bridge in an attempt to dislodge the Danes from London.

Even so, a good deal of scaldic poetry is simpler, and easy to enjoy even today. The Icelander Egil Skall-Grimsson, of all the scaldic poets, most successfully mastered his medium. Egil's greatest poem is the *Sonatorrek* (The Irreparable Loss of Sons). After many adventures, including two successful encounters with his enemy Eric Bloodaxe, king of Norway, he eventually returned to Iceland and settled down. But then he lost his two eldest sons within a very short space of time. One is taken away by illness, the other, his favourite, was drowned in the fjord near home. At first Egil is inconsolable. He takes to his bed and refuses to touch food and drink, intending to starve himself to death. But his daughter persuades him to tell his sorrow in poetry rather than succumb to it. This is the occasion for the *Sonatorrek*. The poem begins slowly, with an expression of grief and loneliness:

Tardily takes
my tongue to move,
and to stir
the steel-yard of song:
hopeless is't
about Odin's-theft,
hard to draw
from the heart's-fastness!

(Odin's theft is poetry.) The pace quickens as the poet declares how he longs to wreak vengeance on the sea-god Aegir and his wife Ran:

Sorely Ran
has smitten me —
left me bare
of bosom-friends;
the sea snapped
my sib's tight links —
a strong strand
is stripped from me.
If my suit
with sword I could press,
all over
for the ale-smith were it:
could I kill
the storm's kinsman,

THE HEAVENLY MAIDENS

Viking-Age metal figures such as those in the drawing above represent the Valkyries, the legendary beings whose duty it was to carry the souls of warriors killed in battle to their last resting-place, Valhalla, and who feature frequently in Viking poetry. These stout, homely and apparently middle-aged ladies bear little resemblance to the popular, heroic Wagnerian conception of Valkyries.

Aegir's might
I would meet as foe.

(The ale-smith was Aegir, who was also the brewer of the gods.) But, the poet realizes, he is too weak for this: he is just a luckless old warrior. All that is left for him is to find consolation in poetry, and await death cheerfully:

Hard my lot;
for Herian's-foe's-
stern-sister
stands on the ness.
Gladly, though,
and ungrudgingly,
with light heart
Hel I will bide.

" Herian " is a name for Odin, and his " foe " is the Fenris-Wolf who swallowed him in the Ragnarök, as is related in the *Völuspá*. The Fenris-Wolf's sister is Hel, the death goddess. The allusion to the fate of the god of poetry is particularly appropriate here. " The ness " is Digranes, where Egil's father and sons were buried.

A WOMAN ON A BUCKLE

It is true that the Vikings were notable craftsmen, but they seldom went further than purely ornamental art within a fixed framework. The unique buckle on the right is therefore all the more remarkable, for it represents human beings in an almost naturalistic form. Fashioned in bronze, the buckle shows the strong face, powerfully carved, of a woman with a carefully elaborate hair arrangement apparently held in place by a frontlet.

DAILY LIFE — DOMESTIC ARTS, TOOLS, CLOTHES, AND CRAFTSMANSHIP FOR PEACE AND WAR

Much modern knowledge of the Vikings' daily life has been reconstructed from the rich finds at Oseberg and Gokstad. They provided a full range of utensils for kitchen and table, tools for spinning and weaving, shoes, combs, wagons, and sledges. Hunting and fishing supplied the food that the farm did not yield, while the skins and wool of animals reared on the farm supplied material for clothes and shoes. Buildings, tools, shoes and cloth were made on the farm. The Eddic poem *Rigsthula* provides evidence which helps piece together the daily life of the Vikings. The thrall had unskilled duties: carrying burdens, fetching firewood, spreading dung, feeding and herding pigs, cattle and goats, digging peat. The freeman worked as ploughman, smith and carpenter, among other jobs. Nobles passed the daylight hours practising with weapons, swimming, riding, hunting to hounds, playing chess, making war and winning wealth. Most houses had a single room, where people cooked, ate, slept and worked. The Vikings cultivated oats, barley, rye, and probably wheat and peas. Cereals were used for porridge as well as baking, and malted barley for brewing beer. They had milk, and so, no doubt, cheese and butter. They ate beef, mutton, bacon, fish, game and poultry. *Rigsthula* tells us of some of the dishes typical of the different classes — meat broth and hard bran bread for the thrall: boiled veal for the freeman farmer; white wheaten bread, chicken and wine for the nobles. The centre of family life was, as described in *Rigsthula*, the open hearth, which was probably placed in the middle of the floor. The fire provided most of the heat and gave light for the household, but oil lamps existed for extra illumination. People retired indoors as daylight faded, and gathered around the fire. *Rigsthula* describes a typical indoor occupation of the freeman — making the warp-beam for a loom — while the earl in his house is shafting arrows and making a bowstring.

One Gotland picture-stone includes the little illustration above of the workshop of the legendary smith Völund or Wayland. The tongs and hanging hammers are, however, realistic enough.

THE TRAIL OF VIKING RELICS

The most important of the finds which have helped scholars to build up a composite picture of daily life among the Vikings are concentrated in Scandinavia, as the map opposite shows. Among them are the ship-burials at Oseberg, Gokstad and Tune near Oslo, at Ladby and Skuldelev in Denmark, and at the towns at Birka, Hedeby and Kaupang. The ship-finds at Hjortspring and Nydam in south Jutland are pre-Viking. Rich Viking finds are conspicuous by their absence in the areas of Nordic settlement in the British Isles, probably because of the strength of the native English culture. Even Iceland, a place where the Vikings found no competing culture, has produced little in the way of spectacular finds from the Viking period, perhaps because Icelandic Vikings were settlers rather than notable plunderers and traders like their relations in Scandinavia, and never had kings and other men as rich as these.

Viking-Age houses in Scandinavia were built mainly of timber. Since wood is perishable, archaeologists usually find only "negative" traces of early Norse houses: holes where posts had been sunk, grooves where walls had been, the remains of stone foundations. Little that is definite can be proved, except on the basis of a few instances where, under special circumstances — like dampness of soil — large sections of house timbers have been preserved. Hedeby, a characteristic Viking-Age site including houses where this was the case, has already been mentioned (page 55).

In the pre-Viking Iron Age, the most common type of house in Scandinavia was a hall-like building, sometimes more than 150 feet long, with a double row of wooden supports to carry the roof, and with walls of earth, turf or so-called "plaited work". This consisted of a frame of vertical posts through which rods and brushwood were woven, the whole being then coated with mud: in other words a sort of wattle-and-daub construction. These were all-purpose houses, with both human beings and animals under one roof.

With the coming of the Viking Age, buildings began to be grouped together to form towns at certain geographically favourable places, to promote trade and industry. Hedeby was such a place. Individual houses also underwent a change. There was specialization, each building being designed for a specific purpose, so they were therefore made smaller. The biggest verifiable house in Hedeby is about 15 × 50 feet. Most of the other houses there are considerably smaller. Because of this, only in exceptional cases was it necessary to have posts inside to help to support the roof. All the houses are four-sided, and have straight walls into which support posts are built. These carry the roof, and were probably connected by longitudinal beams. The largest of the Hedeby houses have wattle-and-daub walls, and in this respect they differ little from the normal practice of the early Iron Age. They also had an entrance in each gable. But instead of using the old Iron Age solid-post construction, builders seem to have experimented at Hedeby with several sorts of plank work. The idea seems to have been to form a framework of sufficient stability by joining upright planks, set in the earth, to horizontal planks at ground level and roof level. The spaces between the upright timbers were then closed by walls of mud-coated wattle-work. The roof was presumably covered with straw. The hearth, simply a pit dug in the floor, sometimes plastered with mud or stone-lined, is situated in an unusual position, the centre of the house, where two pairs of vertical posts — presumably roof-supports — sometimes also occur. Smaller wattle-and-daub houses are also found at Hedeby, the smallest

A WARLIKE WEATHER-VANE

Before being used as a weather-vane on a Swedish church, the gilt bronze standard opposite flew at a warship's prow.

HOW HOUSES WERE BUILT

At left is a detailed reconstruction of the interior of one type of Viking house, divided into rooms. The hearths are in the centre of the floor. Above one, food is being cooked in a large hanging cauldron. Smoke from the fire escapes through an open gable. The walls have sleeping recesses. The drawings directly above show what the gables of a house in Hedeby probably looked like. The top drawing shows the exterior, where wattle-and-daub has been applied over planks. Below it is a sketch of the internal construction of the gable. Horizontal and vertical timbers were joined by wooden nails.

measuring 10 × 13 feet. A special type of Viking construction had wattle-and-daub walls faced on the inside with boards — the walls having a layer of stones as a foundation. This wattle-and-daub construction, incidentally, is an ancestor of that used in the half-timbered houses of Elizabethan England.

The walls of some houses at Hedeby were built entirely of timber. They are all very small. Presumably it was too wasteful of material to build big houses in this way. Two types of wooden construction occur. One used a frame which, in principle, is the same as in the plaited-work construction, but the actual wattle-work is replaced by horizontal planks nailed or pegged to the vertical timbers. In the other method of construction — called stave-construction — the whole wall consists of upright planks or staves standing side by side, with their ends sunk into the ground. The Hedeby house thus constructed measures only 10 × 10 feet, with a hearth in one corner and an entrance at the other. Similar construction made its appearance in western Europe as early as the New Stone Age, at Aichbühl in Germany for example. Then it seems to have disappeared until it turned up again at Hedeby, but was mostly used for much larger buildings like the stave-churches dating from the end of the Viking Age, which exist at Lund in Sweden and at Urnes in Norway. In these later buildings, the staves are usually jointed into one another, which helped to make the building more windproof.

Curiously enough, during the late Viking Age a strikingly severe standardization of house-types sometimes occurred, when individual houses were all built according to one standard pattern and show a quite amazing resemblance to each other. Such houses are found in the great Danish military camps excavated at Trelleborg, Aggersborg and Fyrkat (page 63). The houses in each of these camps are exactly the same size, but house-sizes differ somewhat from camp to camp. In Trelleborg the houses are exactly a hundred Roman feet long. At the widest point they measure twenty-six feet across. The gables are straight, and the long sides are sections of an extremely regular ellipse. The construction of the walls, as was the case in one of the houses found at Hedeby, is double: there is the wall proper, and then, outside it, at a distance of three feet, a row of posts running parallel with it. At Fyrkat and Aggersborg the actual house walls consisted of wattle-work, and the outer posts leaned inwards, thereby strengthening the wattle-work and helping buttress the weight of the roof.

The builders at Trelleborg evidently felt a real need for houses with a large open space in the middle. This was achieved by eliminating the series of support posts inside, which had been obligatory in the older design, and by giving the walls their ellipse-like shape. Questions of economy may have dictated

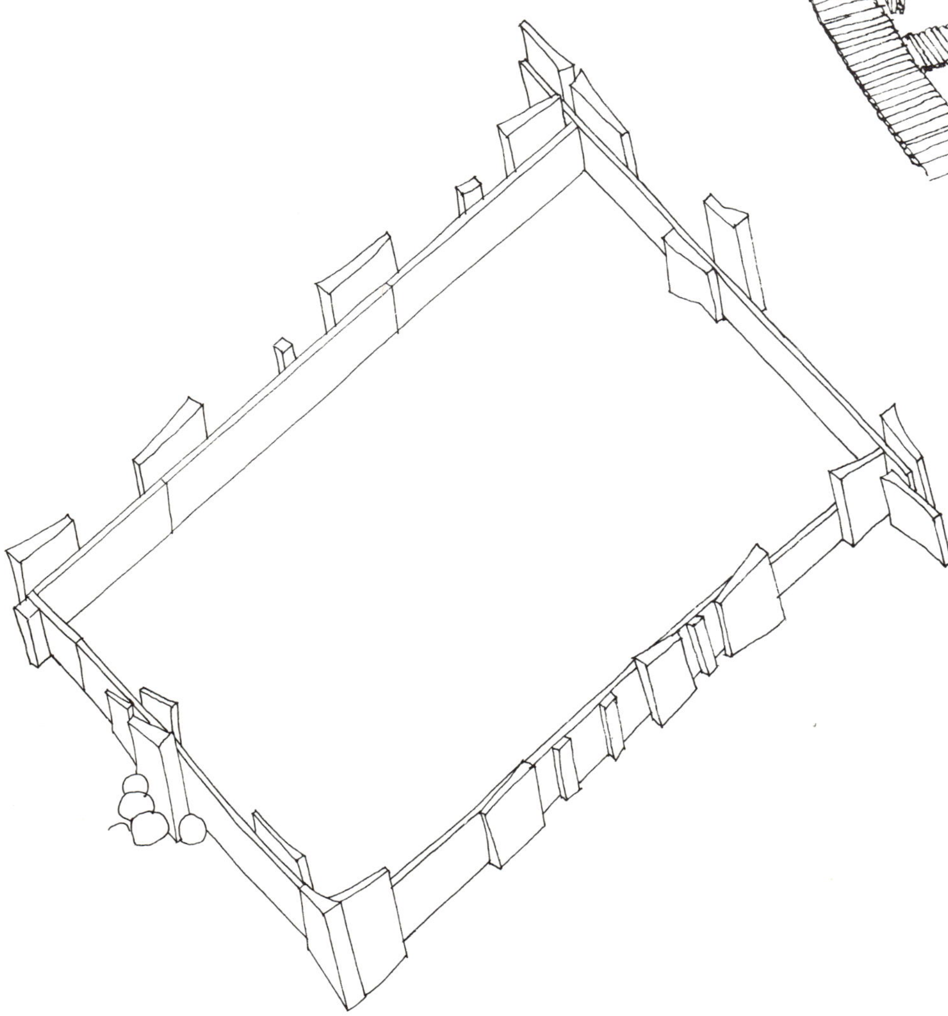

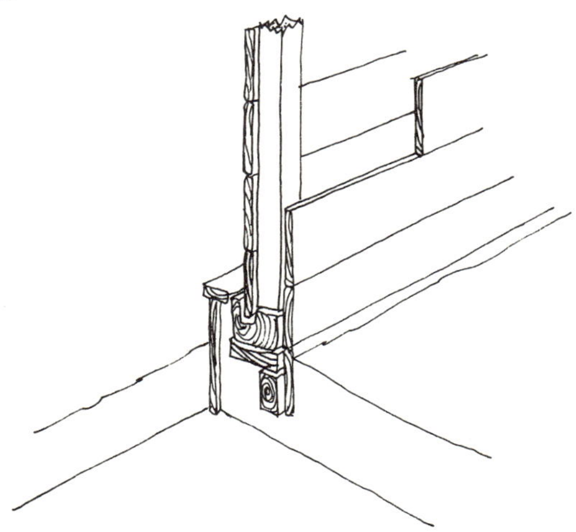

THE PATTERN AND THE PIECES

The dampness of the earth at Hedeby helped to preserve the traces not only of houses, but also of wells and fences between plots of land, making it possible to reconstruct groups of structures like those at the top of the page. At left is a plan of the groundsill and foundations for the roof supports of a house. The double walling, found in one house at Hedeby, is illustrated in the detail above.

the new house-design, for it allowed a saving in timber. But the need for a free space in the middle of a house was evident earlier in the Iron Age, and was achieved by construction on the same principle used in Trelleborg houses. What seems to have been a sixth-century ship-house — a so-called *naust* — has been excavated to the south of Bergen in Norway. Ninety-two feet long by twenty-three feet wide, the house had to be big enough to hold an entire longship. The building material most readily available dictated the building methods used. In the coastal areas of north-western Europe suitable timber was scarce, and as a result wattle-and-daub construction predominated there until superseded by half-timbering. In more heavily forested areas such as eastern and central Europe, it was not only possible, but usually necessary, because of the severe winters, to build houses that were more solid. Construction methods requiring an abundance of timber — such as cross-timbering — naturally occur in these areas. No cross-timbering exists at Hedeby, however. It is still not known when this technique first gained a foothold in Scandinavia. It is found in the burial chambers in the early Viking Age graves at Oseberg and Gokstad in Norway, but no other definite instances of early cross-timbering are known. One difficulty is that houses so built are not sunk in the earth, so that it is virtually impossible to be sure when traces of them have been found. The investigation of farms undertaken recently on Helgö island in the Mälar district of Sweden may help clear up the question. The main period of settlement on this site was, as noted earlier, immediately before the Viking Age. Though the houses generally are long and hall-like with rows of posts inside, foundations of stone have been found which can hardly be anything but bases for cross-timbered houses. Their excavation, however, is not yet complete.

HOMES IN HEDEBY

Danish houses at the Viking town of Hedeby included several designs and types of construction. Above, a house with holes under the roof-peak to let out smoke. Below, a house built wholly of timber. The horizontal planks are fastened to vertical ones.

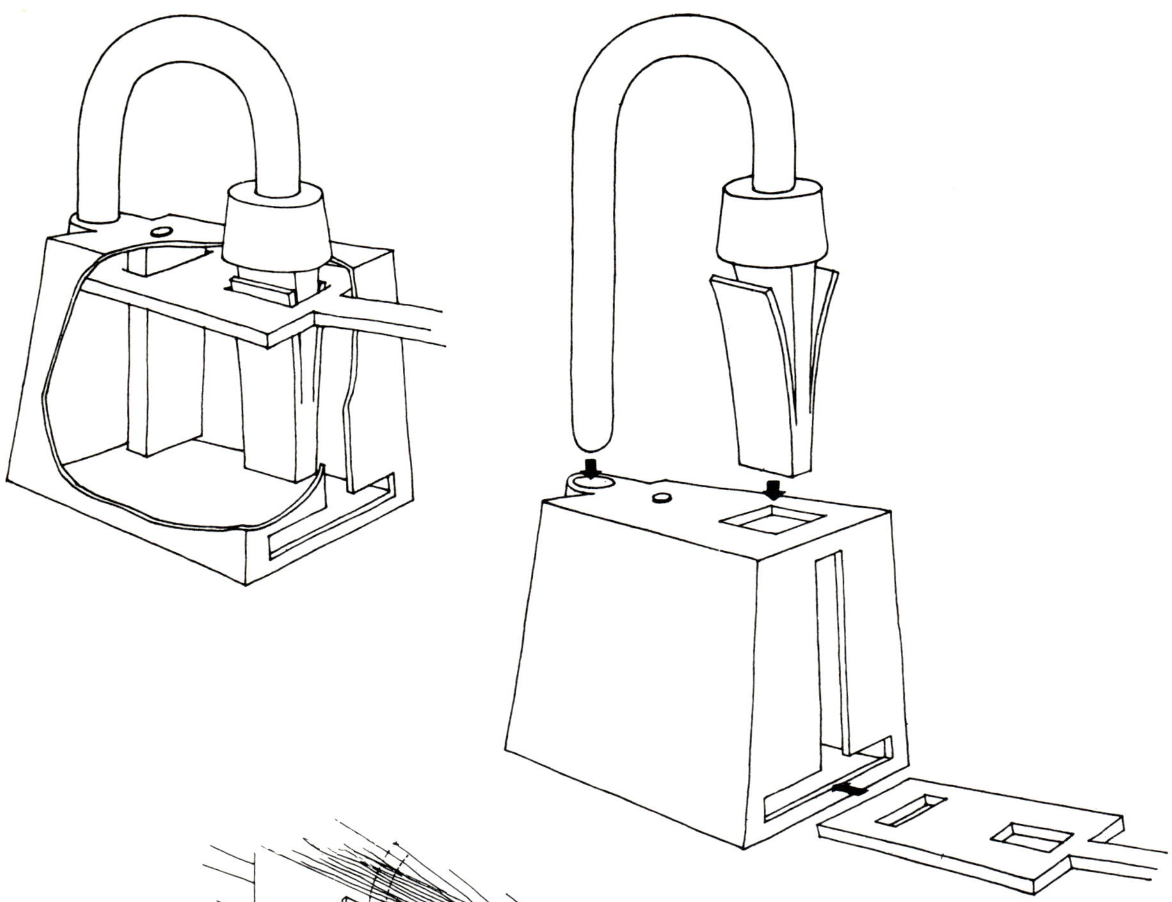

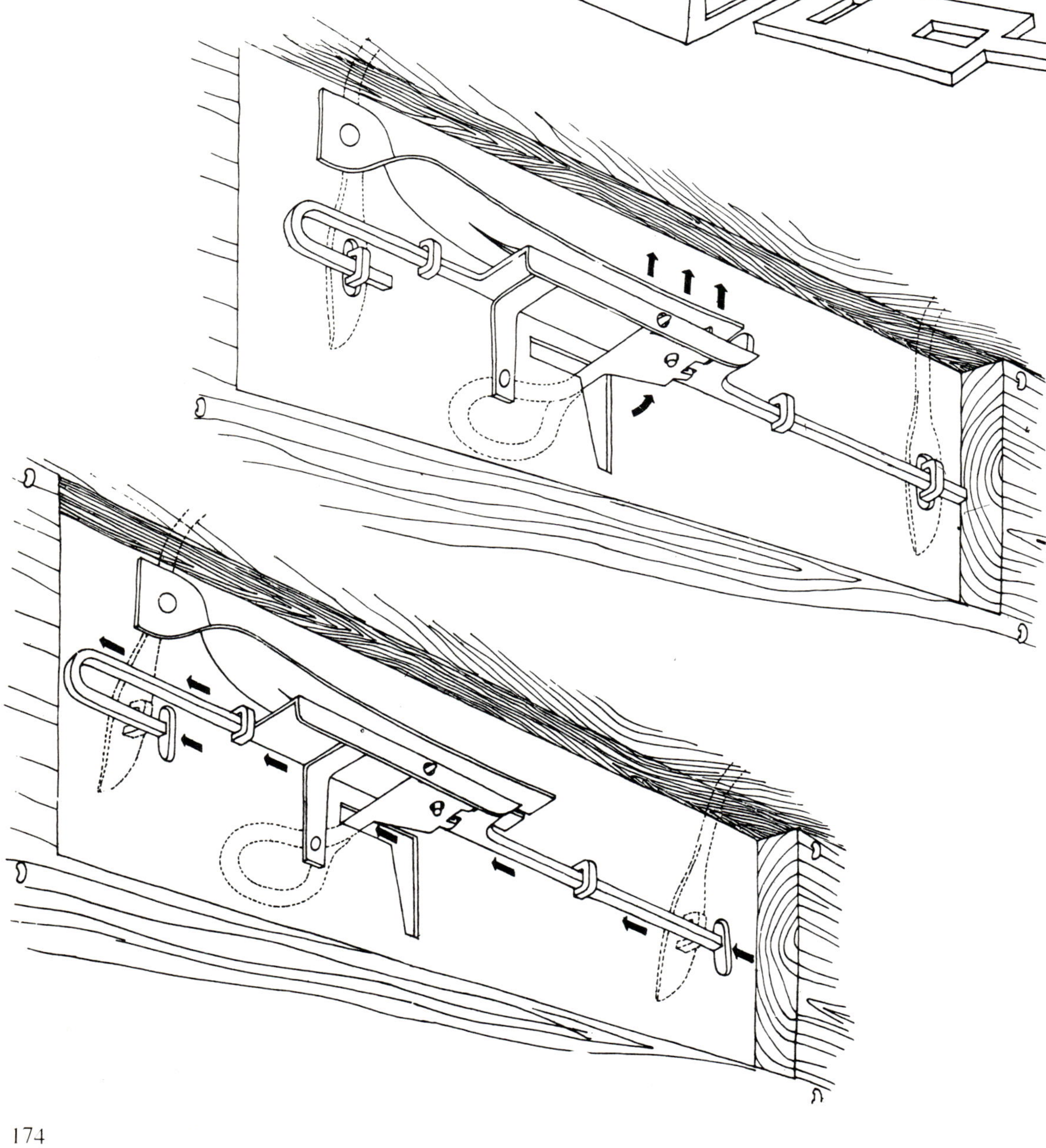

DETERRING THE THIEF

The Vikings had much more need of locks than did their forefathers. In their new trading towns, there were more expensive objects to steal, and many strangers to steal them. Viking locks are skilful adaptations of the Roman locks preserved in western Europe. Roman locks, however, had far too many details requiring precision work to be easily and cheaply manufactured. The Vikings very cleverly simplified their construction, as is shown in the two drawings of locks on the right. The lids of Viking chests were locked in much the same way as a modern suitcase: there were hinged mounts which had eyes or little lugs fitting into the lock proper. But whereas modern man has to use both hands to unlock his suitcase, because it has two separate locks, the Viking could unlock (or lock) his chest in one operation. Padlocks were common during the Viking Age. Their method of construction was well adapted to the abilities of a country smith. As in the case of the chest-lock, a maximum of security was achieved with the minimum of intricately-shaped details. Viking smiths, in fact, provide an object-lesson in how to construct an entirely adequate padlock while using nothing but plain pieces of iron. When found nowadays Viking padlocks are almost always locked. The reason for this is that the bow or hoop of a Viking padlock — like most other early locks of the type — is not hinged or pivoted as it would be in a modern one, but is a separate, removable piece. To avoid losing this piece, one had, therefore, to lock a Viking padlock immediately after use.

TWO CLEVER LOCKS

The spring mechanism of a Viking padlock (top drawings) seems simple, but was an irritating deterrent to anyone without the right key. The hole at the shaft end of the blade of the spadeshaped key engages and compresses the double-bladed spring on the bow, so that the bow can be withdrawn and removed. The slot at the end of the blade fits over a specially-shaped piece of iron inside the lock, thus preventing the use of unauthorized keys. The chest-lock (shown below) works in another way. The key is shaped more like a modern one, and is intended to be twisted. When this is done, its prongs slip through the holes of the locking bar, and lift the spring on the upper side. A lateral movement of the key in the keyhole, and the chest is open.

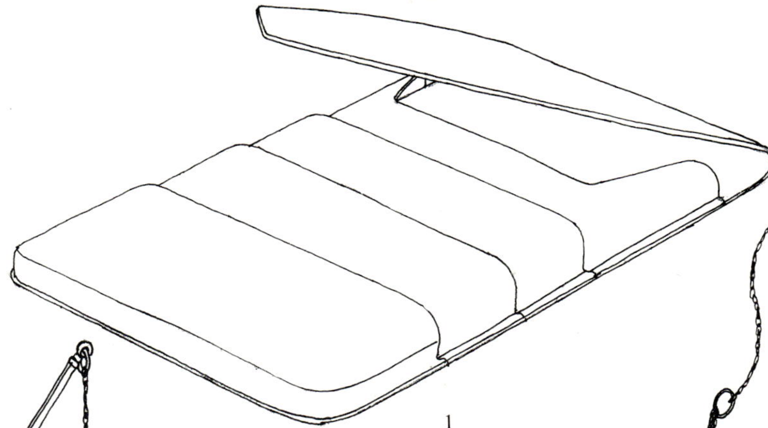

1

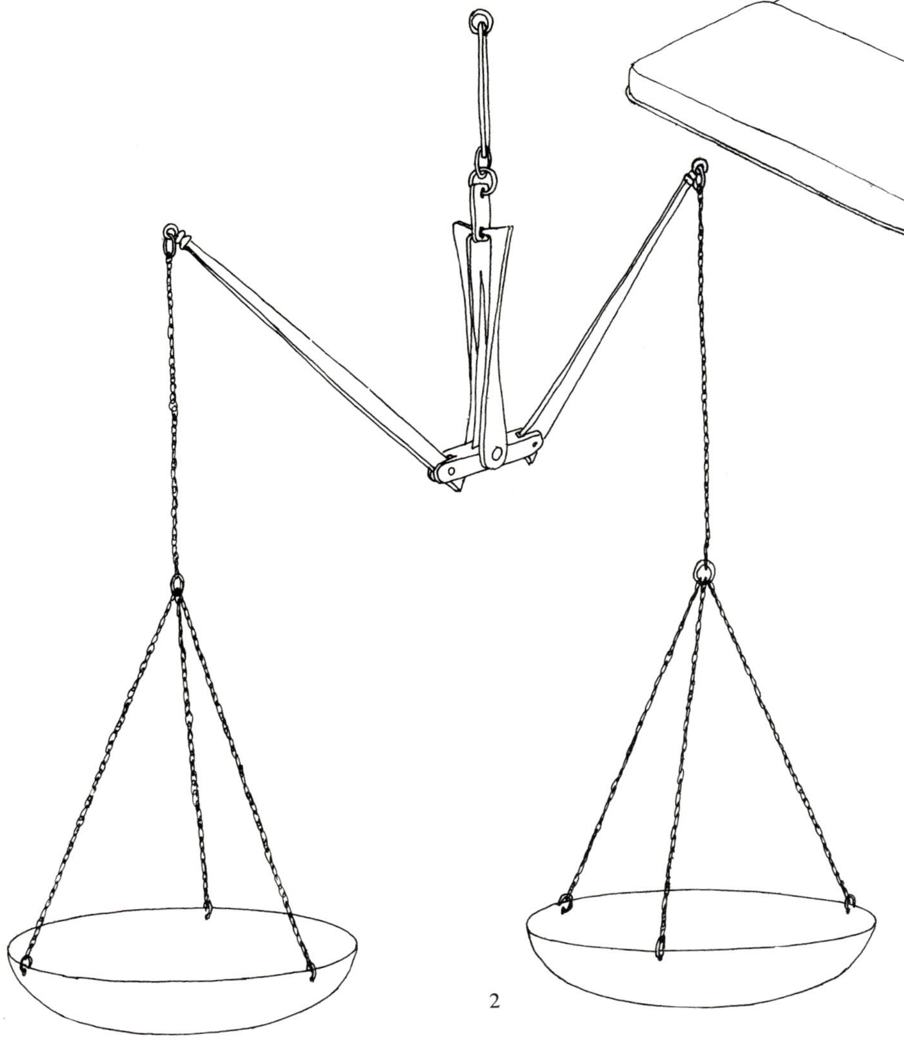

2

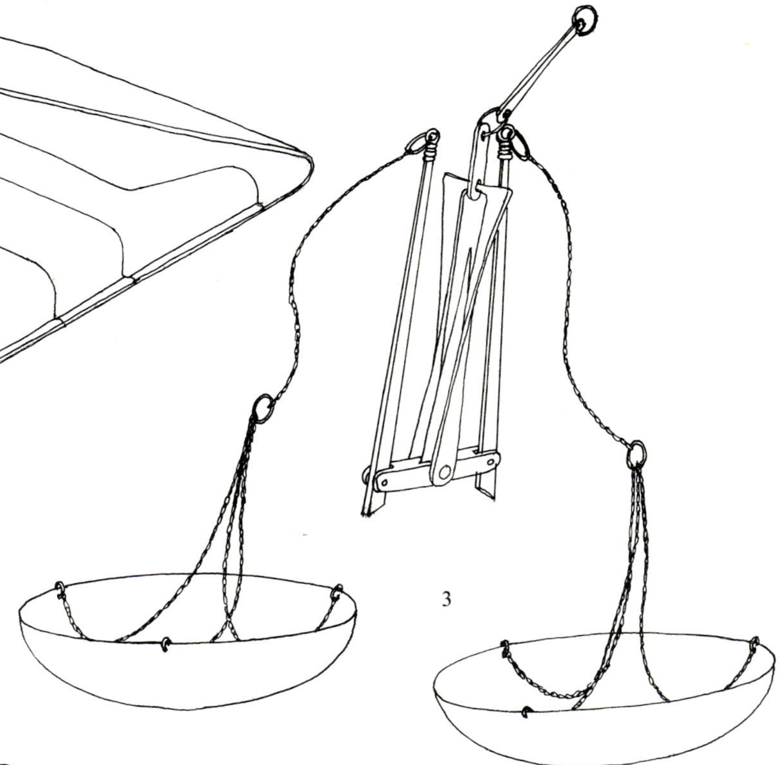

3

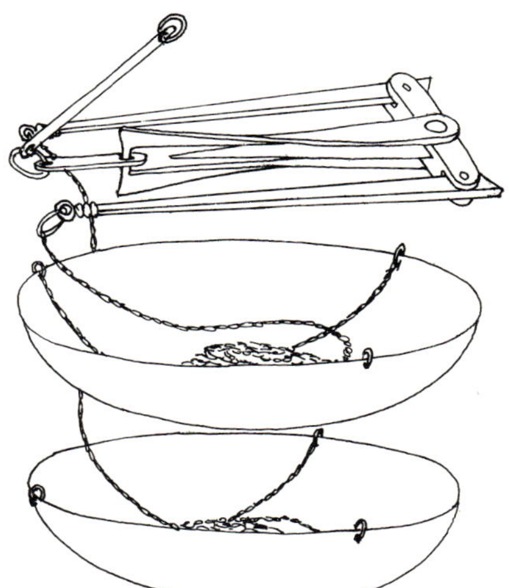

4

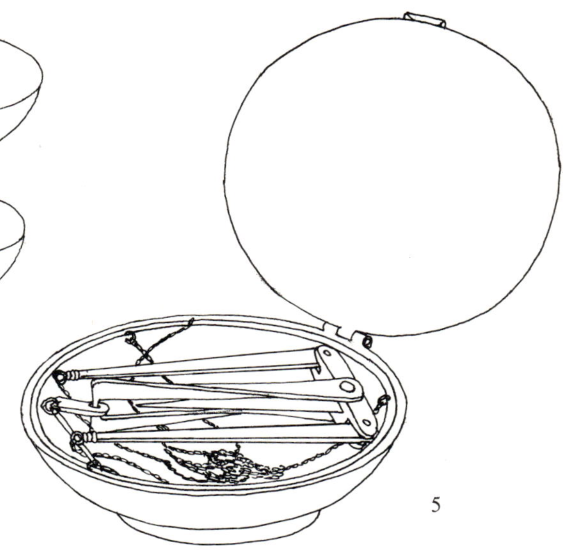

5

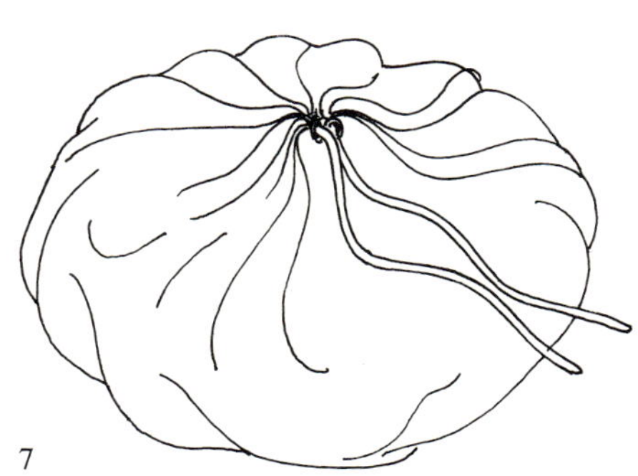

7

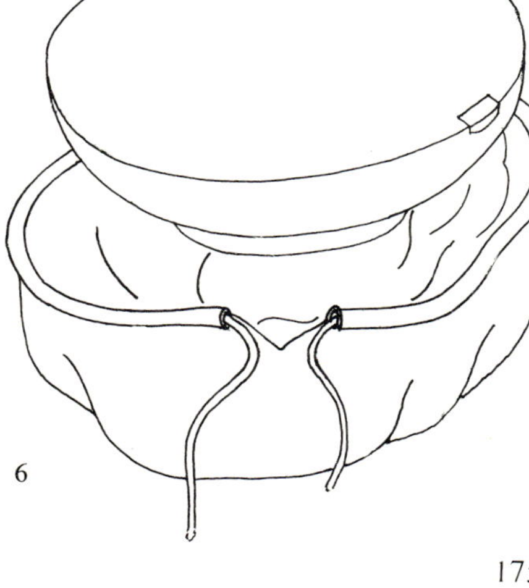

6

WALLET, WEIGHTS AND MEASURES

This skin wallet of fine workmanship (1), with many practical pockets, was needed by its owner, a Birka merchant, to keep silver coins of different values separate. When found, it contained a few of these, and also some small weights. A small portable set of scales (2) was part of the necessary equipment of the tradesman in Viking times — not for weighing merchandise but for weighing the payment, silver. But such scales were sensitive articles which had to be stored and transported carefully. This illustration shows how the scales were folded up (3), the pans placed inside one another (4), the whole thing put in a round metal box with a cover (5), and, finally, the box stowed in a skin bag (6, 7).

SIGNS OF WORLD-WIDE TRADE - AND LOOT

In the tenth century hundreds of thousands of coins like those on the left poured into the Baltic region, and their presence bears witness to Viking skill at trading, and fighting, in the farthest reaches of the known world. Some coins are from as far away as Samarkand, Tashkent, Bokhara and other Muslim mints more than 2,000 miles away across the forests, steppes and deserts of Central Asia. With the rare exception of coins minted at Birka and at Hedeby, the Scandinavians did not produce currency themselves until the eleventh century. Instead they continued to use this imported coinage in its original form. At present, about 85,000 Islamic and Persian coins have been found in Scandinavia, mostly struck by the Samanid dynasty which ruled in Turkestan in the tenth century. There are only slightly fewer German coins, mostly of the eleventh century, and from England there are at least 50,000, almost all minted between 990 and 1050 A.D. Most consist of tribute extorted from the English. The Anglo-Saxon Chronicle reports the payment of over 200,000 pounds weight of silver to the Vikings between 991 and 1018.

MAKING CHANGE - AND WEIGHING IT

Barter was no longer the only means of exchange, but pure-metal weight, assessed on scales like those illustrated at right, was the only wholly reliable monetary standard. To the dealer of skins in Birka or Kaupang, a silver coin was worth exactly the same as an equivalent weight of uncoined silver — unlike today, when silver is worth considerably more uncoined than coined. Therefore, he did not hesitate to split the coins into small segments when change was needed. Arm bracelets or unworked silver rods, spirally shaped and securely fitted around the wrist — for pockets did not exist — were another form of working capital. A piece could simply be cut off and weighed when needed. The box at the lower edge of the picture is a case for a folding balance of this kind — functional, elegant, and not much larger than a pocket watch. Marked weights of iron and bronze of oriental design, the property of the merchants, are often found in Birka graves.

In Viking houses, most of what little furniture there was, was built permanently into the house, and consisted mainly of fixed benches on which to lie on to sleep. Large decorated beds were used in the royal households of Gokstad and Oseberg, as can be seen from the finds, but it is not known if they were common. The benches and beds were furnished with heavy blankets like those found at Oseberg. There, and in a few other instances, the remains of feather pillows have been found, so it is possible that the Vikings sometimes slept under eiderdown covers.

A rich Danish grave from the late Viking Age contained fragments of a small wooden table. On the table was a shallow bronze dish, and the whole may have served as a wash-stand. The ordinary household table of the Vikings would probably look like the long narrow tables known from the Middle Ages, and depicted on the Bayeux Tapestry. In the Oseberg ship burial was found the only known chair of the period.

Articles not in use were kept in wooden chests and boxes. Several splendid chests were found in the Oseberg ship, and locks, keys and hinges have survived in many graves even when the wood has long since crumbled away. The locks are often of ingenious construction, and many of the small boxes must have been intended for valuables. Some of the Oseberg chests are veritable strong-boxes, heavily iron-bound, while others have only the minimum of iron mounts to hold them together. The keys to the various locks would hang from the housewife's belt, as a symbol of her social status. In old Norse laws, it is stated that a woman has the right of divorce if her husband denies her the keys of the house.

A large trough from the Oseberg ship still contained remains of cereals, and was surely used for kneading dough. Flour for bread and porridge was ground in hand-mills, a tedious task taking up much of the time of the domestic servants. Bread was probably baked on small round pans, which are often found in Viking graves. Many of them can be rotated on a central rivet to avoid burning the bread: see illustration on page 180. Kettles were hung from chains above the open hearth. Viking-Age kettles were of riveted iron or copper sheet, or carved from soapstone. Most of them have a capacity of between seven and eleven pints. Soapstone is soft and easily carved, and retains heat for a very long time, so it is a good material for cooking vessels. The soapstone vessels, at any rate, must have been very popular, for a great many have been found. Wooden ladles were used for stirring and pouring, and several have been found in the Oseberg ship.

A BUCKET WITH BRONZE TRIMMINGS

This bucket from the Oseberg find contained wild apples when found — part of the food for the voyage to the land of the dead. The engraved openwork hoops do not resemble the decorative style generally used by the Vikings, and the bucket is probably imported. It may have come from the British Isles. A richly decorated object like this was probably part of the "tableware" used in the Oseberg household.

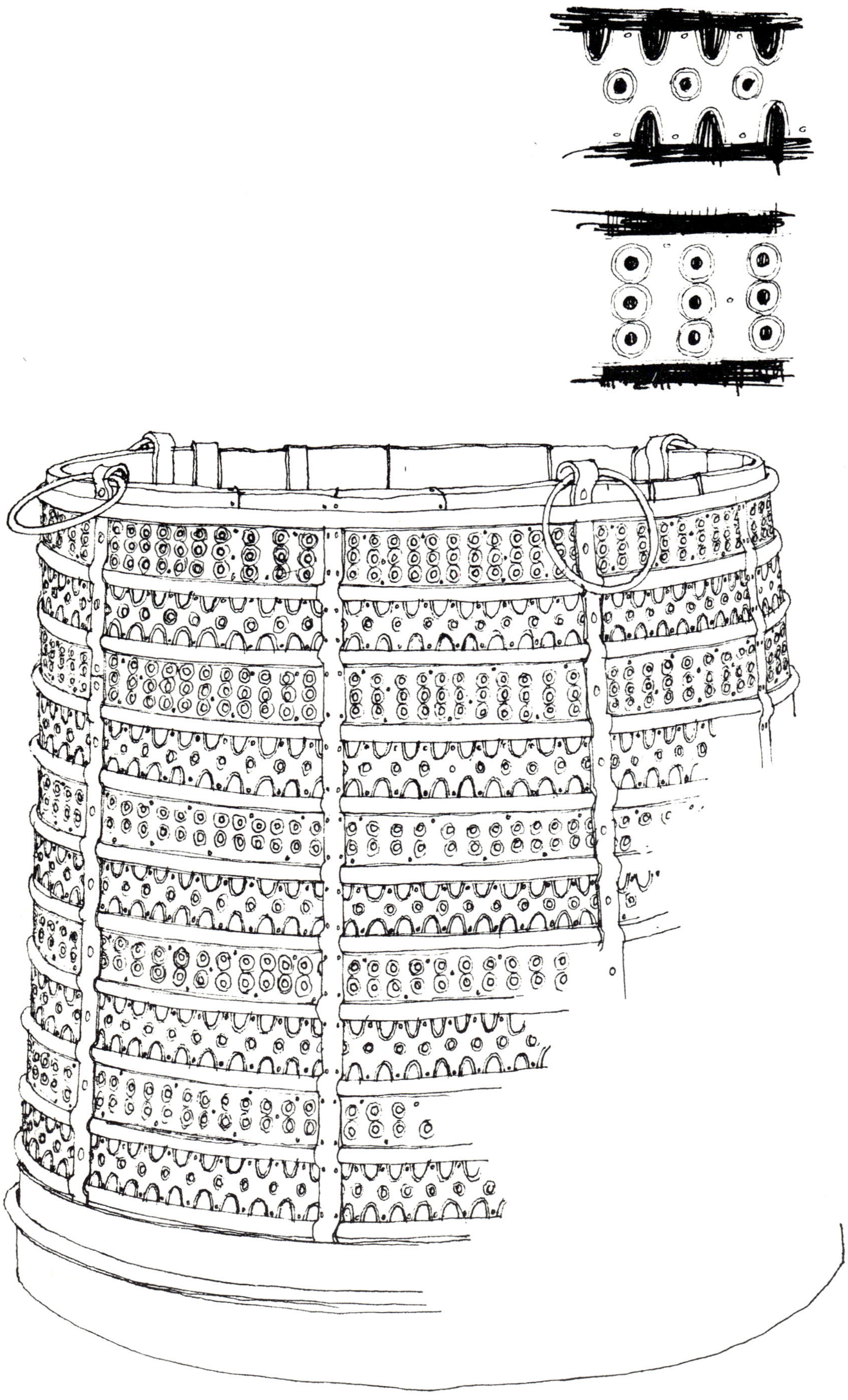

1

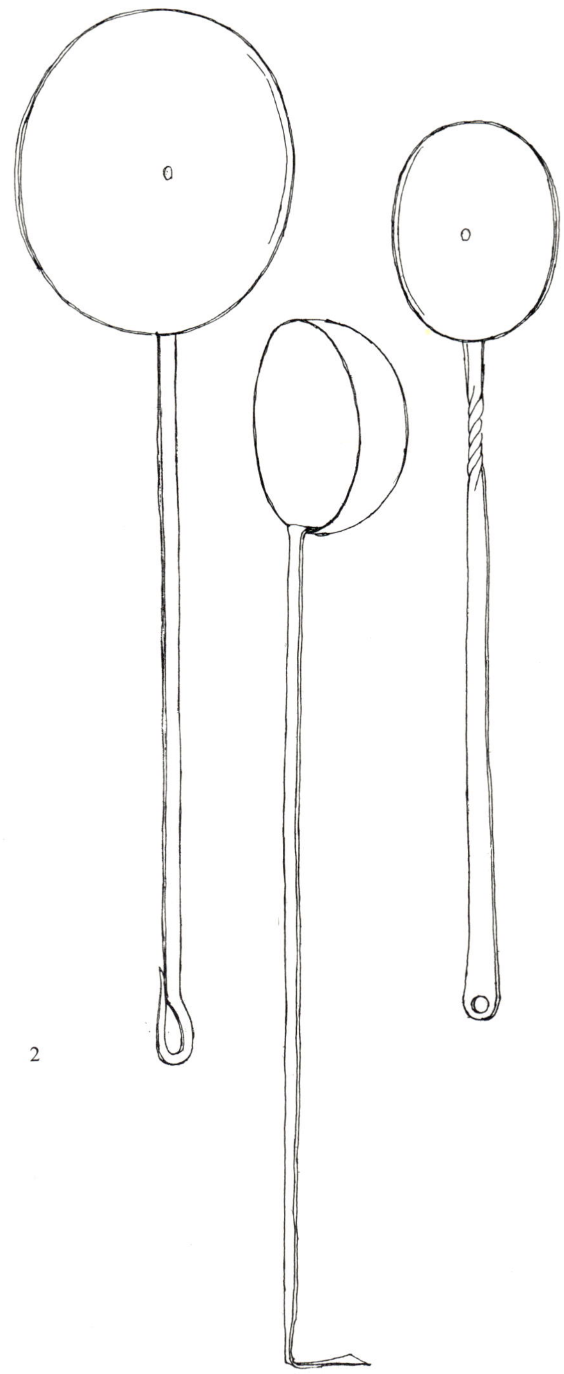

2

DOMESTIC IMPLEMENTS

1. Details of the bucket found at Oseberg (see page 178).
2. Simpler than the bucket, but very practical, are the two frying irons with their revolving discs, and the long-shafted scoop, which could also be used for heating drinks.
3. Iron implements for frying meat and fish.
4. This iron kettle, with a collapsible stand supported by clawed birds' feet, was probably used as a camping utensil only. It stood firmly on the ground over a fire at a temporary camp-site.

Meat and fish could be grilled or boiled. The grill forks and spits found in many graves point to the popularity of grilled food, then as now. Some graves have large forks, for picking choice pieces of meat or fish from the cooking-pot. Much fish and meat was undoubtedly preserved for use in winter or on long sea voyages, in much the same ways as those used in later times: by salting, smoking and drying. Well-worn carving-boards for cutting up dried fish or meat were found in the Gokstad ship, and in the Oseberg ship a large table knife lay among the other cooking implements. For eating, every man, woman and child had his or her own knife, and spoons of horn or wood. Otherwise, they ate with their fingers. Ordinary axes were used for butchering animals and cutting up meat. Two such axes were found in the Oseberg ship. Well-made, decorated troughs and trays from the Oseberg find were probably the "table-ware" of the royal household. In the Gokstad ship were flat round wooden disks, which probably served as plates.

By the standards of the modern housewife, used to stainless steel and electricity, a Viking housewife's kitchen equipment would seem appalling. But though the implements were few, even in the Viking Age their shape and function had been tested for many centuries, and they are as practical as anything of the sort made today. Some of the large buckets found at Oseberg and Gokstad may have been used for brewing beer, and others as containers for salt meat. One smaller bucket is fitted with a lock in the lid, and must have been intended as a container for other things than food. When found, it held weaving tools.

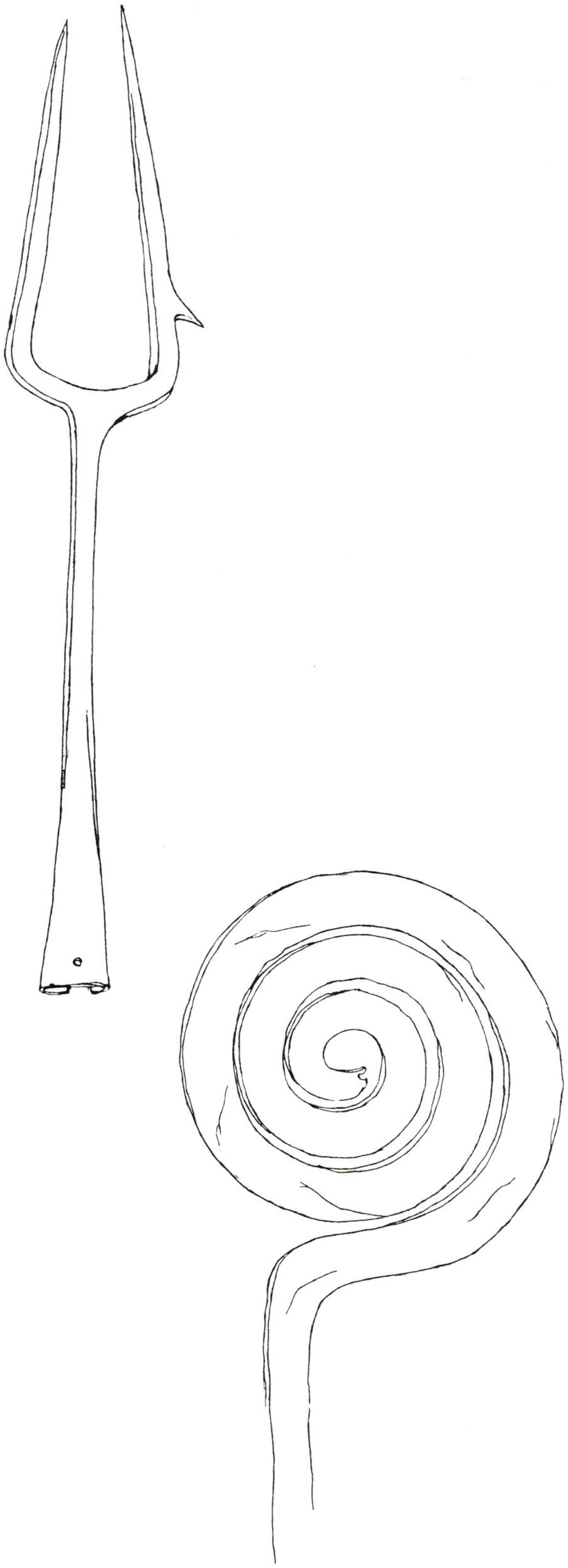

3

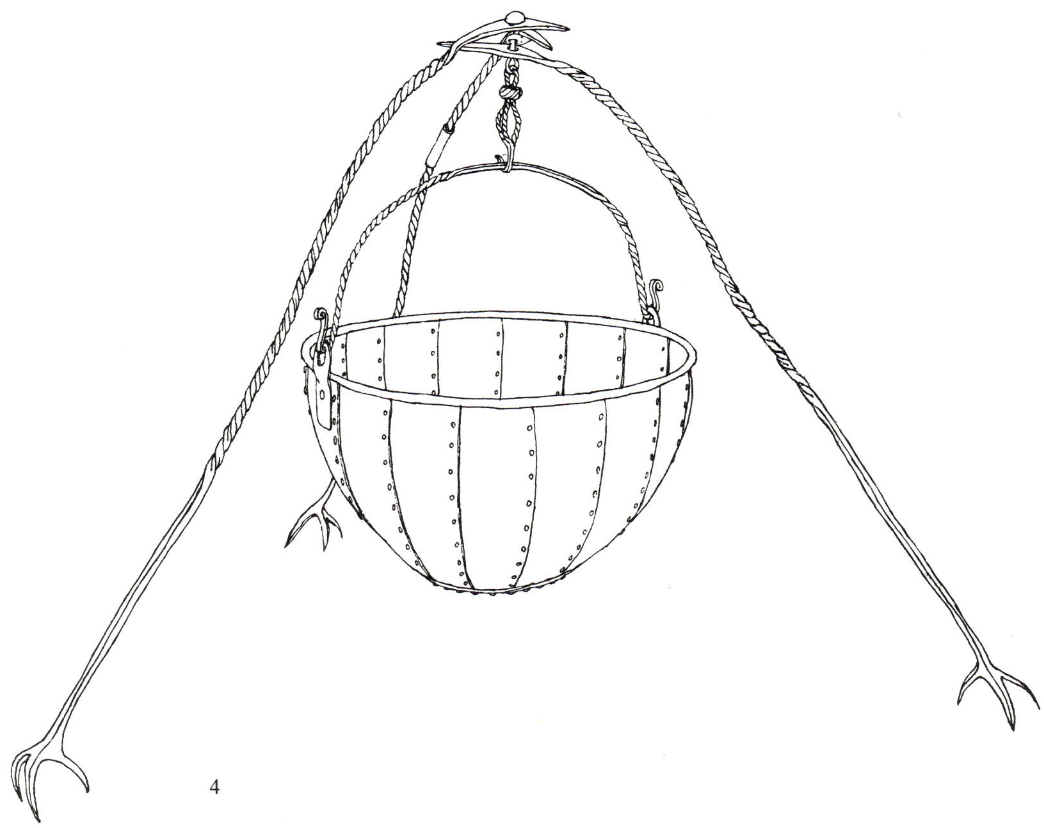

4

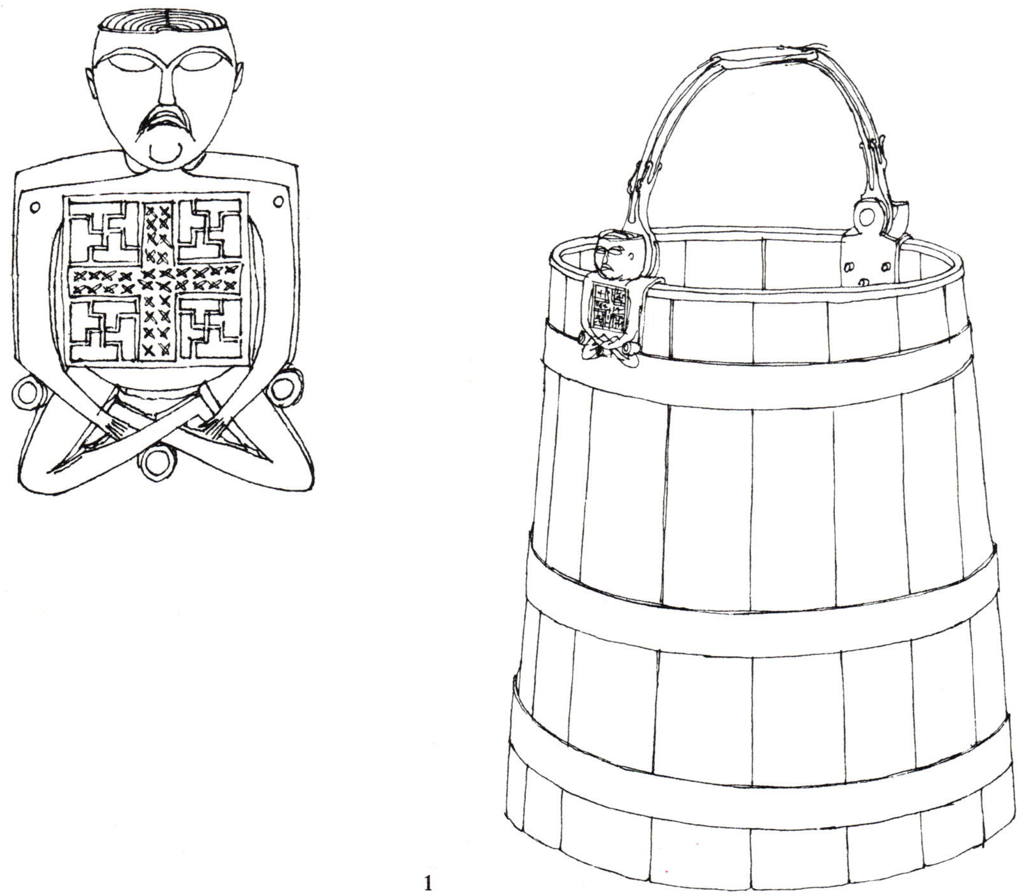

1

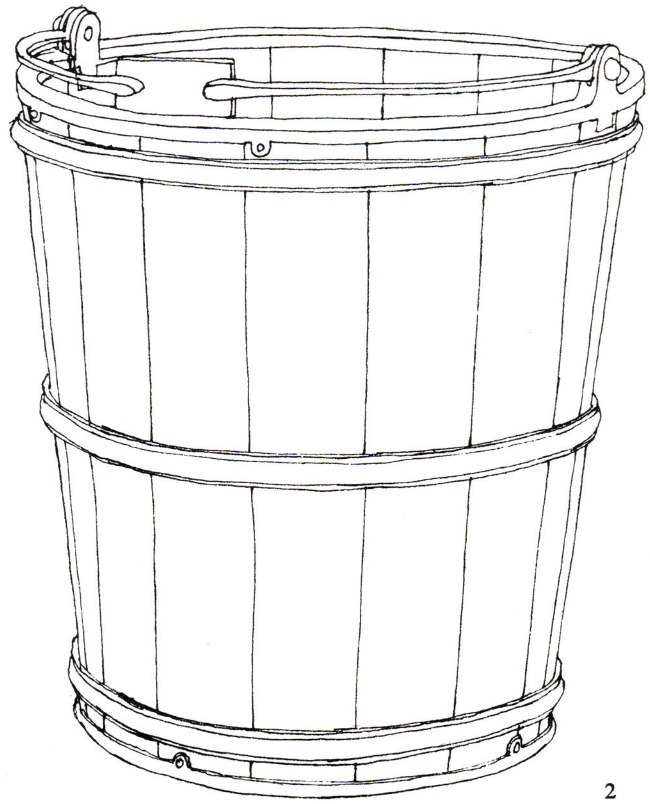

2

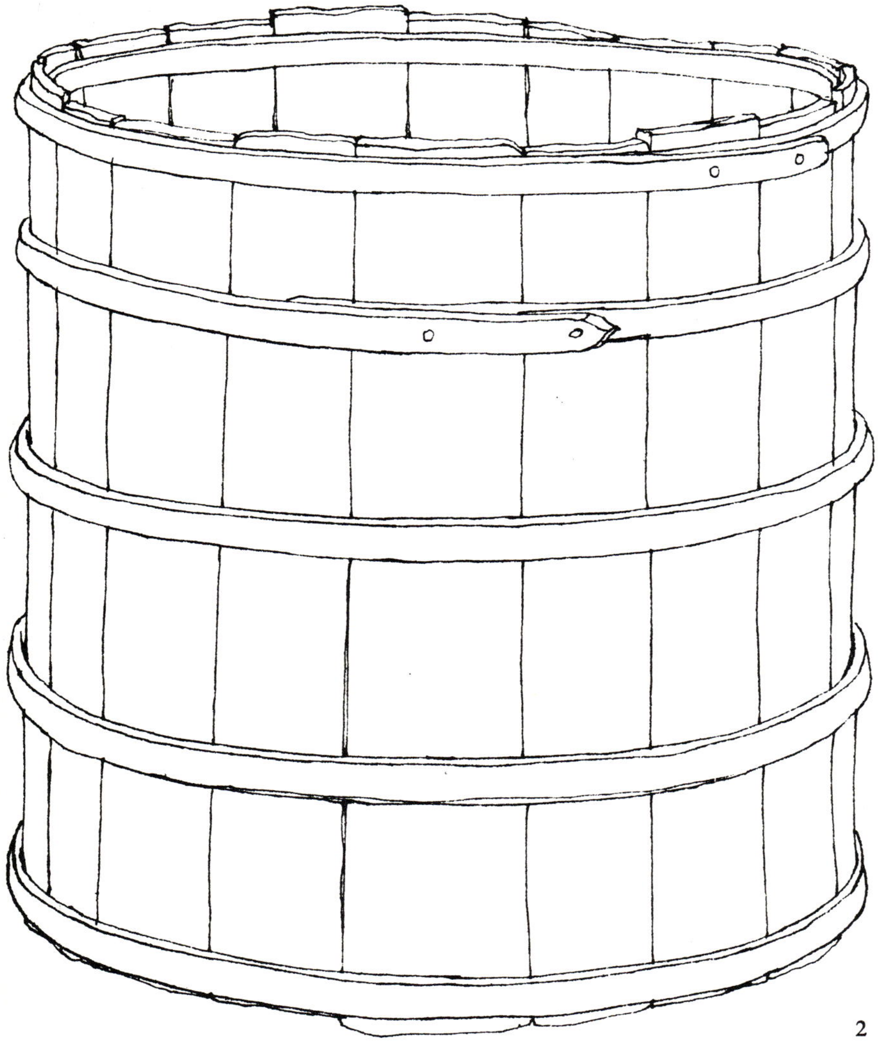

2

TROUGHS AND A BUCKET

1. Wooden bucket from the Oseberg ship. Made of yew-wood, with hoops and mountings of yellow metal, probably brass. The small male figures have enamel inlays. The bucket was most probably made in Ireland. It is the finest ever found and was obviously a prized possession of its Viking owner.
2. Other buckets from Oseberg.
3. Wooden containers from the Oseberg ship. The lower one, which in the grave held weaving tools, has a lid that can be locked in place. The upper one is decorated with criss-cross knife marks.
4. Details of the decorations on two small troughs. It is characteristic of the Viking's love of show and ornamentation, that even simple everyday articles were decorated.
5. Troughs from the Oseberg ship. Both have been cut from single blocks of wood. The large one was used for kneading dough. When it was found, there were still remnants of dough in it. Several small decorated troughs, probably used for serving food, have also been found.

A CHEST FROM THE OSEBERG SHIP

This chest, of a type the Vikings used to store domestic implements, is about four feet long, and sixteen inches high. It is made of oak reinforced with iron bands. The end battens, or "legs", on which the chest stands are pegged into the bottom plank. The lid is secured by a padlock, which has survived, though the key has been lost. Each of the lock hasps is shaped like an animal's head. The decoration of the chest consists of iron plates ornamented with tinned nail-heads.

IRON CAULDRONS

That Viking smiths could handle sheet-iron is proved by the two iron cauldrons shown here. The smaller one is fashioned by hammering a flat piece of sheet iron into shape. The larger is composed of several hammered sheets riveted together. Iron cauldrons are less frequent in Viking-Age graves than soapstone ones, presumably because they were more expensive to manufacture.

BLACKSMITH'S TOOLS

Anvils, hammer and tongs; the favourite tools of the smith. Such tools developed a functional shape long before the Viking Age, and they have barely changed today. If the smith is handy and has a sure eye, he does not need other tools for much of his work. The Viking smith's work was based on 1,000-year-old traditions in the handling of iron, and his best craftsmanship can hardly be copied to-day.

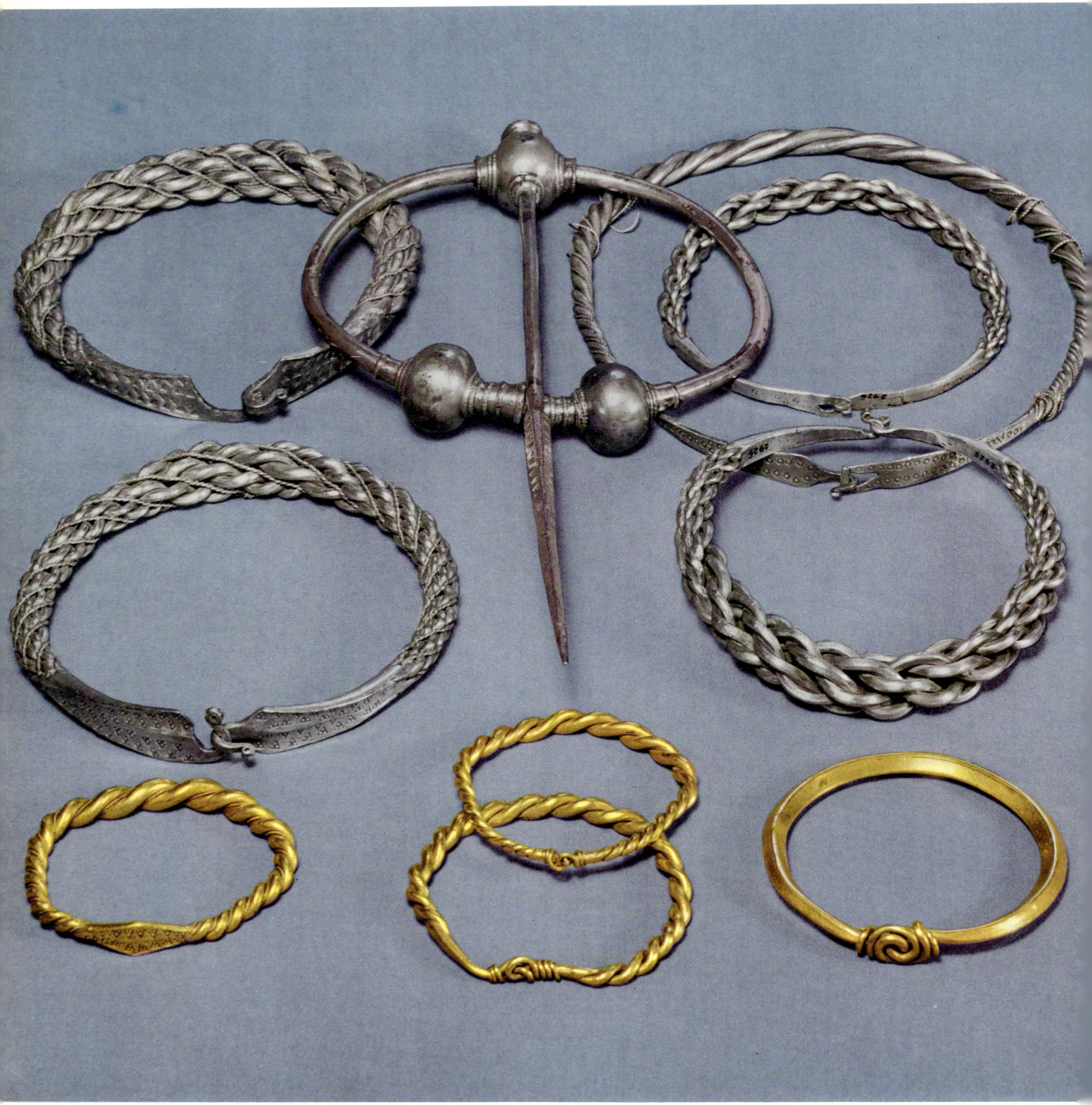

TREASURE FROM NORWAY

In 1834 this remarkably rich collection of jewellery was found in a grave at Hon, not far from Oslo. The treasure consists almost entirely of golden objects and weighs more than 5½ pounds. The biggest of the neck rings alone weighs more than 2½ pounds. Arabian, Byzantine and Frankish coins, all equipped with loops for use as ornaments, are represented, though most of the articles in this treasure are of Frankish origin. The central object, not only in this picture, but also of the treasure itself, is the large three-tongued mounting from a Frankish sword-belt. In Scandinavia such mountings were often remade into shawl clasps by simply adding a pin at the back. The Franks thus indirectly set the pattern for the native three-tongued clasps with purely Nordic ornamentation, which are common grave finds from the Viking Age.

THE BOW IN BATTLE

The Vikings made great use of archers in battle, mainly to open an action before settling down to the serious business of hand-to-hand fighting. Norman descendants of the Vikings continued to employ bowmen, as shown in this illustration from the Bayeux Tapestry.

A SAMPLING OF SWORD HILTS

When it came to weapons, only the best was good enough for the Vikings. In the case of swords, the best were the Frankish swordsmith's damascened blades, which were both sharp and supple. The sword hilts on the left, with their sombre, inlaid ornamentation, precious metal shining against the dark iron, must have afforded great pleasure to their owners. The actual grips, of wood or other perishable material, have, of course, long since rotted away.

The objects which the archaeologist usually lumps together under the single heading "spearheads" should probably be divided into two groups according to the diameter of their shafts. The thinner, lighter weapon was the javelin, which was thrown, while the heavier lance was used for thrusting. In histories of Western European warfare and of feudalism, lances have been closely connected with the first use of the stirrup — a post-Roman idea introduced by Eastern horseman like the Avars. According to this theory it is necessary to have stirrups in order to be able to thrust one's lance into an opponent without being lifted out of one's own saddle by the force of the collision. Thus, it is said, with the introduction of stirrups heavy feudal cavalry, which depended on the lance, first became possible. But the first people known to have employed heavy cavalry, the Parthians and Sassanids of Persia, are often shown on their stone reliefs as throwing their enemies out of the saddle with lances, without the aid of stirrups. Conversely, on the Bayeux Tapestry, the stirrup-equipped, heavily-armed Norman cavalry at Hastings (1066 A.D.) is still shown throwing javelins as well as charging with the lance. These Normans are also wearing chain-mail armour covering arms and legs to the knee as well as the body — a form of protection that did come to northern Europe from the Sassanids, via the Romans. So are some of their English opponents, though they are foot-soldiers. The Viking ancestors of the Normans had mail-coats too, but only the richer warriors could afford them, unless they captured them in battle. The Vikings used foot-archers, as the Bayeux Tapestry and written sources prove. (see page 223).

The Bayeux Tapestry, so reliable in matters of detail, also shows the rightly-dreaded Viking axe. This triangular-bladed weapon (which, incidentally, is still borne as insignia by the Yeomen Warders at the Tower of London), is shown being wielded not by the Norman horsemen, but by their English enemies, who fought on foot. They had probably adopted the Viking weapon at the time when the Scandinavians conquered England at the beginning of the eleventh century. It is just because they fought on foot that they were able to use this broadaxe. It took two hands to wield this axe, and no rider could spare more than one hand for his weapon. Accordingly the broadaxe remained an infantry weapon and disappeared with the final domination of the battlefield by feudal cavalry. The blow of such a cutting edge fixed to the end of a long handle must have been terrible indeed. There is little doubt that it was the thing with which to kill a horse; though the ranks of the axebearers would have to be kept unbroken in order to withstand the weight of a cavalry charge.

SPEARHEADS OF DIFFERENT PATTERNS

These iron spearheads have shaft sockets decorated with inlaid silver. This decoration is comparable with that on the sword hilts seen on page 222, but is more distinctly Nordic in character. The third head from the left has two mysterious projections on the shaft socket. No one knows what they were for. The wooden shaft was so long that they can hardly have acted as protection for the owner. They are not barbs, either. Perhaps their function was to allow the spearhead to penetrate an enemy's body just deeply enough to wound him mortally, while preventing this elegant and expensive weapon from becoming too far imbedded for easy withdrawal. The idea may have been derived from the hilt of a dagger.

A GOLDEN SPUR

The golden spur from Rød in south-east Norway, shown above, is one of the most costly survivals of the Viking Age, with its rich ornamentation in filigree and granulation. Even the mountings on the stirrup are made of gold. It must be borne in mind, however, that such a piece of jewellery — and in this case a spur can rightly be classed as jewellery — was not found on every Viking heel. Most horsemen had to be content with much simpler accessories.

THE OSEBERG STEERING OAR

The function and construction of the Oseberg ship's steering oar is identical to those of the Gokstad ship, but the dimensions were considerably slighter. The tiller was never found, but it was presumably as richly decorated as the rest of the ship. The thong which holds the rudder to the ship's side is of artistically plaited leather.

The small boats from the Gokstad find carry side rudders of the same type as the large ships. On small boats, however, the rudder was probably used under sail only, not when rowing. The upper picture shows how the withy used for lashing is fastened through holes in the "rudder-rib". The fastening was kept taut with the help of a couple of small wedges. In the lower picture, the rudder is hoisted, to keep it from grounding in shallow water.

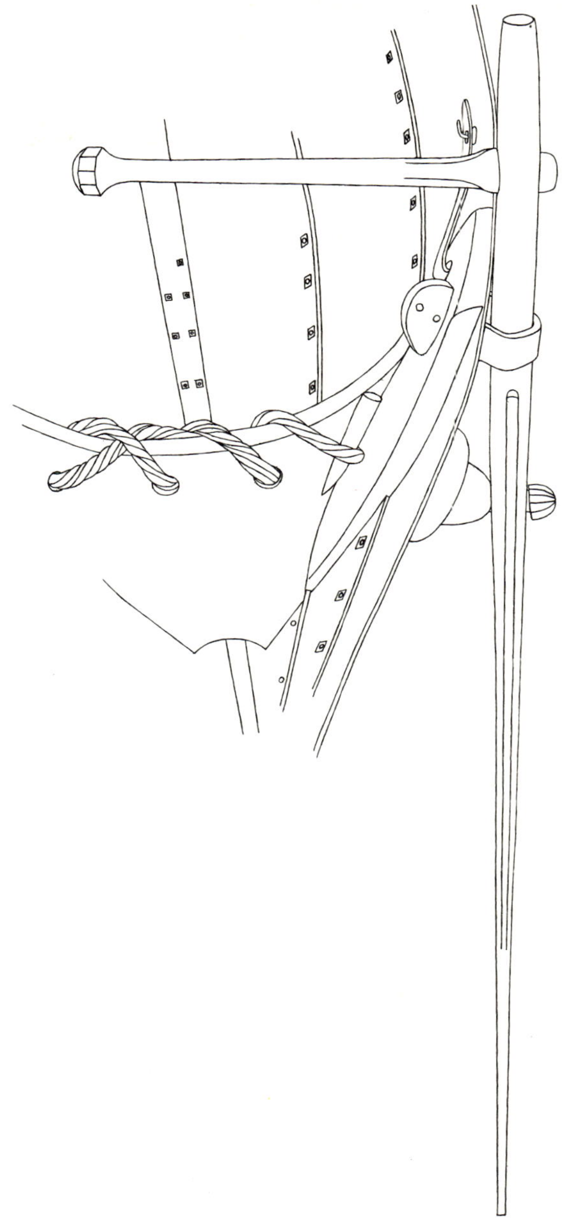

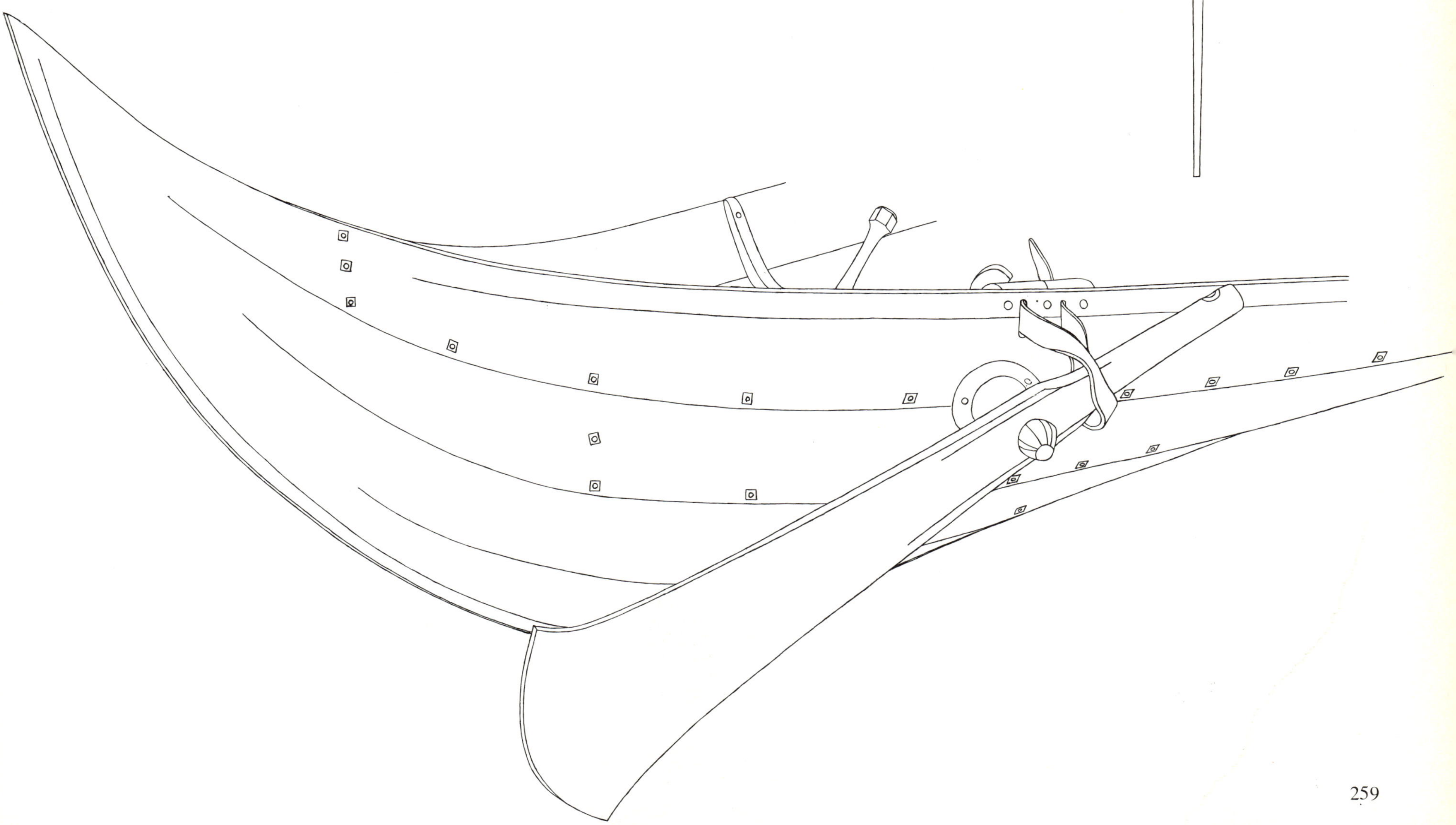

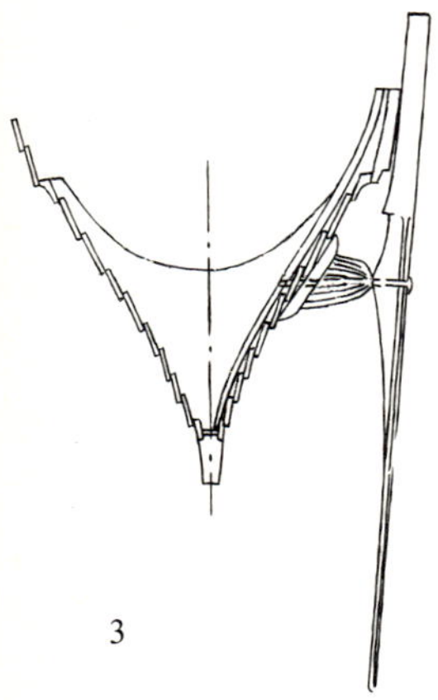

3

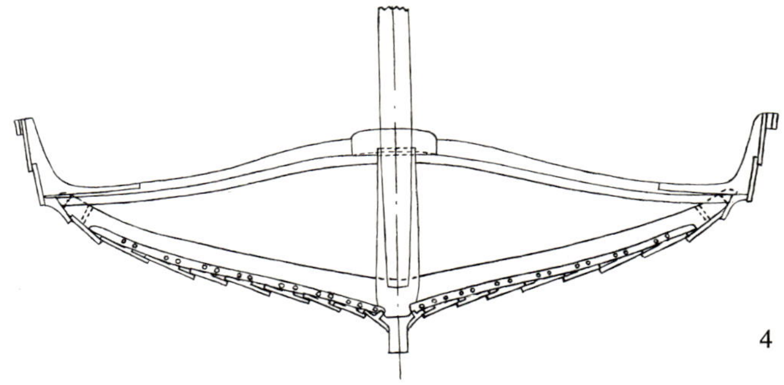

4

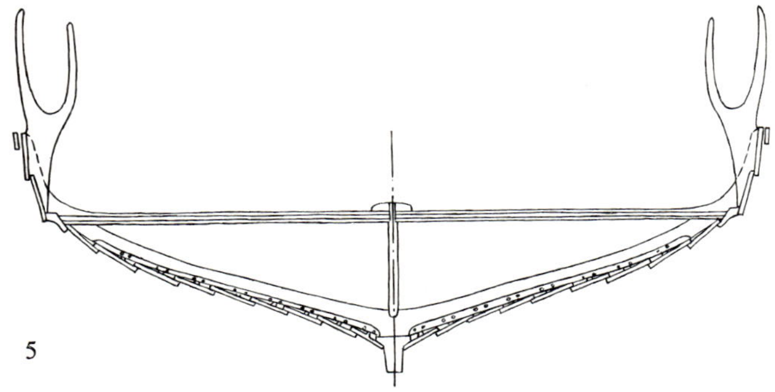

5

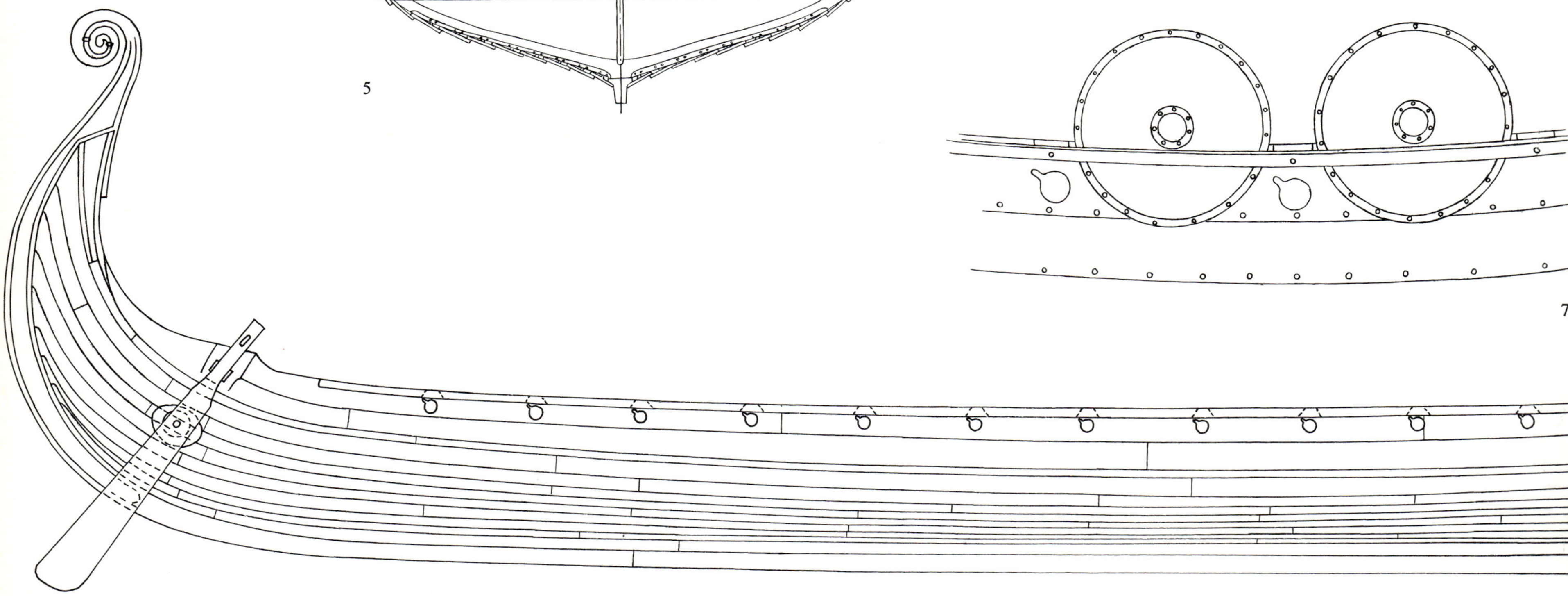

7

1

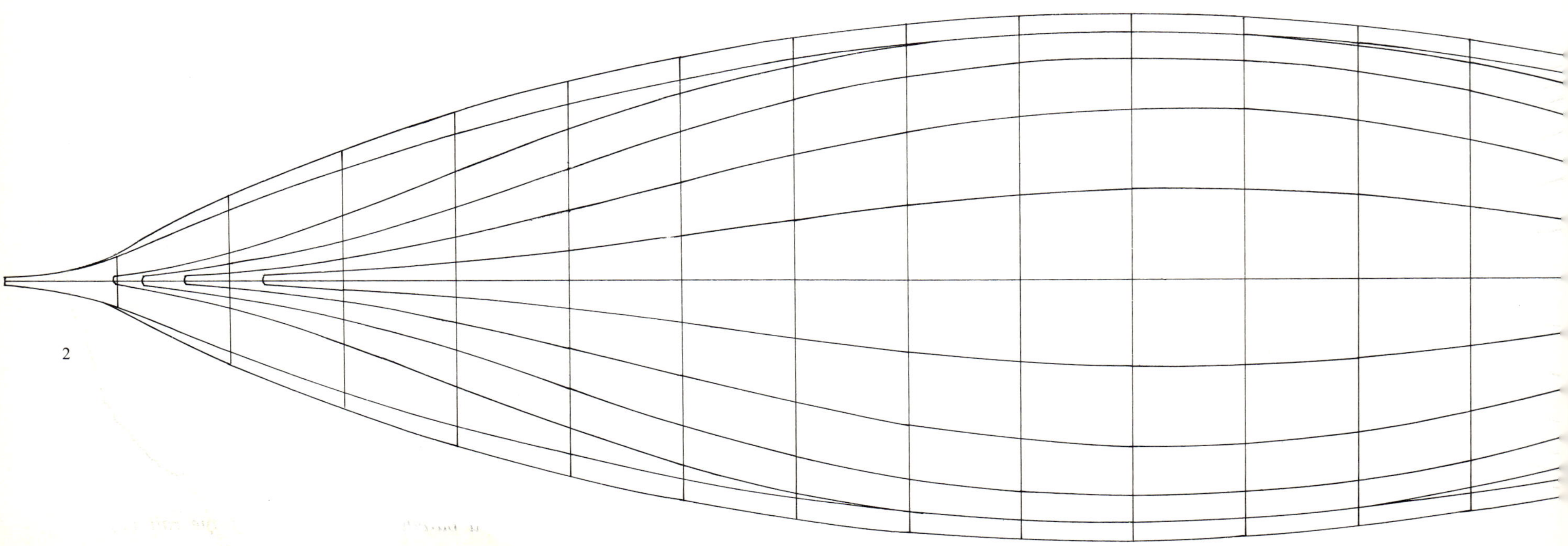

2

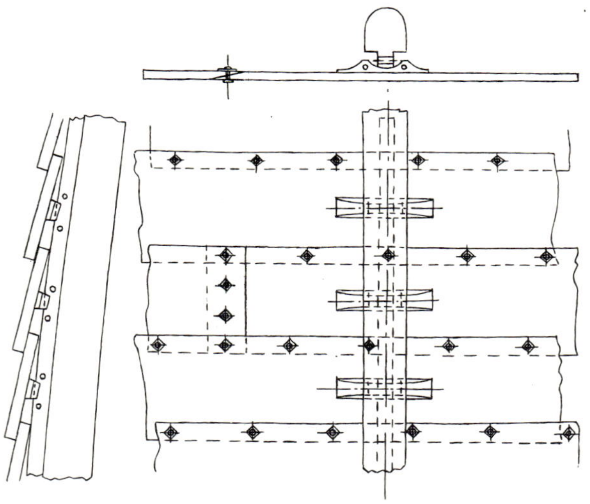

6

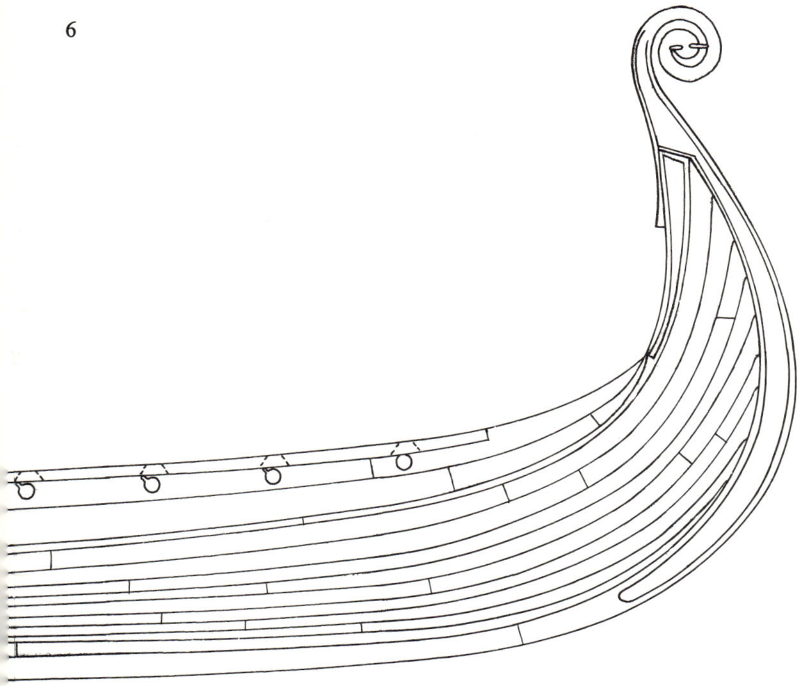

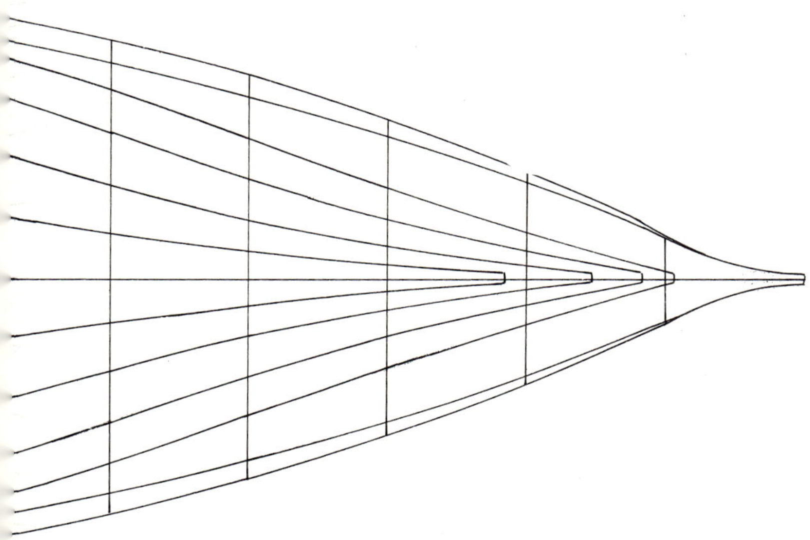

8

A comparison of the ships found at Oseberg, Gokstad and Tune soon reveals that the Oseberg ship differs from the other two in many details. Not only is it between fifty and a hundred years older than the others, but it was also a comparatively luxurious pleasure vessel. The Gokstad ship and the Tune ship, although of outstanding design, were nonetheless clearly intended for purely practical use.

Diagrams of the Oseberg ship (1, 2) include sections through the steering oar (3), at the mast (4) and abaft the mast (5). The ship lay low in the water and must have been a rather dangerous ship under sail. Whether this is because it was meant for use in shallow coastal waters, or because Scandinavian ships had not reached a more advanced stage of development when it was built around 800 A.D., cannot yet be decided with certainty. The timber supporting the lower part of the mast (known as the mastfish), is much less solidly built than on the other two ships, and even bears traces of old repairs. The rivets and the cleats of the planking, and their positions in relation to the rib, are illustrated in three projections (6). Evidently the oss beams of the Oseberg ship were not an organic part of its hull framework: they still show signs of having been developed from loose thwarts. The heavy plank, meginhúfr, *found at the waterline, resembles in form the rail timber found in older ships. It has a projection along the outside, and in cross-section most resembles an inverted letter L (4). The two rows of planking above the* meginhúfr *give the impression of being little more than a pair of splashboards which were added on, but had not yet become a permanent part of the planking. Even in matters of shape alone there is a rather important difference between the Oseberg and the Gokstad ships.*

The Oseberg ship has the same type of high, turned-back prow and stern which was found in the Kvalsund ship and in representations on coins and stone carvings. While very elegant, this must have been a real wind-catcher. In addition, finding suitable timber for it must have been difficult. The vertical ends of the Gokstad ship, with their more restrained curves, were undoubtedly more practical. The stems of the Oseberg ship are all decorated from the waterline to the top in a animal ornamentation — see detail (8) and photograph p. 256. The shields were fitted into a batt on the outside of the rail (7).

The equipment and gear found in the Oseberg and the Gokstad ships provide a fairly detailed picture of life on board a Viking vessel. According to the sagas the Vikings liked to moor their ships close to land at night, and pitch a tent on shore. The remains of one such tent were found in the Gokstad ship and two in the Oseberg ship. They consist of a light framework of timber over which a covering was spread. Unfortunately, the actual covering was not preserved. On the verge-boards of the Oseberg tents, magical symbols like the coiled serpent were painted. Possibly these were intended as protection against the evil powers of the night. In each of the two ships a large, splendid bed with carved posts was found, along with several simpler beds. All the beds could be dismantled and stowed on board. They may therefore have been field beds which could be set up for the use of the Viking leaders when they went ashore for the night. From the sagas it appears that during the early Middle Ages, it was usual to carry large skin bags called *hudfat* to store gear and weapons during the day and to serve as two-man sleeping bags at night. Little is known about the food the Vikings ate on long voyages. It was impossible to light even a cooking fire at sea, so that on open stretches of water the crew had to live on cold food. Dried and salted fish or meat with water, and sour milk or beer to drink must have been their staple diet. In both the Oseberg and Gokstad ships large cauldrons, perhaps for cooking on shore, were found. At Oseberg, in addition to cauldrons, a real piece of camping equipment turned up, a collapsible iron tripod for hanging the pots over a fire (see illustration page 181). The Gokstad cauldron is bronze and holds thirty-two gallons. Even assuming a ship carried as many as fifty men, a cauldron that large could supply ample portions of porridge or soup for everyone. On longer voyages large supplies of water were obviously necessary. It was probably carried in skin bags like those still used for wine in Mediterranean countries. Long, narrow boards with steps hewn out of them have been found on many burial ships, and these obviously served as gangplanks.

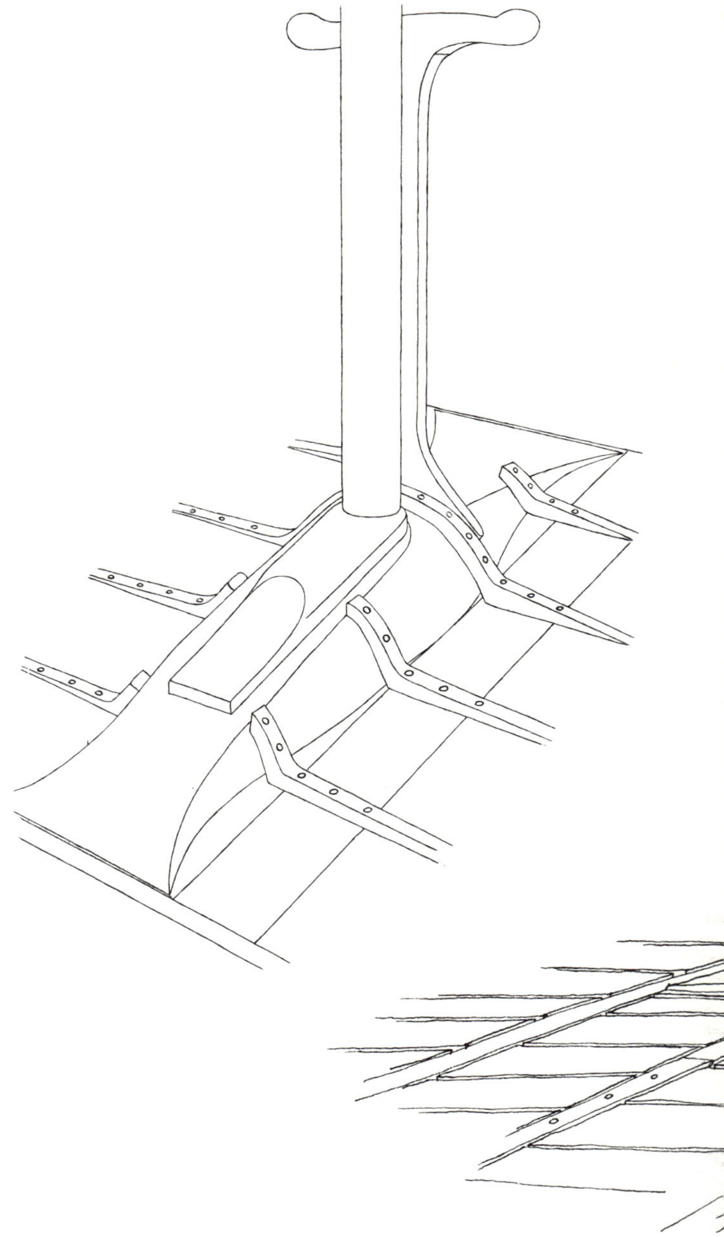

RAISING THE MAST

Raising the mast, as illustrated here, must have been heavy work. It has been reckoned that the mast of the Gokstad ship weighed about 800 pounds. While part of the crew lifted the mast bodily, walking it up, several men hauled on a stay attached to the bow of the ship, to help with the lifting and to hold the mast if the others lost their grip. When the mast was upright, the slot in the mast partner (above) was closed by the oak block lying on the decking. Then the stay and shrouds were tightened. The lower drawing shows how a short mast fitted snugly within the cross timbers in the stern of the ship when lowered.

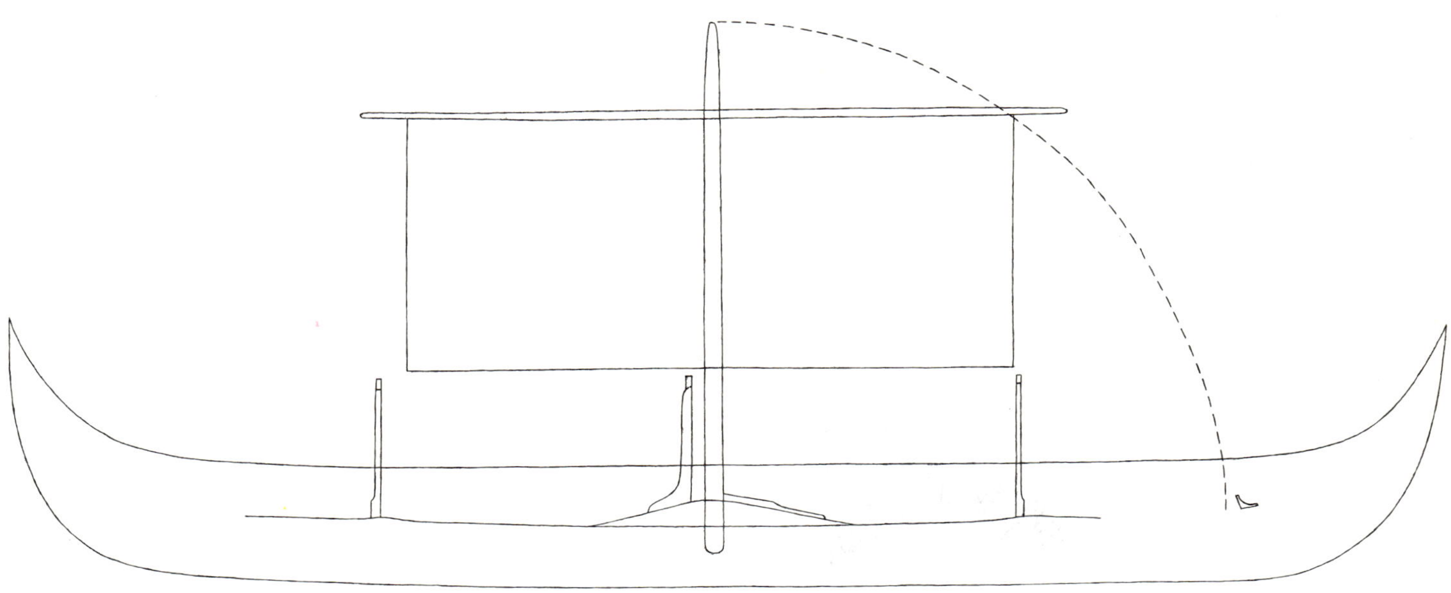

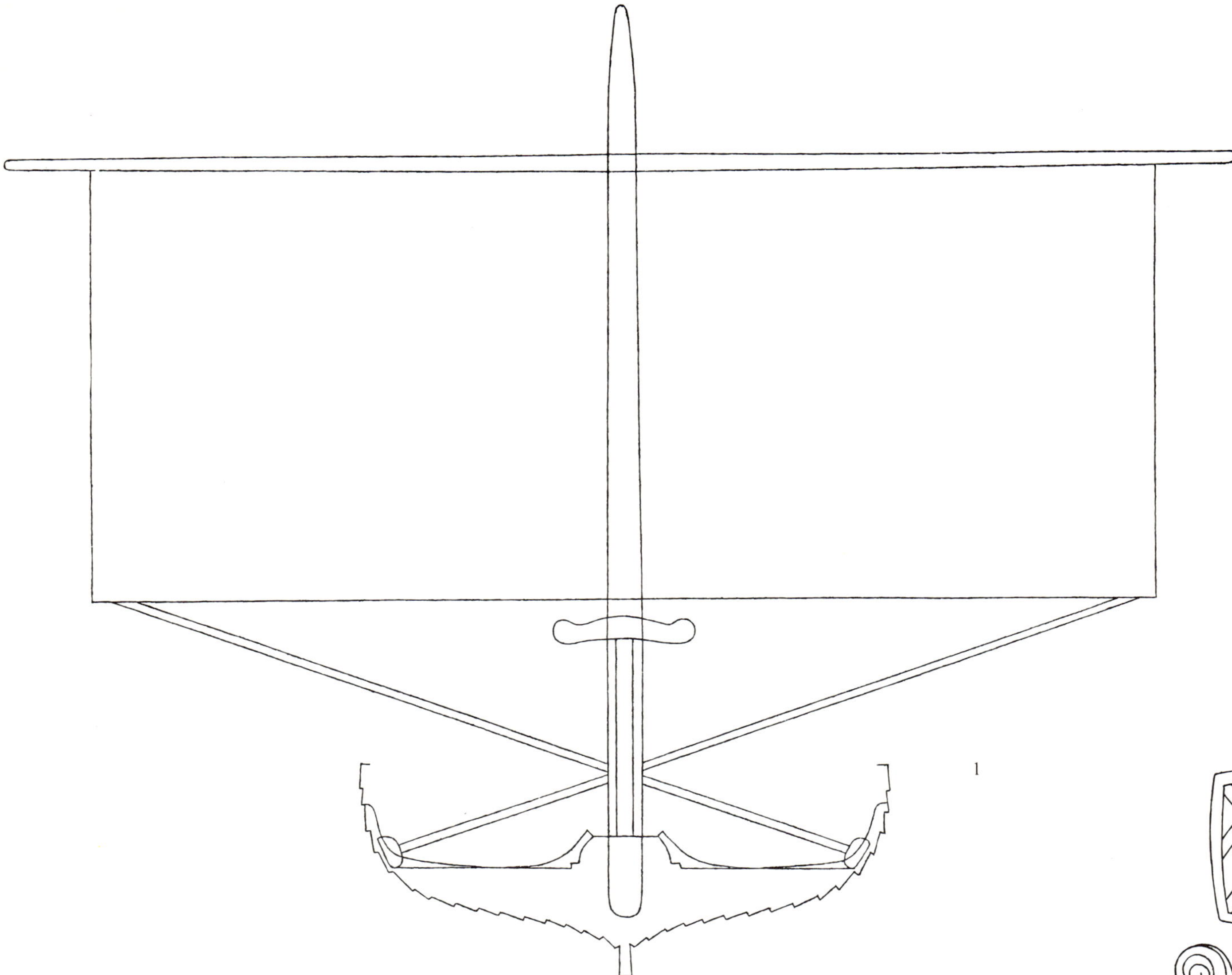

1

2

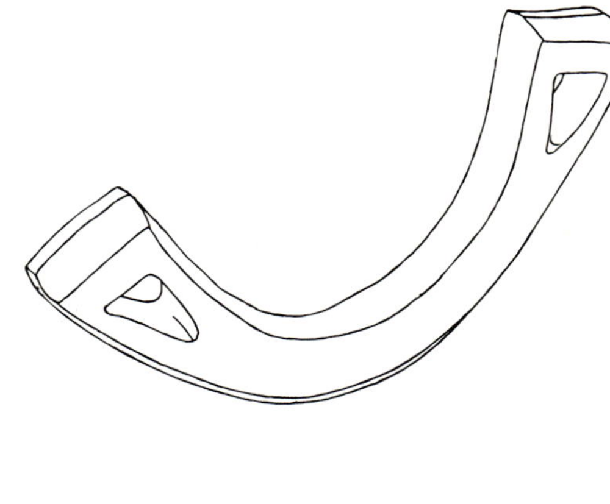

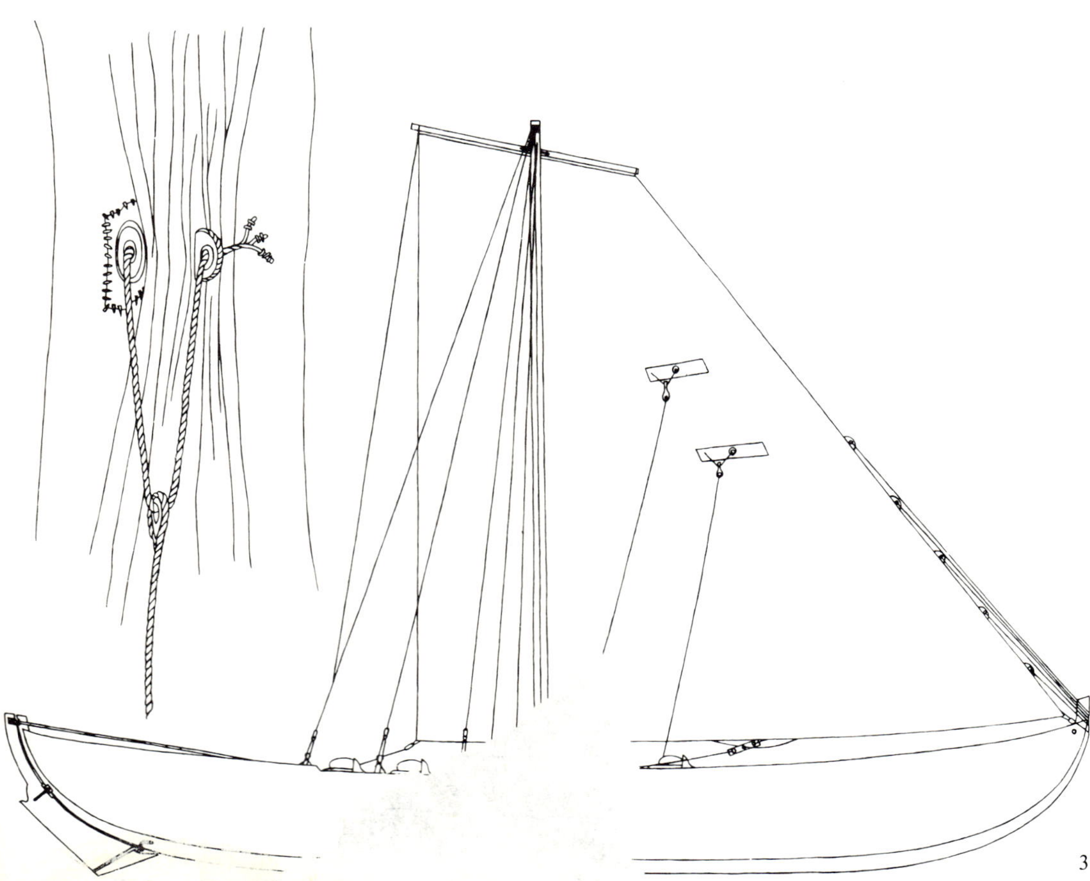

3

It is not known for certain when sails were first used in Scandinavian shipbuilding. It seems likely, however, that by about 700 A.D. hulls had developed far enough for ships to carry sails. Though all three Norwegian Viking ships used about the same method of mounting the mast, the mounting on the Oseberg ship, which is earliest, gives the impression of being still unsure and tentative in workmanship and design. The mounting on the Gokstad and Tune ships is fully developed.

The foot of the mast stands in a socket in the kjerringa. *In the Oseberg ship it only extends the distance between two ribs, but in the Gokstad ship it stretches over four ribs and is further strengthened by knees (see page 251). Above the* kjerringa *is the mastfish, a massive piece of oak laid over the cross beams at deck level. In the Oseberg ship it spans four cross beams, in the Gokstad ship, six. On the Gokstad ship it is very solidly fixed, being recessed to fit the cross beams and further supported on each side by strong knees. The mastfish of the Oseberg ship, by contrast, is fastened only by trenails at the front and the back, though it does also get some support from an extra thick cross beam in front of the mast, into which it is partly rebated. But this construction was obviously not adequate, as is shown by the fact that the mastfish split under the pressure of the sail and had to be repaired with iron bands. There is a large opening or slot in the mastfish behind the mast, so that the mast could be raised and lowered. When the mast was in position, it was held fast by a piece of oak, known as the mast-lock, placed in the slot.*

It has been said that this construction is so solid that no further support for the mast was necessary — that the Vikings sailed without stays, "on the bare timber" as the old expression has it. Indeed no physical traces of any means of securing standing rigging to support the mast have yet been found. However, there are two main objections to the "bare timber" theory. The first is that, among ships past and present about whose rigging we have complete knowledge, no ship carrying a square sail has been found where the mast is without supporting rigging. Second, all known representations of ships of the Viking Age without exception show stays and rigging helping to support the mast. It is possible, moreover, that this rigging was not fixed in any one position all the time, but moved to suit wind direction. If so, it may be that the fastening was effected by using the holes bored in the knees of both the Oseberg ship and the Gokstad ship. When sailing before the wind, the sail may have been stretched by poles (1). The U-shaped pieces seen attached to

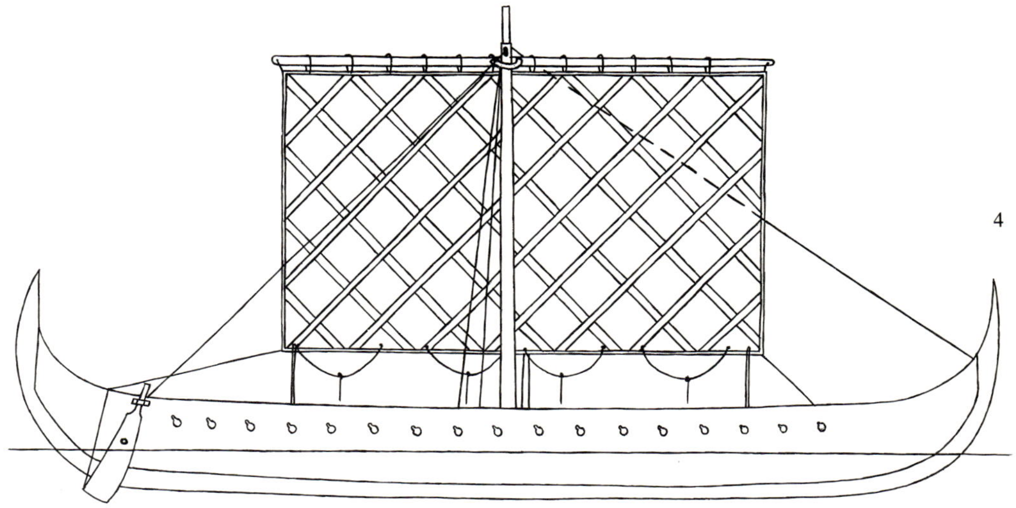

4

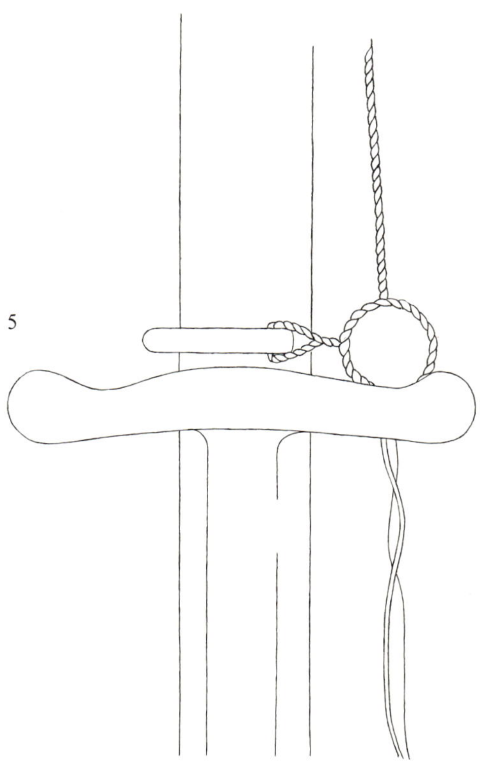

5

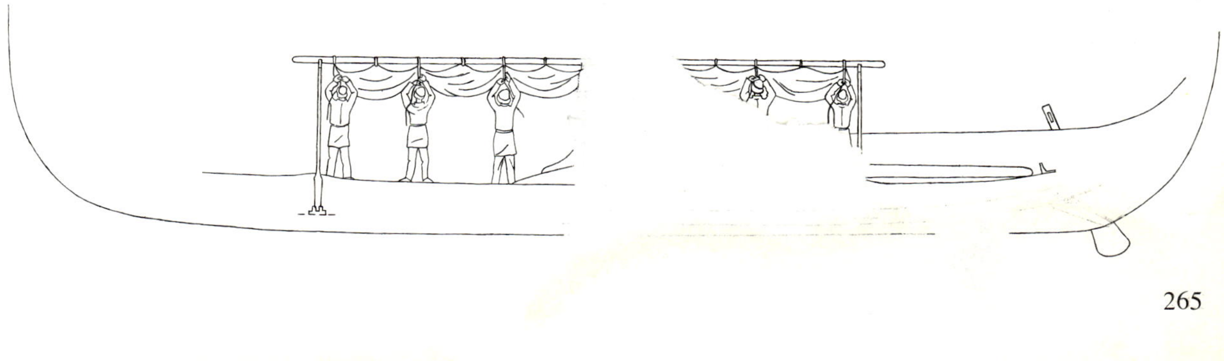

6

No known remains of sails have been found in the Norwegian ship-burials. Neither has the top part of a mast or any means of attaching rigging. But it is obvious from contemporary depictions like those on the Gotlandic picture-stones, as well as on rune-stones and coins, that Viking ships did carry a square sail. In fact what is probably a whole yard, forty-one feet long, is preserved in perfect condition at Oseberg. This large piece of timber cannot be a mast, because its diameter at both ends is much smaller than the diameter of the socket for the foot of the mast. Moreover the length of this yard corresponds well with the distance — 35½ feet — between the two outermost of the three T-shaped supports placed down the middle of the Gokstad ship. These must have been intended for carrying the yard when it was lowered. Laid along them, the yard would project about three feet at each end, a suitable margin of safety when the ship was under way. The supports are so constructed that yard and sail could be quickly hauled down on them on whatever side of the mast it happened to be. Two large spars were found lying along the three supports at Gokstad. One of these, twenty feet long, broken at the widest part, may be exactly one half of a broken yard. How broad would the sail have been? On the evidence of the existing yards, not more than forty feet. But it may have been as broad as the distance between the two outer yard supports, 35½ feet. Unhappily even the smaller of these measurements suggests that with a tall mast, Viking ships must have carried far more canvas than any of the reconstructions of Viking sails indicate. The answer to the problem lies in the height of the mast, which is difficult to determine, in view of the fact that, except for short fragments, no mast has been preserved. The mast was thick (a foot through in the case of the Gokstad ship and eight inches at Oseberg), and heavy. Yet all the evidence provided by surviving arrangements for mounting suggest that masts were quite clearly intended to be frequently and speedily raised and lowered. This being so, it is rather unlikely that they can have been so long that they stuck out backwards over the strong curves of the stern when being lowered. To manoeuvre a mast weighing 800 pounds *outside* the ship when under way would have been extremely dangerous. The mast must, therefore, have been just long enough so that it would clear the beams in the stern when lowered, that is, not more than thirty-three feet. A low sail and short mast on a Viking ship would have considerably lessened the need for special stays or ballast, because the lateral force of the wind was thereby afforded less leverage. Viking ships may therefore have been still lighter and faster than has hitherto been assumed.

the sail in picture-stones were probably used for altering the sail's profile to suit various wind conditions (2). (3) illustrates a method of reefing by gåthering sail-cloth, applied to a type of ship used in Norway until recent times. Picture-stones suggest that the Vikings also used it. Little standing rigging would have been necessary when the mast was held fast by kjerringa *and mastfish. As the mast on these Viking ships was obviously intended to be raised and lowered frequently, the mastfish would have given the necessary support while the rigging was being raised.*
Judging by the evidence of the Gotland picture-stones, the mast was supported by a line to the prow and two or three lines — shrouds — from the mast top to the ship's sides, just aft of the mast (4). In addition to supporting the mast when the ship was under sail, this rigging must also have helped when the mast was being lowered and raised. When rowing or in harbour, the yard and sail, and perhaps the mast as well, could be laid along the T-shaped uprights seen on the Gokstad ship, giving more free deck space (5) and (6).

THE GOKSTAD SHIP VIEWED FROM THE HELMSMAN'S POSITION, AND DETAILS OF PLANKING ON THE STARBOARD QUARTER

In the rough oak mastfish stand the remains of the mast, and a T-shaped trestle for raising the yard. The ridged gang-plank is on the right, and two wooden tubs on the left. Picture at right: the two upper planks, the wedge-shaped repair and the cleat are reconstructions from preserved parts; most of the rivets, washers and planking are original.

A CARVED ROWLOCK

The rowlocks of the largest of the ship's boats (left) are decorated with carved line patterns. The rowlocks acted as stops for the oars during the pull, whilst they were held in place by rope thongs which passed through the upper holes in the rowlocks.

THE LITTLE SHIP'S BOAT

Amongst the Gokstad discoveries were three small boats, thirty-two feet, twenty-six feet, and twenty-two feet long with five, three and two pairs of oars respectively. Their shape is similar to that of the large ship, with the same elegant construction and workmanship. The smallest (left), which was most suitable as a ship's boat, is built of oak with planking up to three-fifths of an inch thick. The boat is rather narrow, but fast and easy to handle.

SHIPS' GEAR

The flexible hulls of even the best-built and best-tended Viking vessels clearly shipped water sometimes, and it must have been very difficult to keep them absolutely water-tight. The crew of the Oseberg ship had a bailer shaped like a large wooden shovel. The ship carried an iron anchor, very well made (and well preserved), but rather small for a ship of its size. It is possible that it was only meant for holding the stern fast when the ship lay moored.

When it was uncovered in the burial mound, the Gokstad ship had thirty shields hanging in rows along either side outside the gunwale. They were held in position by cords drawn through the handles of the shields and through rectangular holes left for the purpose in a batten, the shield rack, attached to the underside of the gunwale on the inside. Painted alternatively black and yellow, the shields formed a continuous line from prow to stern, and overlapped each other so that one shield covered half of the shield aft of it. When hung like this, the shields completely covered the oar holes, and so they could not have been displayed when the ship was being rowed. This view is supported by the sagas, which make it clear that the shields were hung up when the ship was in harbour, but lay inside while at sea. On the other hand, several of the Gotland stone carvings show ships under sail with the shields hanging out. In the Oseberg ship they were placed in slots cut in a timber attached to the outside of the gunwale. Like this it would have been possible to row with the shields on display, and serving as a protective screen for the rowers.

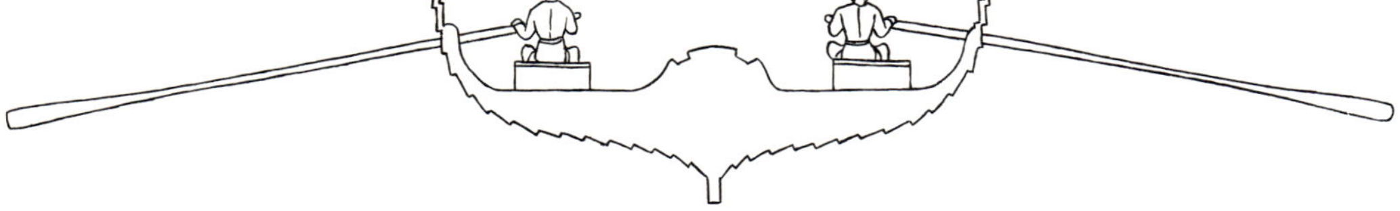

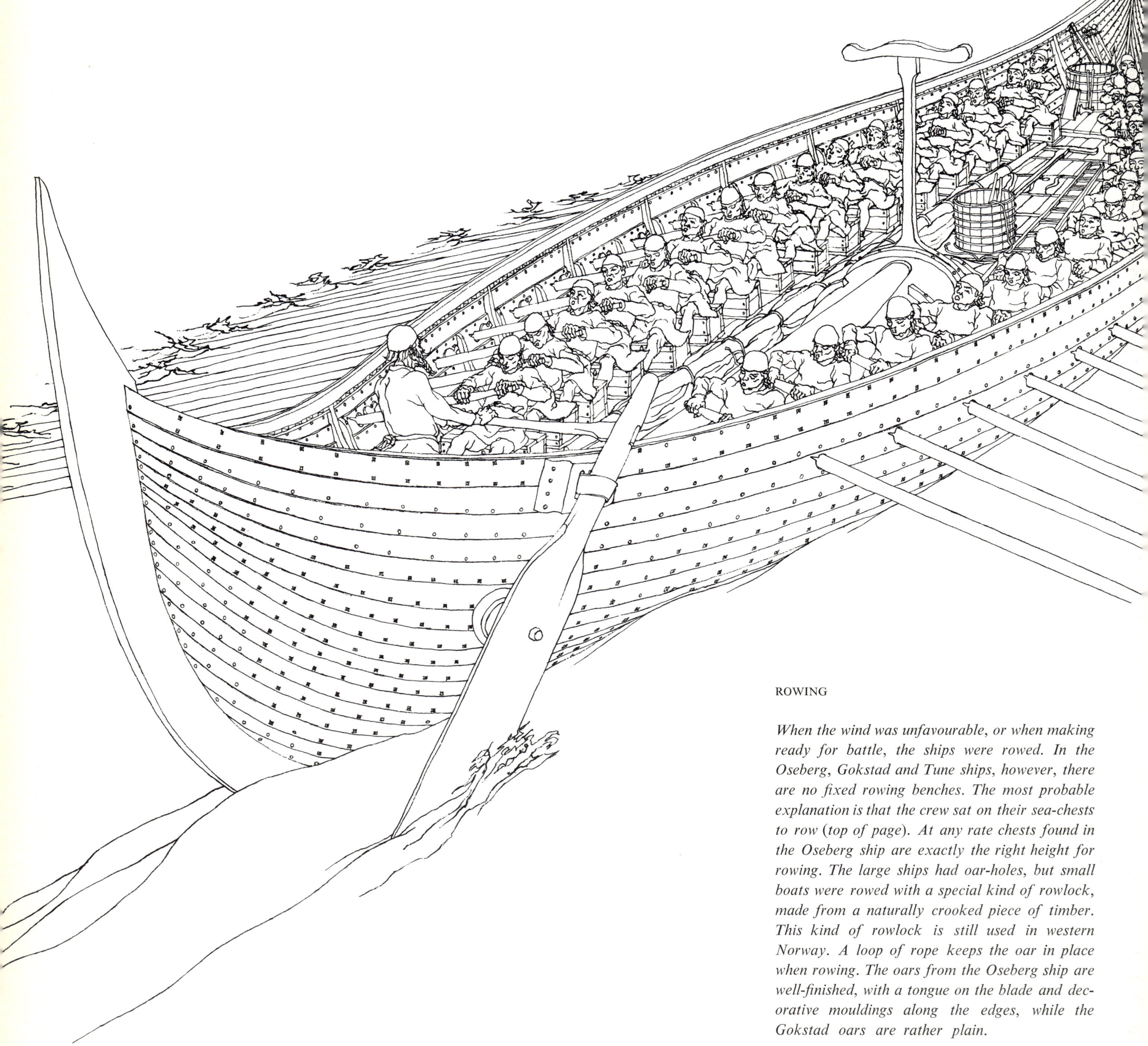

ROWING

When the wind was unfavourable, or when making ready for battle, the ships were rowed. In the Oseberg, Gokstad and Tune ships, however, there are no fixed rowing benches. The most probable explanation is that the crew sat on their sea-chests to row (top of page). At any rate chests found in the Oseberg ship are exactly the right height for rowing. The large ships had oar-holes, but small boats were rowed with a special kind of rowlock, made from a naturally crooked piece of timber. This kind of rowlock is still used in western Norway. A loop of rope keeps the oar in place when rowing. The oars from the Oseberg ship are well-finished, with a tongue on the blade and decorative mouldings along the edges, while the Gokstad oars are rather plain.

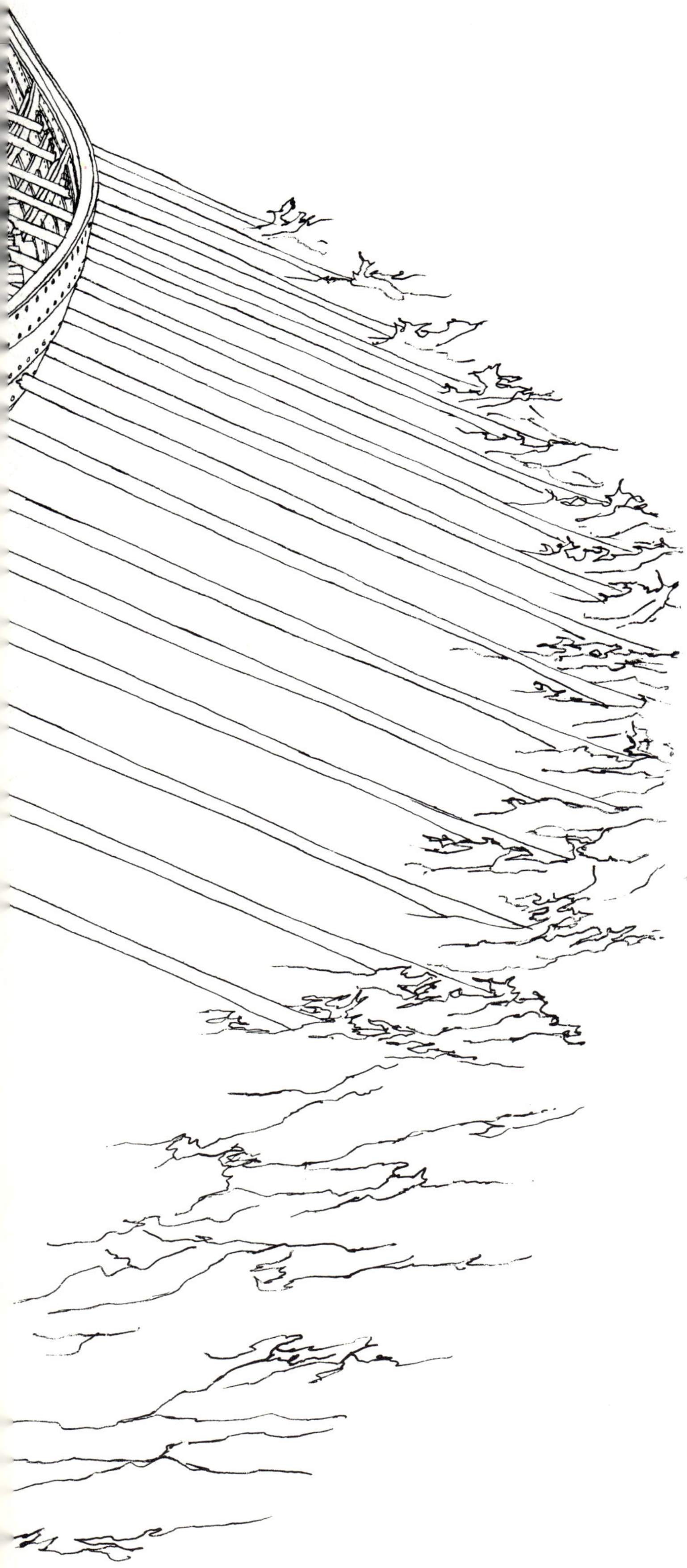

In poems from the close of the Viking Age, and in sagas of the Middle Ages, many different names for different types of ship occur. But all these ships belonged to two main categories: merchantmen and warships.

The merchantman was designed to carry a large cargo and a relatively small crew. Built broad and deep with the emphasis on cargo capacity and seaworthiness rather than speed, the merchantman was a sailing ship with only a few pairs of oars for use during calms or when manoeuvering in narrow harbours. Warships, on the other hand, obviously had to be built for speed, with or without wind. They had places for many oarsmen, and were, in fact, most often used in sheltered coastal waters, where seaworthiness was not as essential as it was in the case of merchantmen.

No one knows when the distinction between merchantman and warship first began to be made, but by about 1000 A.D. an established difference existed. It seems reasonable to associate the origin of a special type of ship intended for commerce with the growth of the first towns. Obviously, too, there must have been a period when shipbuilders tried to combine warlike and commercial vessels in a single vessel. The Gokstad ship, for example, is probably one that had not yet acquired a distinct character, one that could be used as warship and which could also carry sufficient cargo to make sea transportation profitable.

During the tenth century the first large kingdoms were consolidated in Scandinavia, and the military organization called *ledungen* was finally established. According to this organization each district was required to build and maintain a ship, and to man her in the event of war. This allowed kings to build ships for purely military purposes, and naturally led to the development of a ship intended specifically for war.

The early medieval sagas about the last years of the Viking Age often describe very big ships. Greatest of all was the ship of Cnut the Great, reputed to contain sixty *spantrum*, as the spaces between the deck beams were called. It is probable that there is a good deal of exaggeration in these accounts of giant ships. To enable the oarsmen to use the oars properly, the oar holes should have been more than three feet apart. If the oars of Cnut's ship were spaced like those of the Gokstad ship, it would have been about 230 feet long. Knowing the Viking methods of shipbuilding, this would have meant a very weak hull. There is, therefore, reason to believe that such colossal dimensions existed only in the world of the sagas.

A VIKING CAMP FOR A LONG STAY ASHORE

All of the objects seen in the picture were actually found in a grave ship. In the foreground are several wooden tubs, a spade, a pitchfork, some washing implements, a soapstone cauldron, and a chain. Beyond are two types of portable cooking equipment. On the left preparations for baking are being carried out, and at right two tents have been put up. The foot of a bed is protruding from one of them. An oil lamp has been stuck into the ground outside the nearest tent, and the man sitting nearby is surrounded by tools and simple wooden objects, such as plates, trays, and bowls. The boats in the background have been beached.

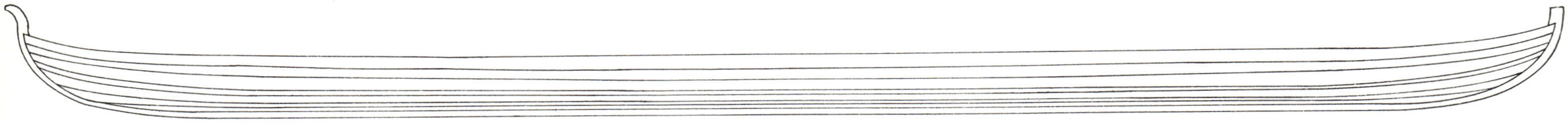

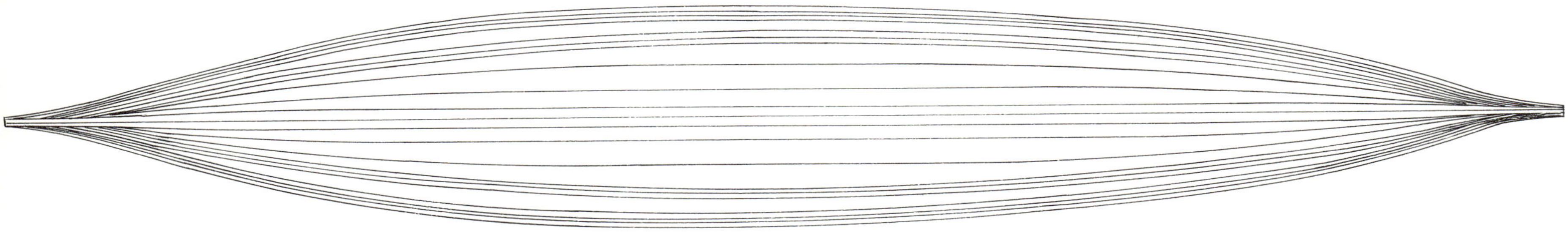

OTHER SHIP FINDS, AND WHAT THEY TELL

For a long time the three Norwegian Viking ships were the only known remains of ships from the Viking period. In 1936, however, excavations at Ladby on the island of Fyn in Denmark uncovered another ship, and in 1962 five more were found in a unique "underwater" excavation in a natural channel in the middle of the extremely shallow Roskilde Fjord at Skuldelev, Denmark, west of Copenhagen. All six ships proved to be quite different from the earlier Norwegian remains. At Ladby only the iron rivets and minute fragments of timber had in fact been preserved, but by carefully recording the position of the rivets, it was possible to make a reliable reconstruction. The Ladby ship is narrow, shallow-draught, and with a less defined profile or sheer. Although probably not particularly seaworthy, it seems admirably suited to the relatively calm Danish coastal waters. It was, moreover, fast and easily propelled because of its narrow shape. That oars were not its only means of power is indicated by the presence of four large iron rings which were found on each side of the ship, fastened to the ribs aft of amidships. These rings were probably for fastening the lines that supported the mast. The ship is dated to the period 900-950 A.D. A large anchor was found with the Ladby ship, fastened to thirty feet of iron chain which was, in turn, tied to the remains of a hawser. The five ships from Skuldelev were built later than the Ladby ship and the three from Norway. They probably date from shortly after the year 1000. Three were merchantmen, but of different sizes and construction. The others were probably warships. One, shaped much like the Ladby ship, was very likely a coaster.

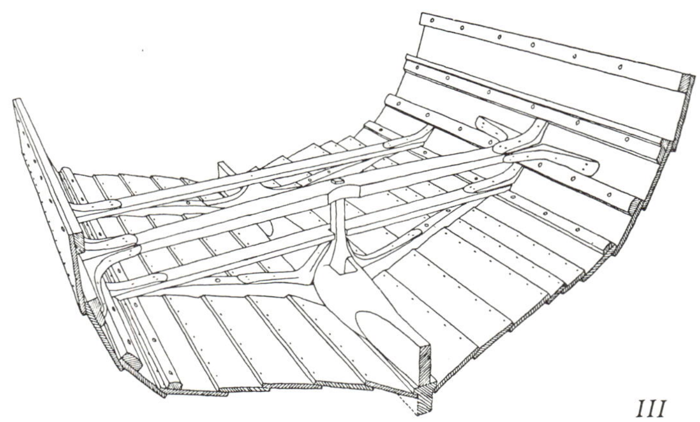

III

DESIGN DEVELOPMENTS FROM DENMARK

These drawings of the ships found at Ladby and at Skuldelev show developments in ship building and design that took place in the 150 years between the building of the Gokstad ship and the Danish vessels. In one of the later models, known as Wreck III (above and opposite page) the planking is no longer lashed to the ribs, but fastened by trenails: a rigid construction has replaced a flexible, elastic one.

The discovery of the Skuldelev ships made it possible to study for the first time, especially in Wreck III, the mounting of the mast in a merchant ship of the Viking period. The mastfish which held the lower part of the mast in the Gokstad ship has been replaced in the Skuldelev ship by a cross beam placed higher up above the ordinary cross beam (above, this page). This beam supports the mast and also strengthens the sides of the ship. The knees fastened to the cross beams on other Viking ships, and their extra ribs, have disappeared. Instead, by way of compensation, the upper planking is reinforced lengthwise on the inside. The ship

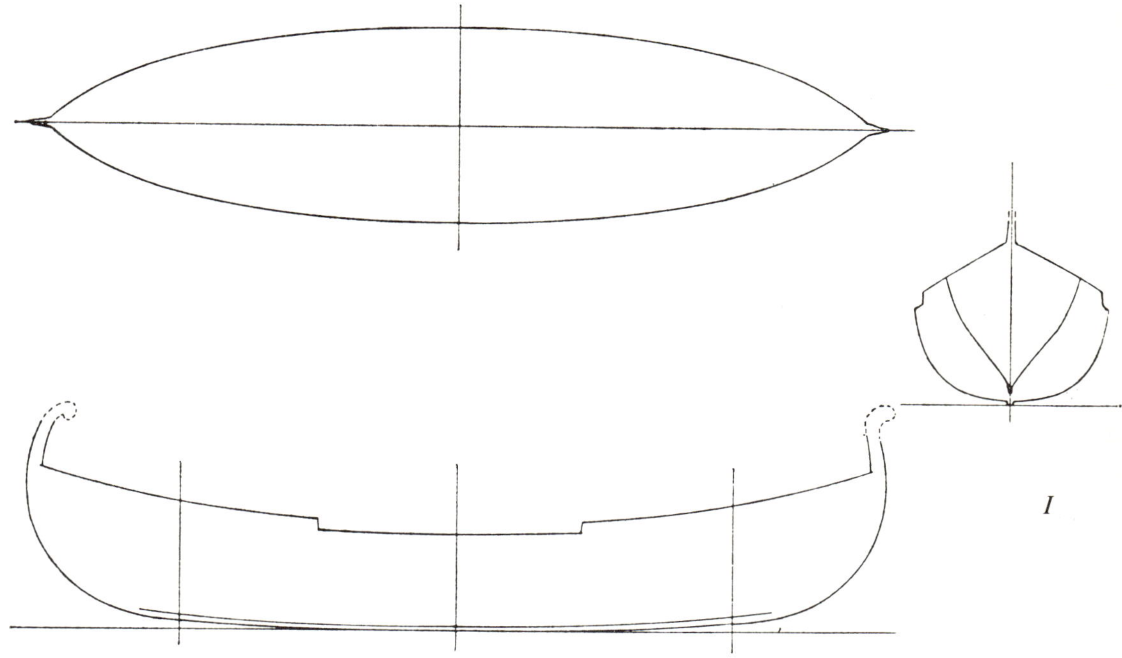

I

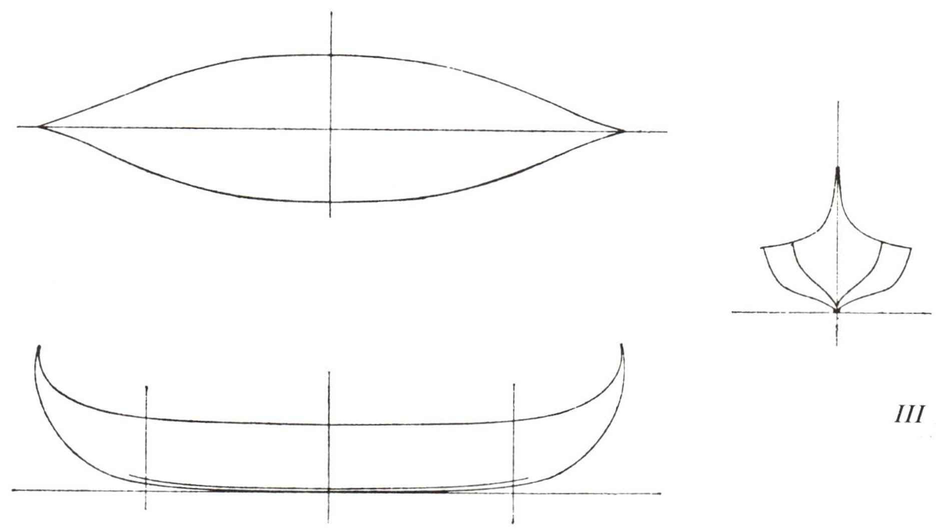

III

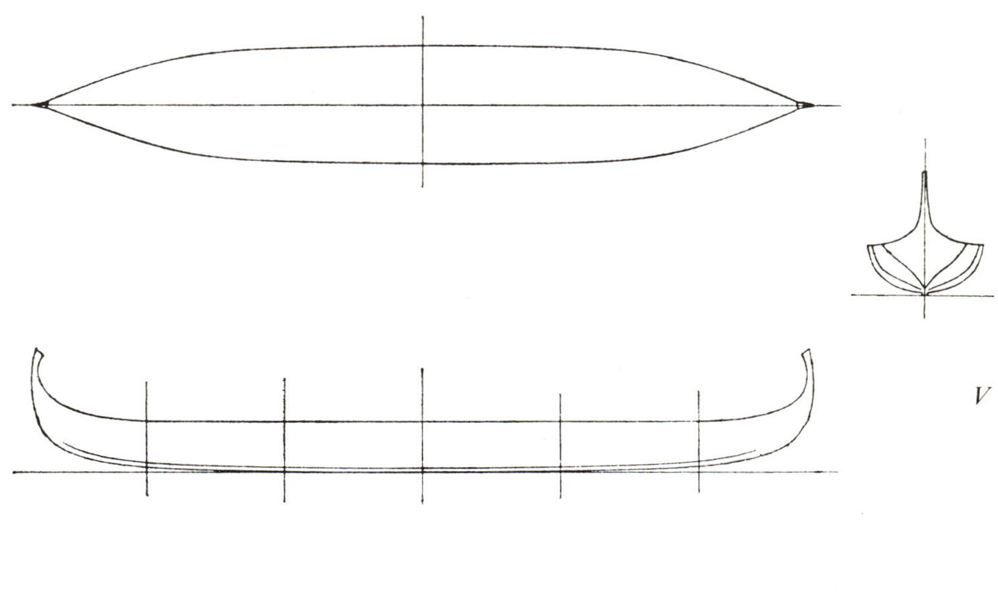

V

had an open hold around the mast, with decking fore and aft of it. The stern unfortunately was destroyed, so the interesting details of the bracing of the steering equipment were missing. The prow, on the other hand, was preserved intact, and it is a remarkable piece of work. The illusion of overlapping timbers is retained but, in fact, the prow is only imitation clinker-built, the whole being carved out of a single block of timber.

Although primarily a sailing ship, oars seems to have been used, though holes for them appear only fore and aft, not amidships. Wrecks I and II from Skuldelev were also merchantmen, but larger and more crudely built than Wreck III. It is probable that they are examples of the great ocean-going merchant ships from the end of the Viking Age. Because the remains of these ships are still being studied, it is not yet possible to be specific about dimensions and constructional details.

Wreck V has holes for oars along the whole length of the ship and like the smaller Wreck IV, was presumably a coastal warship.

THE ARCHAEOLOGICAL SENSATION OF THE TURN OF THE CENTURY.

The Oseberg grave-mound was not as impressive as most of the other grave-mounds, which were normally placed on high and open ground. It is on a flat piece of ground near a stream which runs through a valley. The Gokstad site is similar, leading to the conclusion that such places were chosen because it was comparatively easy to transport the ships to them, using the nearby stream. For both ships ditches were dug deep in the clay, which proved a very good medium for the preservation of the wood; in fact only the prow, which protruded above the clay, decayed.

At Oseberg a large pile of rocks was placed over the ships and on top of the pile the mound was built with turves; as these sank down, the mound formed an airtight covering over the ship, thus preserving it intact. At the same time the colossal weight of the rocks bore down on to the ship and the damp floor of the grave gave way, so that over the centuries the entire grave-mound sank. The ship was crushed to pieces and thus changed shape, so that the keel came to be higher than the sides of the ship. A short while after the ship had been buried, marauders managed to break into the grave-mound. They made a tunnel into the mound, destroyed the prow, which blocked their way, and broke through the ceiling of the burial-chamber. The position of the skeletons was disturbed and the bones were scattered. It is supposed that the marauders were in search of booty, for no jewels were found in the graves. But perhaps they were prompted by superstitious or religious motives, to prevent the dead man returning as a ghost. But in any case the vandals carried off all the precious metals. However, the other objects found give us an overall picture of the art and everyday life of the Vikings.

The building of the grave-mound at Oseberg was a long and arduous task, and we can imagine that the preparations were started while the Oseberg queen was still alive. Perhaps she herself decided where the grave should be. The state of preservation in the grave-mound was so good that even the grass and the plants remained intact. During the excavations it was possible to ascertain, on botanical evidence, that the grave was constructed in early spring, while the burial took place in late autumn.

THE GRAVE-MOUND AT OSEBERG, NORWAY

When the excavations were begun there in 1904, the grave-mound at Oseberg had concealed for more than a thousand years the richest burial-place of the Viking Age. It had been disturbed only once, by vandals in medieval times. The huge grave-mound rises up, just under 55 yards in diameter, an awe-inspiring monument to the respect of another age for its dead. The grave was restored after the excavations were completed and now blends with the ancient landscape.

A SHIP BROUGHT OUT OF THE GRAVE-MOUNDS AFTER A THOUSAND YEARS

The picture on the opposite page shows the majestic prow of the ship.
Reconstruction work on the Gokstad ship lasted from its discovery in 1880 until a place was found for it fifty years later in the Ship Museum. Especially in the case of the Gokstad ship, photographic records are scarce, since photography was in its infancy in Scandinavia when the ship was discovered.

BROKEN WOODEN CONTAINERS FROM THE GRAVE-MOUND

Cooking utensils were found together in the fore part of the ship at Oseberg. There were pots and frying-pans, ladles of various sizes and several serving-plates made of wood. There was even an implement for grinding grain to make bread or porridge. Some wooden buckets had probably been used to store food. In the centre of the picture can be seen a ladle carved from a single piece of wood. The bucket has been forced entirely out of shape, as have nearly all the containers bound with staves. Originally this was a finely-made bucket, with ornamental staves made of baleen.

FRAGMENTS OF A BUCKET

The work of preparing and reconstructing all the objects found at Oseberg lasted many years. This bucket with staves is a typical detail of the world's greatest puzzle. Even if the wood had been well preserved, every single piece would have needed treatment to prevent it from shrinking or disintegrating entirely.
Before they could be reassembled the pieces had to be boiled in an alum solution and covered with linseed oil and varnish.

THE OSEBERG AND GOKSTAD SHIP EXCAVATIONS

It is difficult to imagine all the problems confronting the archaeologists in their work with these important finds. At Oseberg every single piece of the ship and of the objects found in the grave had to be marked and numbered, taken out of the grave and packed ready for transport to Oslo. The reconstruction of the ship was carried out under the direction of Ing. Fr. Johannessen, who succeeded in achieving the impossible and putting the ship together again. The oak wood used was so well preserved that it was possible to bend it back into its original shape. On the left is shown a stage in the excavation of the ship. The Gokstad ship (page 282) had disintegrated completely. The upper planks had been forced into the centre of the ship, and the extremities of the prow and the stern were decayed. Finally, the ship was divided in two and transported by cart. First of all, the ship was reconstructed only temporarily and left like that until 1930. When it was taken to the Viking Ship Museum at Bygdöy, the ship was taken to bits and the fragments steam-treated to restore their original shape; when the ship was finally reconstructed, new pieces of wood were used to replace those which were quite decayed.

THE SLEDGES OF THE OSEBERG QUEEN

The four sledges of the Oseberg queen had suffered much deterioration from their long storage in the grave-mound. One of them was broken into nearly a thousand pieces. The simple everyday sledge was so poorly preserved that it was not possible to put it together again, while the three resplendent sledges, for special occasions, could be exhibited after much careful and time-consuming work had gone into restoring them. Even after careful scientific treatment the wood was so fragile that it could hardly withstand its own weight, and extensive technical problems had to be solved before the sledges could be exhibited. In the state in which the sledges were found during the excavations, their reconstruction must have appeared practically impossible. They had been crushed to such an extent that they had quite lost their shape, and in many places the damp wood had taken on the shape of the stones which lay beneath them.
During the excavations it was possible to discern traces of paint on the box-frames. Black, brown and red had been used to emphasize the lines of the carving. The sledges were made in two parts: the box-frame was fixed on top of the lower section, consisting of the legs and runners. An examination of the ornamentation revealed that the carving had been carried out by several craftsmen, and that the box-frame and the lower section were not carved by the same person.
At one time sledges were used all the year round in Norway. The roads were bad and the sledges could run over grass as well as over snow. We can therefore presume that the Oseberg sledges were not only for winter use.

FRAGMENTS OF THE WAGON FOUND DURING THE EXCAVATIONS

Two of the wheels as they were found on the ship. Even these solid fragments, enormous and made of oak, were crushed to pieces and had lost their original shape. During the burial ceremony the wagon was dismantled. The wheels, the body and the undercarriage had been taken apart. The construction of the wagon was technically rather primitive, and it is clear that the making of wheels and carts at that time was difficult and that capable craftsmen were hard to find.
Fragments of wagons were found in various places in the graves and several wagons can be seen on the Gotland picture-stones, so that it is certain that the Oseberg wagon was not unique, but wagons were far from common in Viking times.

THE PRINCIPAL DRAWINGS OF SCENES RECONSTRUCTED ACCORDING TO THE IDEAS AND THEORIES OF VARIOUS COLLABORATORS.

Animals over the sea, Bertil Almgren: 26–27

Warriors land on an enemy coast, Bertil Almgren: 28–29

Battle tactics, Thorkild Ramskou: 30–31

The living town, Bertil Almgren: 38–39

A Birka woman's grave, reconstructed from a grave in Birka: 42–43

A Birka warrior's grave, reconstructed from a grave in Birka: 44–45

The thronging water-front at Hedeby, Bertil Almgren: 60–61

A king's reeve dies, Peter Sawyer: 82

A rune-stone bridge, Inga Henning: 150–151

Feminine fashions: 200–201

How brooches were worn, Bertil Almgren: 202–203

Men's dress: 204–205

Borrowed plumage: A composite portrait of a Viking rider, Bertil Almgren: 229

A precursor of the Viking, Bertil Almgren: 230

A Viking shipyard, Bertil Almgren: 250–251

Raising the mast, Arne Emil Christensen Jr and Bertil Almgren: 263

MAPS

Population distribution. This map shows the distribution of population in Viking-Age Scandinavia, Kjell Lundholm, Uppsala, Sweden: 15

Birka: 32

Kaupang: 47

Gotland: 51

Hedeby: 55

Military bases in Denmark: 63

The Vinland map—the scholars argue: 67

The world the Vikings voyaged: 68–69

The British Isles in the Viking Age. The most important features and places: 70

Viking attacks against England. The three phases of Viking attacks: 74

Mobility: the main Viking weapon. The Viking progress back and forth across the Channel: 83

Viking England. English parishes which still have Scandinavian names: 88

The neighbours. Part of the East Riding of Yorkshire with Scandinavian placenames: 89

Ireland and the Irish Sea: 93

The Faroes: 96

Iceland: 98

Greenland: 113

Newfoundland: 116

The Norse settlement in Normandy: 112

France: the river raiders: 129

Into North-Western Europe. How ninth-century Viking raiders were able to make use of the rivers to penetrate into the heart of Germany. Max Roosman, Uppsala, Sweden: 130

Treasure buried in forest and steppe. Viking Age trade in eastern Europe: 135

The trail of Viking relics. The most important finds which have helped the scholars build up a composite picture of daily life among the Vikings: 163

COLOURED PHOTOGRAPHS

The Gokstad Ship, Per Maurtvedt, Oslo, Norway: 9

The Dangerous Road, Artur Nilsson, Gothenburg, Sweden: 12–13

The Island Shield, Stig Sjöstedt, Gothenburg, Sweden. By permission of the Swedish Defence Staff: 17

A Blend of Land and Water, Denmark, Jörgen Jensen, Aalborg, Denmark: 19

A Haven from the Atlantic, Skei in Jölster, Norway. Wideroe Flight Company Ltd.: 20–21

Forest, Lake and River, Kuopio, Finland. Finnish Tourist Association, Stockholm, Sweden: 22

Birka, Sweden, Karin Eriksson, Stockholm, Sweden. By permission of the Swedish Defence Staff: 33

The Rich Trade-Goods of Birka, Prof. Bertil Almgren, Uppsala, Sweden: 36–37

Birka's Oldest Fortification, Sweden, Åke Grundström, Stockholm, Sweden: 40

The Bay of Kaupang, Norway, Knut Einar Oskarsen, Sandefiord, Norway: 49

The Cliffs and Shoals of Gotland, Sweden, Prof. Sten Rudberg, Gothenburg, Sweden: 52–53

The Hedeby Area from the Air, Schleswig-Holstein, Germany. Dr. Uwe Muus, Kiel, Germany. By permission of the Ministry of Defence: 56

An Ancient Island Landmark, Shetland, Prof. Bertil Almgren, Uppsala, Sweden: 73

The Holy Island. Lindsfarne, England. Brian Seed, London, England: 76–77

A Holy Book Ransomed, Sixten Sandell, Gothenburg, Sweden: 80

The Islands of Sheep, the Faroe Islands, Scandinavian Press Photo Service Ltd., Copenhagen, Denmark: 97

The Islands of Murder, The Westman Islands, Iceland, Karin Eriksson, Stockholm, Sweden: 100–101

Runic Influence in Icelandic Art, Museum of Antiquities, University of Oslo, Norway: 104

A Strange Site for a Parliament, Thingvellir, Iceland, Gudmundur Hanneson, Reykjavik Iceland: 108–109

Signs of Life at the Edge of the Ice, Brattahlid, Greenland, Museum inspector Jörgen Meldgaard, Copenhagen, Denmark: 114–115

The "Wonderful Beaches", Cape Porcupine, Labrador, Helge Ingstad, Oslo, Norway: 118

The Waterway That Led to Plunder, Les Andelys, France, French Tourist Association, Stockholm, Sweden: 124–125

A Gateway to the East. River Don, Russia, APN, Stockholm, Sweden: 137

Freyr, the God of Fruitfulness, Åke Grundström, Stockholm, Sweden: 144

The Serpent's Secret, Åke Grundström, Stockholm, Sweden: 144

A Woman on a Buckle, Carl E. Rosenberg Ltd, Copenhagen, Denmark: 161

A Warlike Weather-Vane, Åke Grundström, Stockholm, Sweden: 168

Making Change and Weighing It, Prof. Bertil Almgren and Åke Grundström, Sweden: 177

A Bucket with Bronze Trimmings, Per Maurtvedt, Oslo, Norway: 178

A Chest from the Oseberg Ship, Per Maurtvedt, Oslo, Norway: 187

Iron cauldrons, Per Maurtvedt, Oslo, Norway: 188

Blacksmith's Tools, Per Maurtvedt, Oslo, Norway: 188

A Fragment of History, Per Maurtvedt, Oslo, Norway: 197

A Norwegian Treasure, Per Maurtvedt, Oslo, Norway: 198

A Goldsmith's Masterpiece, Carl E. Rosenberg Ltd, Copenhagen, Denmark: 207

Four Fine Brooches, Åke Grundström, Stockholm, Sweden: 208

A Gilded Gotland Speciality, Åke Grundström, Stockholm, Sweden: 211

Treasure from Norway, Per Maurtvedt, Oslo, Norway: 212–213

Viking Jewellery, Åke Grundström, Stockholm, Sweden: 214

A Decorated Battle-Axe, Carl E. Rosenberg Ltd, Copenhagen, Denmark: 219

Infantry and Cavalry Equipment Shown in the Bayeux Tapestry. By permission of the town of Bayeux: 220

A Sampling of Sword Hilts, Åke Grundström, Stockholm, Sweden: 222

Spear Heads of Different Patterns, Per Maurtvedt, Oslo, Norway: 225

Golden Spur, Per Maurtvedt, Oslo, Norway: 226

Harness Bows, Carl E. Rosenberg Ltd., Copenhagen, Denmark: 235

The Richly Carved Oseberg Wagon, Collection of Antiquities, University of Oslo, Norway: 236

Craftsmanship in Wood, Prof. Bertil Almgren, Uppsala, Sweden: 245

The Gokstad Ship, Per Maurtvedt, Oslo, Norway: 246

A Dragon's Head on the Tiller, How Steering Oars Were Attached, Per Maurtvedt, Oslo, Norway: 255

The Oseberg Ship—Seaworthy Lines and Symbolic Stern-Posts, Per Maurtvedt, Oslo, Norway: 256–257

The Oseberg Steering Oar, Per Maurtvedt, Oslo, Norway: 258

The Gokstad Ship from the Helmsman's Position, the Inside of the Planking on the Starboard Quarter, Per Maurtvedt, Oslo, Norway: 267

A Carved Rowlock, the Little Ship's Boat, The Viking Ship House, Bygdöy, Oslo, Norway: 268

INSTITUTES AND MUSEUMS

Gratitude is due to many research institutes and museums in European and other countries.

Bergen Maritime Museum, Bergen, Norway.

British Museum, London, Great Britain.

Gothenburg Maritime Museum, Gothenburg, Sweden.

Gothenburg University Library, Gothenburg, Sweden.

Gotland Collection of Antiquities, Visby, Sweden.

Iceland National Museum of Antiquities, Reykjavik, Iceland.

Musée de Normandie, Caên, France.

National Museum, Helsinki, Finland.

National Museum of Antiquities, Copenhagen, Denmark.

Norwegian Maritime Museum, Bygdøy, Oslo, Norway.

Royal Library of Sweden, Stockholm, Sweden.

Schleswig-Holstein Museum of Prehistory and Protohistory, Schleswig Schloss Gottorp, Germany.

Swedish State Historical Museum and Royal Coin Collection, Stockholm, Sweden.

University of Oslo Museum of Antiquities, Oslo, Norway.

University of Uppsala, Coin Collection, Uppsala, Sweden.

Oxford University Press / Prof. Gwyn Jones, and their book The Norse Atlantic Saga.

LITERATURE

THE HISTORICAL AND ARCHEOLOGICAL BACKGROUND

G. Arwidsson, *Vendelstile, Email und Glas.* Diss. Uppsala 1942.
——, Valsgärde 6. *Die Gräberfunde von Valsgärde I.* Uppsala 1942.
——, Valsgärde 8. *Die Gräberfunde von Valsgärde II.* Uppsala 1954.
A. Dopsch, *Wirtschaftliche und soziale Grundlagen der europäischen Kulturentwicklung aus der Zeit von Cäsar bis auf Karl den Grossen, I-II,* Wien 1923-24.
R. H. Hodgkin, *A History of the Anglo-Saxons, II,* Oxford 1939.
W. Holmqvist, Die eisenzeitlichen Funde aus Lillön, Kirchspiel Ekerö, Uppland. *Acta Archaeologica XXV* 1954. Copenhagen.
——, Grävningarna på Helgö i Mälaren. Summary. *Viking* 21-22. Oslo 1958.
——, Helgö, en internationell handelsplata. *Proxims Thule.* Stockholm 1962.
——, B. Arrhenius & P. Lundström, *Excavations at Helgö I.* Stockholm 1961.
——, B. Arrhenius, *Excavations at Helgö II.* Stockholm 1964.
B. Nerman, Grobin-Seeburg, *Ausgrabungen und Funde.* Stockholm 1958.
H. Pirenne, Un contrast économique: Mérovingiens et Carolingiens. *Revue belge de philologie et d'histoire,* 1922-23.
H. Pirenne, *Mahomet et Charlemagne.* Bruxelles 1935. German ed.: *Geburt des Abendlandes.* Leipzig 1939.

HISTORICAL SOURCES

Adam Bremensis, magister, *Gesta Hammaburgensis ecclesiae pontificum,* ed. H. B. Schmeidler, Hannover-Leipzig 1917.
H. Birkeland, Nordens historie i middelalderen efter arabiske kilder. *Norske Videnskaps-Akademis skrifter.* Oslo 1954.
A. Bugge, *Vikingerne, I-II.* Christiania 1904-06.
G. N. Garmonsway, *The Anglo-Saxon Chronicle.* Everyman Library 1953.
G. Jacob, Arabische Berichte von Gesandten an germanische Fürstenhöfe aus dem 9. und 10. Jahrhundert. *Quellen zur deutschen Volkskunde,* I. Berlin-Leipzig 1927.
C. H. Robinson, *Anskar, the apostle of the north. (Vita Anskarii).* London 1921.
Alexander Seippel, *Rerum Normannicarum fontes Arabici, I-II.* Oslo 1876-1928.
Johannes Steenstrup, *Normannerne, I-IV,* Copenhagen 1876-82.
H. Sweet, King Alfred's Orosius, *Early English Text Society* 1883.
V. Vogel, *Die Normannen und das fränkische Reich bis zur Gründung der Normadie,* Heidelberg 1906.
D. Whitelock, *English Historical Documents.* (500-1042) London 1955.
A. Zeki Validi Togan, Ibn Fadlan's Reisebericht, *Abhandlungen für die Kunde des Morgenlandes XXIV:3.* Leipzig 1939.

GENERAL WORKS ON THE VIKINGS

J. Adigard des Gautries, Études de toponymie normannique 4. *Études Germaniques* 15. 1960.
Jean Adigard des Gautries, *Les noms de personnes scandinaves en Normandie de* 911 *à* 1066. Lund 1954.
W. E. D. Allen, *The Poet and the Spae-Wife. An Attempt to Reconstruct Al-Ghazal's Embassy to the Vikings.* London 1960.
B. Almgren, Vikingatåg och vikingaskepp. Summary: Viking raids and viking ships. *Tor VIII.* Uppsala 1962.
B. Almgren, Vikingatågens höjdpunkt och slut. Summary: The peak and the end of Viking raids. *Tor XI.* Uppsala 1963.
C. G. Andrae, *Kyrka och frälse i Sverige under äldre medeltid.* Diss. Uppsala 1960.
H. Arbman-M. Stenberger, *Vikingar i västerled,* Stockholm 1935.
H. Arbman, *Svear i österviking,* Stockholm 1955.
H. Arbman, *The Vikings.* London 1960.
H. Arbman, Sverige och östern under vikingatiden. *Proxima Thule.* Stockholm 1962.
H. Arbman, Zur Frage der Verbindungen zwischen Ost und West in IX.-X. Jhdt. *Atti del VI Congresso Internat. Prehist. Protohist. Vol. I.* Roma 1962.
T. J. Arne, *La Suède et l'Orient.* Diss. Uppsala 1914.
T. J. Arne, Ibn-Fadlans resa till Bulgar. Résumé: Le voyage d'Ibn Fadlan à Bulgar. *Fornvännen.* Stockholm 1941.
T. J. Arne, Die Varägerfrage und die sovjetische Forschung, *Acta Archaeologica XXIII,* Copenhagen 1952.
Fritz Askeberg, *Norden och kontinenten i gammal tid,* Uppsala 1944.
F. Askeberg, La Guerche. Ett bidrag till Loirevikingarnas historia, *Namn och Bygd* 1944. Uppsala.
A. L. Binns, The Viking Century in East Yorkshire. *East Yorkshire Local Historical Society* 1963.
S. Bolin, Mahomet, Charlemagne and Ruric. *Scandinavian Economic History Rewiew* 1954.
S. Bolin, Die Anfänge der Münzprägung in Skandinavien. *Settimane di studio del Centro italiano di studi sull'alto medioevo VII. Moneta e scambi nell'alto medioevo.* Spoleto 1961.
Johannes Brøndsted, *Nordboer i Amerika før Columbus?* Copenhagen 1951.
J. Brønsted, *The Vikings.* London 1960.
A. Bugge, *Vesterlandenes indflydelse paa nordboernes og særlig nordmændenes ydre kultur, levesæt og samfundsforhold,* Christiania 1905.
P. Enemark, Om problemer vedrørende friserhandelen. *Jyske Samlinger.* Aarhus 1959-1961. (Frisian Trade, extensive bibliography.)
R. H. C. Davis, East Anglia and the Danelaw. *Transactions of the Royal Historical Society, 5th ser. V.* 1955.
R. Ekblom, Ortnamnens vittnesbörd om svenskarnas tidiga förbindelser med slaver och balter. Zusammenfassung. *Språkvetenskapliga Sällskapets i Uppsala Förhandlingar* 1940-1942.
E. Ekwall, Scandinavians and Celts in the North-West of England. *Lunds Universitets Årsskrift* 14:27. Lund 1918.
E. Ekwall, The Scandinavian Element. *Introduction to the Survey of English Place-Names I.* Cambridge 1924.
E. Ekwall, The scandinavian settlements. *An historical geography of England before A. D.* 1800. ed. H. C. Darby. Cambridge 1936.
E. Ekwall, *Concise Oxford Dictionary of English placenames.* Oxford 1960.
E. Ennen, *Frühgeschichte der Europäischen Stadt.* Bonn 1953.
K. O. Falk, Dneprforsarnas namn i kejsar Konstantin VII Porfyrogennetos' De Administrando Imperio. *Lunds Universitets Årsskrift N. F. Avd. 1, 46:4.* Lund 1951.
G. Hasselberg, *Studier rörande Visby stadslag och dess källor.* Diss. Uppsala 1953.
H. Hermansson, The Problem of Wineland. *Islandica 25,* 1936.
W. Hovgaard, *The Voyages of the Norsemen to America,* New York 1915.
Lis Jacobsen, *Svenskevældets fald,* Copenhagen 1929.
H. Jankuhn, and others. Die Zeit der Stadtgründung im Ostseeraum. *Acta Visbyensia I.* Visbysymposiet för historiska vetenskaper 1963. Visby 1965.
A. Janzén, Scandinavian Place-Names in England I-VI. *Names 1957-1963.* Berkeley, California.
E. Joransson. *The Danegeld in France.* Rock Island, Ill. 1924.
T. D. Kendrick. *A History of the Vikings.* London 1930.
E. Kivikoski, Studien zu Birkas Handel im östlichen Ostseegebiet. *Acta Archaeologica VIII.* 1938 Copenhagen.
Kulturhistoriskt lexikon för nordisk medeltid från vikingatid till reformationstid. I-XI seqq. Malmö 1956-1966 seqq.
A. R. Lewis, *The Northern Seas,* Shipping and Commerce in Northern Europe A. D. 300-1100. Princeton 1958.
H. Lindkvist, *Middle English Place-Names of Scandinavian Origin.* Diss. Uppsala 1912.
G. J. Marcus, The norse emigration to the Faroe Islands. *English Historical Review LXXI,* 1956.
I. Martens, Vikingetogen i arkeologisk belysning. Summary: The Viking Raids seen in the Light of Archeology. *Viking, XXIV.* Oslo 1960.
A. Mawer, The Scandinavian Settlement in England as Reflected in English Place Names. *Acta philologica Scandinavica 7.* Copenhagen 1932.
J. Meldgaard, *Nordboerne i Grønland.* Copenhagen 1965.
A. Melvinger, *Les premières incursions des vikings en Occident d'apres des sources arabes.* Uppsala 1955.
V. Minorksy, Rus. *Encyclopedia of Islam.* 1936.
L. Musset, Relations et échanges d'influences dans l'Europe du Nord-Ouest. (Xe-XIe siècles). *Cahiers de civilisation médievale.* 1958.
L. Musset. Les invasions: Le seconde assaut contre l'Europe chrétienne. *Nouvelle Clio XII B.* Paris 1965.
B. Nerman, Die Verbindungen zwischen Skandinavien und dem Ostbaltikum in der jüngeren Eisenzeit. *Kungl. Vitterhets Historie och Antikvitets Akademiens Handlingar 40:1.* Stockholm 1929.
P. Nörlund, *Viking settlers in Greenland and their descendants during five hundred years.* Cambridge 1936.
E. Oxenstierna, *Norsemen.* New York 1965.
S. U. Palme, Vikingatågen i väst - deras förutsättningar och samhälleliga följder. *Nordish-Tidskrift.* Stockholm 1962.
H. Paszkiewicz, *The Origin of Russia,* London 1954.
——, *The making of the Russian Nation.* London 1963.
S. Piekarczik, *Studia nad rozwojem structury spoleczno-gospodarczej wczesnosrednrowiecznej Szwecji.* Warszawa 1962.
B. A. Rybakov, Problèmes en cours sur la formation de la Russie de Kiev. *XIe Congrès International des Sciences Historiques, Stockholm 21-28 août 1960,* Résumés des communications. Uppsala 1960. With discussion in: *Actes du Congrès.* Uppsala 1962.
P. H. Sawyer, *The age of the vikings.* London 1962.
A. H. Smith, *The Place-Names of the East Riding of Yorkshire and York.* Cambridge 1937.
A. H. Smith, *The Place-Names of the West Riding of Yorkshire 1-8.* Cambridge 1961-1963.
Carl V. Sølver, *Vestervejen. Om Vikingernes sejlads.* Copenhagen 1954.
Johannes Steenstrup, Normandiets Historie under de syv første Hertuger 911-1066. *Det kgl. danske Vidensk. Selsk. Skrifter 7.* Række, Copenhagen 1925.
J. Stefansson, Vikings in Spain. *Saga-Book of the Viking Club,* VI, 1909.
A. Stender-Petersen. *Varangica.* Aarhus 1953.
——, Das Problem der ältesten Byzantinisch-Russisch-Nordischen Beziehungen. *Relazioni III: Storia del Medioevo,* ed. *Comitato internaz. di scienze storiche, X congresso internaz.* Roma 1955.
——, Varaegerspörgsmålet. *Viking, XXIII.* Oslo 1959.
F. M. Stenton, The scandinavian colonies in England and Normandy. *Transactions of the Royal Historical Society. 4th ser. XXVII.* 1945.
——, *Anglo-Saxon England.* Oxford 1947.
——, *The Bayeux Tapestry.* London 1957.
M. Strömberg, Neue Schwedische Beiträge zur Geschichte der skandinavisch-slawischen Beziehungen während der Wikingerzeit und das frühe Mittelalter. *Slavia Antiqua VII.* Warszawa-Poznán 1960.
V. Thomsen. *The relations between ancient Russia and Scandinavia and the origin of the Russian state.* Oxford 1877. Also in: *Samlede skrifter I.* Copenhagen 1919.
W. Vogel, *Die Normannen und das fränkische Reich.* Heidelberg 1906.
E. Wadstein, *Norden och Västeuropa i gammal tid.* Gothenburg 1925.
A. Walsh, *Scandinavian Relations with Ireland during the Viking Period.* Dublin 1922.
R. E. M. Wheeler, *London and the Vikings.* London Museum Catalogue. London 1927.
S. Wikander, Orientaliska källor till vikingatidens historia. *Historisk Tidskrift.* Stockholm 1963.

TOWNS AND SETTLEMENTS

B. Ambrosiani, Birka-Sigtuna-Stockholm. Ett diskussionsinlägg. Zusammenfassung. *Tor 1957.* Uppsala.
H. Andersen & O, Klindt-Jensen, Det aeldste Århus. Summary: Oldest Århus. *Kuml.* Århus 1963.
E. Aner. Das Kammergräberfeld von Haithabu. *Offa 10.* Neumünster 1952.
H. Arbman, *Birka, Sveriges äldsta handelsstad,* Stockholm 1939.
H. Arbman, *Birka I. Die Gräber.* Uppsala-Stockholm 1940, 1943.
Charlotte Blindheim, *Kaupang, markedsplassen i Skiringssal,* Oslo 1953.
Ch. Blindheim, En amulett av rav. Summary: An amber amulet (Kaupang). *Universitetets i Oslo Oldsaksamlings Årbok 1958-1959.* Oslo.
Ch. Blindheim, The Market Place in Skiringsal. *Acta Archaeologica XXXI* 1960. Copenhagen.
Ch. Blindheim, New Light on Viking Trade in Norway. *Archaeology 13:4.* New York 1960.
Ch. Blindheim, En barre av bly. Summary: An ingot of lead (Kaupang). *Universitets i Oslo Oldsaksamlings Årbok 1960-1961.* Oslo.
T. Capelle, Die Ausgrabungen im innern des Halbkreiswalles. (Haithabu). *Offa 21-22.* Neumünster 1964-65.
Vilh. la Cour, *Danevirkestudier. En arkæologisk-historisk Undersøgelse.* Copenhagen 1951.
Ejnar Dyggve, Gorm's Temple and Harald's Stave-Church. *Acta Archaeologica XXV.* 1954. Copenhagen.
S. Erixon (ed.), Byggnadskultur. *Nordisk Kultur XVII.* Stockholm-Oslo-Copenhagen 1953.
B. Fritz, Stadshistoria och arkeologi. *Historisk Tidskrift.* Stockholm 1965.
A. Geijer, *Birka III. Die Textilfunde.* Stockholm (Diss. Uppsala) 1938.
G. Hatz, Münzfunde aus Haithabu 1962. *Offa 21-22.* Neumünster 1964-65.
I. Heltoft, *Kongesædet i Jelling,* København 1957.
A. Herteig, Marknadsplatser-stadsbildningar. Summary: The origin of towns in the north. *Tor X.* Uppsala 1964.
Bjørn Hougen, *Fra seter til gård. Studier i norsk bosetning-historie.* Oslo 1947.
E. K. Hougen, Tinnfoliert keramik fra Kaupang. Summary: Tin-foiled pottery from Kaupang. *Universitetets i Oslo Oldsaksamlings Årbok 1958-1959.* Oslo.
——, Kaupang-keramikken. Summary: The pottery from Kaupang. *Universitetets i Oslo Oldsaksamlings Årbok 1960-1961.* Oslo.
W. Hübener, *Die Keramik von Haithabu.* Neumünster 1959.
H. Jankuhn, *Die Wehranlagen der Wikingerzeit zwischen Schlei und Treene.* Neumünster 1937.
——, *Die Ausgrabungen in Haithabu* (*1937-39*). Berlin 1943.
——, Die Frühgeschichte vom Ausgang der Völkerwanderung bis zur Ende der Wikingerzeit. *Geschichte Schleswig-Holsteins III.* Neumünster, 1955-57.
——, Zur Fortführung der Ausgrabungen in Haithabu, Probleme und Zi. *Zeitschrift der Gesellschaft für Shleswig-Holsteinische Geschichte, Band 87 1962.* Neumünster.
——, *Haithabu. Ein Handelsplatz der Wikingerzeit. 4. ergänzte Auflage.* Neumünster 1963.
——, Überblick über die verschiedene Grabungen. (Haithabu). *Offa 21-22.* Neumünster 1964-65.
J. Larsen. Rekonstruktion af Trelleborg. Summary: The reconstruction of the Trelleborg houses. *Aarbøger for nordisk oldkyndighed og historie.* Copenhagen 1957.
Palle Lauring–A. Hoff-Møller, Trelleborghusets rekonstruktion, *Aarbøger for nordisk Oldkyndighed og Historie 1952.* Copenhagen.
Soph. Müller og C. Neergaard, Danevirke, archæologisk undersøgt, beskrevet of tydet. *Nordiske Fortidsminder I. 1903.*
P. Nørlund. *Trelleborg.* Copenhagen 1948.
O. Olsen, Trelleborg-problemer. Summary: Trelleborg Problems. *Scandia 28.* Lund 1962.
H. P. L'Orange, Trelleborg-Aggersborg og de kongelige byer i Østen. *Viking XVI,* Oslo 1952.
K. Raddatz, Bericht über die Probegrabung auf der Südsiedlung. (Haithabu) *Offa 21-22.* Neumünster 1964-65.
H. Schledermann, Danevirkeundersögelser ved Bustrup 1962-63. *Offa 21-22.* Neumünster 1964-65.
C. G. Schultz, Vikingetidshuset paa Trelleborg, *Fra Nationalmuseets Arbejdsmark 1942.* Copenhagen.
——, Aggersborg. Vikingelejren ved Limfjorden, *Fra Nationalmuseets Arbejdsmark 1949.* Copenhagen.
P. Simonsen, Nord-Norges bosetningshistorie i oldtiden. *Ottar 32-33.* Tromsø, 1962.
K. Skaare, Et myntfunn fra Kaupang. Summary: A coin find from Kaupang. *Universitetets i Oslo Oldsaksamlings Årbok 1958-1959.* Oslo.
——, Nye mynter fra Kaupang. Summary: New coins from Kaupang. *Universitetets i Oslo Oldsaksamlings Årbok 1960-1961.* Oslo.
M. Strömberg, Untersuchungen zur jüngeren Eisenzeit in Schonen. (Völkerwanderungszeit-Wikingerzeit). I, II. *Acta Archæologica Lundensia.* Diss. Lund 1961.
——, Eine siedlungsgeschichtliche Untersuchung in Hagestad, Südost-Schonen. *Meddelanden från Lunds Universitets Historiska Museum 1961.* Lund.
——, Handelsstråk och vikingabygd i sydöstra Skåne. Om Hagestad-undersökningen. *Ale 1963:3.* Lund.
H. Wideen. *Västsvenska vikingatidsstudier.* Summary: Studies on the viking age in West Sweden. Diss. Stockholm 1955.

GRAVE FINDS

E. Aner. Die wikingerzeitlichen Kammergräber am Thorsberger Moor. *Offa 11.* Neumünster 1952.
H. Arbman, Das Årby-Fund. *Acta Archæologica XI 1940.* Copenhagen.
T. J. Arne, Ein bemerkenswerter Fund aus Östergötland. *Acta Archæologica III 1932.* Copenhagen.
——, *Das Bootgräberfeld von Tuna in Alsike.* Stockholm 1934.
C. Bertheussen, Ei gåta frå Gokstadskipet. Summary: An unsolved problem of the Gokstad ship. *Viking 21-22.* Oslo 1958.
Ch. Blindheim, Osebergskoene på ny. Summary: The shoes from Oseberg. *Viking XXIII.* Oslo 1959.
——, Smedgraven fra Bygland i Morgedal. Summary: The Smith's Grave at Bygland in Morgedal, Telemark County, Norway. *Viking XXVI.* Oslo 1963.
A. W. Brøgger & H. Shetelig. *Osebergfundet. Resumé. Vol. I-III, V.* Oslo 1917-1928.
——, ——, The Viking Ships. Oslo 1953.
J. Brøndsted, Danish Inhumation Graves of the Viking Age. *Acta Archæologica VII 1936.* Copenhagen.
A. E. Christensen jr, Gokstadskipets stevner. *Universitetets i Oslo Oldsaksamlings Årbok 1958-1959.* Oslo.
——, Faeringen fra Gokstad. Summary: The Gokstad "faering". *Viking XXIII.* Oslo 1959.
E. Dyggve. La fouille par le Musée National danois du tertre royal sud à Jelling en 1941. *Acta Archæologica XXIII 1942.* Copenhagen.
E. Hinsch, Gokstadshövdingens jaktrensel. Résumé: La gibecière du seigneur de Gokstad. *Viking XXI-XXII.* Oslo 1958.
Bjørn Hougen, Osebergfunnets billedvev. *Viking IV.* Oslo 1940.
E. Kivikoski, *Kvarnbacken. Ein Gräberfeld der jüngeren Eisenzeit auf Åland.* Helsinki 1963.
S. Marstrander, Et nytt vikingetidsfunn fra Romsdal med vesteuropeiske importsaker. *Viking, XXVI.* Oslo 1963. English edition in *"Lochlann" Vol. III* (*Norsk tidsskrift for sprogvidenskap Suppl. VIII*).
N. Nicolayesen, *The Viking Ship discovered at Gokstad.* Christiania 1882.
O. Olsen & O. Crumlin Pedersen, The Skuldelev Ships. A preliminary report on an underwater excavation in Roskilde Fjord, Zealand. *Acta Archæologica XXIX 1958.* Copenhagen.
K. G. Peterson, Ett gravfynd från Klinta, Köpings sn, Öland. Summary: A grave from Klinta, Öland. *Tor IV.* Uppsala 1958.
Th. Ramskou, Viking Age Cremation Graves in Denmark. *Acta Archæologica XXI 1950.* Copenhagen.
T. Ramskou. Lindholm. Preliminary report of the 152-53 excavations. *Acta Archæologica XXIV 1953.* Copenhagen.
——, Lindholm Höje. Second preliminary report for the years 1954-55. *Acta Archæologica XXVI 1955.* Copenhagen.
——, Lindholm Höje. Third preliminary report for the years 1956-57. *Acta Archæologica XXVIII 1957.* Copenhagen.
H. Rydh. *Förhistoriska undersökningar på Adelsö.* Deutscher Auszug. Stockholm 1936.
I. Serning, *Dalarnas järnålder.* Malung 1966.
H. Shetelig, Tuneskipet. *Norske Oldfunn II,* Christiania 1917.
Thorleif Sjøvold, *Osebergfunnet og de andre vikingeskipsfunn,* Oslo 1957.
M. Stenberger, Das Gräberfeld bei Ihre im Kirchspiel Hellvi auf Gotland. Der wikingerzeitliche Abschnitt. *Acta Archæologica XXXII 1961.* Copenhagen.
H. Stolpe, *La nécropole de Vendel.* Stockholm 1927.